Love, Sex, Intimacy and Friendsh

Love, Sex, Intimacy and Friendship Between Men, 1550–1800

Edited by Katherine O'Donnell and Michael O'Rourke

First published in hardback 2003
First published in paperback 2007 by
PALGRAVE MACMILLAN
Houndmills, Basingstoke, Hampshire RG21 6XS and
175 Fifth Avenue, New York, N.Y. 10010
Companies and representatives throughout the world.

PALGRAVE MACMILLAN is the global academic imprint of the Palgrave
Macmillan division of St Martin's Press, LLC and of Palgrave Macmillan Ltd.
Macmillan® is a registered trademark in the United States, United Kingdom
and other countries. Palgrave is a registered trademark in the European
Union and other countries.

ISBN-13: 978–0–333–99743–7 hardback
ISBN-10: 0–333–99743–3   hardback
ISBN-13: 978–0–230–54679–0 paperback
ISBN-10: 0–230–54679–X   paperback

This book is printed on paper suitable for recycling and made from
fully managed and sustained forest sources. Logging, pulping and
manufacturing processes are expected to conform to the environmental
regulations of the country of origin

A catalogue record for this book is available from the British Library.

Library of Congress Cataloging-in-Publication Data

Love, sex, intimacy, and friendship between men, 1550–1800 / edited by
Katherine O'Donnell & Michael O'Rourke.
      p. cm
    Includes bibliographical references and index.
    ISBN 0–333–99743–3 (hbk) 0–230–54679–X (pbk)
      1. Gay men – History. 2. Male friendship – History. I. O'Donnell,
Katherine. II. O'Rourke, Michael.

HQ76 .L78 2002
305.38'9664–dc21

                                                              2002026951

10 9 8 7 6 5 4 3 2 1
16 15 14 13 12 11 10 09 08 07

Printed and bound in Great Britain by
Antony Rowe Ltd, Chippenham and Eastbourne

This book is dedicated to the memory of Alan Bray

Contents

Editorial Acknowledgements

Those of us who study early modern sexuality are part of a vibrant community of scholars who know each other largely through the reading of articles, monographs and e-mail bulletin boards. Less frequently we meet at conferences or at research libraries. As both the editors of this volume are at the start of our academic careers, the opportunities to travel widely are not frequent and so the rather audacious idea occurred to us that we would invite our heroes to meet with us in Dublin. To our delighted surprise most of them said "yes" and we had a conference entitled "Queer Men: Queer Masculinities 1550–1800" in July 2001 at Newman House, University College Dublin. This book, inspired by that conference, is a testament to our successful search for a collegial community.

The book's title is significantly different from the original conference as it seemed to us that the concerns of the scholars we brought to Dublin appeared to cohere in a focus on the erotically charged feelings and desires between men, a focus that marks a new moment in the history of male (homo)sexuality, a moment that David M. Halperin contextualizes so well in his introduction, a moment symbolized for us by the most recent work of our late colleague, Alan Bray, whose last public lecture was the final contribution at our conference and to whom this collection is dedicated.

There are a number of people at University College Dublin who were especially supportive of our work on this book: the Academic Conference Committee and the Academic Publications Committee both awarded us generous grants and we would also especially like to thank Dr Danielle Clarke and Professor Declan Kiberd of the Department of English for their interest and support. We will always be indebted for the help and support of the students, researchers, administrators and lecturers at the Women's Education Research and Resource Centre, in particular Ursula Barry, Marie Hammond Callaghan and Jennifer Morawiecki, but most especially the Director, Ailbhe Smyth, who not only gave us the material and financial support for which we asked but who also knew how to give us support we had not realized we would need. Katherine O'Donnell owes a large debt of gratitude to Linda Cullen, who must surely have suffered to have to listen so often to the minutiae of this project but who always had the grace to appear fascinated. Michael O'Rourke would like to acknowledge the support of a Government of Ireland scholarship in the Humanities and Social Sciences and give his particular thanks to Noreen Giffney.

Our more experienced colleagues tell us that our relationship with our publisher, while not unique, is unusually ideal. Luciana O'Flaherty and Janey Fisher, publisher and desk editor respectively at Palgrave Macmillan were always a delight to deal with: prompt, inspiringly efficient, courteous, and even kind.

Our final thanks goes to the contributors to this volume who produced work that yet again confirms why they are among the leading lights in the field. It is rare to have an edited publication produced with such speed and this is due to the generosity of the scholars who made this project a priority.

Thank you all.

Katherine O'Donnell and Michael O'Rourke

Notes on Contributors

Alan Bray was an historian and Honorary Research Fellow of Birkbeck College, University of London. His groundbreaking and influential monograph *Homosexuality in Renaissance England* was published by the Gay Men's Press in 1982 and has proved so indispensable for courses on sexuality, gender and the Renaissance that it was reprinted by Columbia University Press in 1995. His later article "Homosexuality and the Signs of Male Friendship" (*History Workshop Journal*, 1990, reprinted in *Queering the Renaissance*, 1994) is perhaps the single most influential essay on male homoeroticism and Bray's work remains unsurpassed for the historical investigation of this period. His most recent work was on the history of male friendship and his last book *The Friend* is forthcoming with the University of Chicago Press. Alan Bray died in November 2001.

Mario DiGangi is Associate Professor of English at Lehman College and The Graduate Center, CUNY. He is the author of *The Homoerotics of Early Modern Drama* (1997) and of many articles on Shakespeare and his contemporaries. He is editing *The Winter's Tale* for Bedford's *Texts and Contexts* series and *Romeo and Juliet* and *A Midsummer's Night Dream* for the Barnes and Noble Shakespeare. He is completing a book on queer theory, historicism, and sexualities in Shakespeare's England

Jody Greene is Associate Professor of Literature at the University of California, Santa Cruz. She is the author of *The Trouble with Ownership: Literary Property and Authorial Liability in England, 1660–1730* (Penn, 2005). She has edited a special issue of *GLQ* entitled *The Work of Friendship: In Memoriam Alan Bray*, and a special issue of *Eighteenth-Century Studies, Derrida's Eighteenth Century*, will appear in 2007. Her current research, which concerns the relations between poststructuralism and book history, has appeared recently in *PMLA* and *The Eighteenth Century: Theory and Interpretation*.

George E. Haggerty is Professor of English at the University of California, Riverside. His books include *Gothic Fiction/Gothic Form* (1989), *Unnatural Affections: Women and Fiction in the Later Eighteenth Century* (1998), *Men In Love; Masculinity and Sexuality in the Eighteenth*

Century (1999), and *Queer Gothic* (2006). He has also edited *Professions of Desire: Lesbian and Gay Studies in Literature* (1995), *Gay Histories and Cultures: An Encyclopedia* (2000), and *Music and Sexuality in Britten: Selected Essays of Philip Brett* (2006). At present he is writing a book on Horace Walpole and editing, with Molly McGarry, *The Blackwell Companion to LGBTI/Q Studies*.

David M. Halperin is the W.H. Auden Collegiate Professor of the History and Theory of Sexuality at the University of Michigan, where he teaches English, Women's Studies, Classical Studies, and Comparative Literature. He was a founding editor of *GLQ: A Journal of Lesbian and Gay Studies* and is author or editor of eight books, including *Before Sexuality* (1990), *The Lesbian and Gay Studies Reader* (1993), *Saint Foucault* (1995), *What Do Gay Men Want?* (2007), and *Gay Shame* (forthcoming).

Katherine O'Donnell is Head of Women's Studies in the School of Social Justice, University College Dublin. She has published widely on the topic of eighteenth-century Irish literature. She has edited the *Palgrave Guide to Irish History* with Leeann Lane and Mary McAuliffe and *Twenty-First Century Lesbian Studies*, with Noreen Giffney (Harrington Press).

Michael O'Rourke is the editor (also with Katherine O'Donnell) of *Queer Masculinities, 1550–1800: Siting Same-Sex Desire in the Early Modern World* (Palgrave Macmillan, 2006) and (with Noreen Giffney) of *The Ashgate Companion to Queer Theory*. His many articles focus on queer theory, the history of sexuality, and Continental philosophy.

Nicholas F. Radel Professor of English at Furman University, South Carolina, is co-editor of *The Puritan Origins of American Sex*. His editions of *The Taming of the Shrew* and *As You Like It* are forthcoming from Barnes and Noble, and he has published several articles on the history of sexuality in Shakespeare and Renaissance literature in edited collections and in journals such as *Renaissance Drama* and *MaRDIE*. He is currently working on a book-length study of the social effects of the prohibition on speaking sodomy in early modern drama.

George Rousseau has taught at the universities of Harvard, UCLA, Cambridge, Oxford, Leiden, Lausanne, Aberdeen, and is currently a member of the Faculty of History at Oxford University and Co-Director of its Centre for the History of Childhood. His primary interest lies in the interface of literature and medicine, for which his work has been internationally acclaimed, most recently in the award of a three-year Leverhulme Trust Fellowship. His often-cited 1981 article, "Literature and Medicine: The State of the Field," *Isis* LXXII (September, 1981) is said to have charted a new academic field. His article on configurations of same-sex arrangements in the Enlightenment won the James L. Clifford Prize for the best article of the year awarded by the American Society for Eighteenth-Century Studies: His recent books include *The Languages of Psyche: Mind and Body in Enlightenment Thought* (California, 1990), a trilogy entitled *Pre-* and *Post-Modern Discourses: Medical, Scientific, Anthropological* (Manchester, 1991), (with Roy Porter) *Gout: The Patrician Malady* (Yale, 1998), *Framing and Imagining Disease in Cultural History* (Palgrave Macmillan, 2003); *Yourcenar; A Biography* (Haus, 2004), *Nervous Acts: Essays on Literature, Culture and Sensibility* (Palgrave Macmillan, 2004), and *Children and Sexuality: The Greeks to the Great War* (Palgrave Macmillan, 2007).

Alan Stewart is Professor of English and Comparative Literature at Columbia University in New York, and Associate Director of the Centre for Editing Lives and Letters in London. His publications include *Close Readers: Humanism and Sodomy in Early Modern England* (1997), *Hostage to Fortune: The Troubled Life of Francis Bacon* (with Lisa Jardine, 1998), *Philip Sidney: A Double Life* (2000), and *The Cradle King: A Life of James VI and I* (2003). He is currently working on a study of Shakespeare's letters.

Randolph Trumbach is Professor of History at Baruch College and the Graduate School, City University of New York. He is the author of *The Rise of the Egalitarian Family* (1978) and *Sex and the Gender Revolution*, Vol. I (1998). A second volume on "The Origin of Modern Homosexuality" is forthcoming from the University of Chicago Press. He has two chapters in *The Gay History of Britain since the Middle Ages*, ed. Matt Cook (Greenwood International, 2007) which cover the period 1500–1800.

Introduction: Among Men – History, Sexuality, and the Return of Affect

David M. Halperin

> "How is it possible for men to be together? to live together, to share their time, their meals, their living quarters, their pastimes, their sorrows, their knowledge, their confidences? What is it like for men to be among men – 'stripped naked,' outside of institutionalized social relations, family, job, obligatory social life?"[1]

Such are the terms in which Michel Foucault, in a 1981 interview to the French gay magazine *Le gai pied*, represented the "question of existence" posed to him throughout his entire life by his own homosexuality. The point of interest for him, he said, was not his desire for boys but his desire for relations with boys – it was the problem of same-sex relationality, which the lived experience of homosexual desire laid before him. And it was this very problem that Foucault set out to address in the latter volumes of his own unfinished *History of Sexuality*, where he approached historical formations of desire as *modes de vie*, as ways of life or ways of being.[2]

The essays collected in this volume can be read as expressing, without conscious or coordinated planning on the part of their authors (so far as I know), a new impulse to reanimate the spirit of Foucault's late understanding of the history of sexuality as an inquiry that looks beyond the practices or classifications of sex to the ways of being and relating that such a history discloses. They can be understood as rephrasing Foucault's existential question about what it is like for men to be among men. And they take up this project within a historical perspective shaped by Foucault's own approach to the study of sexuality.

Even more important, the various studies assembled here all testify to a new surge of interest on the part of scholars of male sexuality in the history of affect. One senses throughout this volume a growing restiveness among historians of early modern male sexuality at the restrictiveness of the analytic category of "sexuality" itself. Such restiveness has long been apparent in histories of lesbianism. Judith Bennett's recent arguments against limiting the history of lesbian sexuality to the history of lesbian sex, for all their passion, flair, and eloquence, express at least something of the same historiographic impulse that had already, 25 years earlier, animated the boundary-redefining work of Carroll Smith-Rosenberg and Lillian Faderman.[3] A similar chafing against the narrowness of the category of "sexuality" on the part of historians of same-sex relations among men is hardly new or unprecedented, as Foucault's example indicates ("sex is so boring," he once remarked)[4], and as previous work by a number of the contributors to this volume has demonstrated. But I detect in the studies collected here a more specific and innovative preoccupation with the history of subjectivity and with the need to find ways of incorporating previously excluded or ignored kinds of affect into the history of sexuality.

I have argued elsewhere that recent, dominant, public, or "official" definitions of gay identity have had the effect of imposing a blackout on explorations of gay subjectivity.[5] Even within the field of lesbian and gay studies, and despite some notable exceptions, queer theorists have shown a certain reluctance to analyze gay subjectivity for fear of subjecting it to normalizing scrutiny. The only kind of subjectivity that qualifies for "serious" lesbian and gay analysis is that which can be safely theorized in the register of psychoanalytic abstraction (a method rejected by all the contributors to the present volume, not coinciden-tally). Matters of lesbian and gay sensibility, by contrast, have been off the agenda of mainstream lesbian and gay studies for a couple of decades, although some of the most distinguished work in the field has continued to address the topic. The result is that the life of queer affect that is often part of homosexuality – whatever dissident sensibility it is that makes many gay people feel queer in the first place – never comes in for sustained, unembarrassed, analytic attention. It is as if the trans-formation of homosexuality from a sexual perversion into a social identity, and the political requirements of gay pride, have militated against gay inquiry into the inner life of homosexuality. Perhaps we have been afraid that we wouldn't like what we'd find, if we delved too deeply into ourselves, or that what we did find would be used against us. To be sure, gay identity does emphasize certain elements of gay sex-uality, in so far at least as it insists on the fact of same-sex sexual desire, but in claiming public recognition and acceptance of gay *sexual-*

ity it effectively preempts inquiry into homosexual feeling, emotion, sensibility, style, or any specific form of queer *affect*.

The foregrounding of gay identity and the backgrounding of gay subjectivity, or the promotion of gay identities at the expense of gay subjectivities, could be more easily tolerated during the 1980s and early 1990s, when this protective tendency seemed to reflect the urgent demands of a catastrophic political situation. With the rise of the New Right, the increasing devastation of HIV/AIDS, the newly fashionable homophobia unleashed by the moral panic surrounding the epidemic, and the failure of most governments in the industrialized West to react to the disaster afflicting their own citizens, the understandable impulse of the gay movement was to insist on our survival as a people, to defend ourselves as *members of a group* at great collective risk, to feature our common belonging to various social and ethnic identity-categories, and to play down those subjective dimensions of homosexuality, to say nothing of the emotional vicissitudes of gay male life, which in the minds of many people were responsible for the spread of HIV/AIDS in the first place.

But there was a more subtle reason why gay men in particular did not feel constrained by the bracketing of emotion, sensibility, or affect in collective gay representations of gay identity during this period. Far from having been silenced, gay affect seemed everywhere to be triumphant: the public gay response to HIV/AIDS, after all, was positively drenched in affect. Or rather, it was drenched in two particular affects, namely grief and anger, accompanied and amplified by their corollary public expressions, mourning and militancy.

Grief and anger, though they were admittedly, undeniably, passionate emotions, were also politically righteous emotions. They were safe: they did nothing to undermine the public stance of gay pride. They expressed not individual sensibility but the personal experience of collective devastation. The more personal they were, the more exemplary they could come to seem – exemplary of gay men's suffering, loss, and victimization *as a group*. So grief and anger, far from being discreditable emotions, were politically imperative ones, emotions we were politically committed to having. In that sense, grief and anger weren't individualizing or privatizing, however individual or private they might also be; they didn't reduce to matters of personal subjecthood, if that was defined by a unique, unshareable interiority. Far from being limited to the personal, grief and anger propelled gay identity further into the public sphere, they increased its human dignity, they accelerated its transformation into a publicly claimable identity, deserving of recognition, acceptance, and protection. There was no political tension between the emotions of anger and grief and the demands of political visibility.

There were, however, some queer emotions that gay people weren't supposed to have, and that weren't politically respectable. Leading gay writers and intellectuals, such as Larry Kramer and Paul Monette, made the distinction very clear.[6] Bad gay emotions included narcissism, shame, self-loathing, passivity, sentimentality, cowardice, and supposedly "destructive" forms of sexuality. Unlike grief and anger, these emotions were *merely* personal: they expressed individual weakness; they even implied pathology, the lingering effects of centuries of oppression from which we had insufficiently liberated ourselves. HIV/AIDS no longer permitted us the luxury of incomplete political identification, the luxury of not struggling for psychic decolonization. The enemy was not only in the corridors of power but also in our souls. It was more than ever necessary to rid ourselves of whatever affects prevented us from coming together collectively in a newly militant movement.

What distinguished good gay emotion from bad gay emotion was that the good kind was not personally or psychologically revealing. Anger and grief were publicizable precisely because they did not express some peculiar, individual, personal, and possibly pathological inward condition afflicting gay men. Rather, they expressed our collective situation of political oppression and resistance, our collective victimization by an epidemic and by a society that smugly watched it happen; they also expressed our refusal to go quietly, to keep our suffering out of the public eye, to hide our sexuality, to closet our relationships, to let our oppressors off the hook. As such, feelings of anger and grief didn't need to be denied. After all, they originated not in our psyches but in our objective situation. They were psychological responses to an external threat, an external devastation, a reaction to a calamity that had been visited upon us from outside ourselves. HIV/AIDS was precisely *not* the inner truth of homosexuality, not the outward and visible sign of an inward or spiritual illness, not the punishment of gay sin or gay crime, not what we had asked for. Hence the characteristic political tactic of turning our grief into anger, our mourning into militancy. The point was to express our personal and collective insistence that HIV/AIDS was a public-health catastrophe, not the working out of the inner logic of male homosexuality itself. It was a terrible historical accident, and had nothing to do with us or with who we were – and so our emotional response to it also had nothing to do with us or with who we were as gay men, except in so far as we were being collectively blamed for the very epidemic of which we were the victims.

In the long shadow of the HIV/AIDS epidemic, it has been possible for gay men to dodge the awareness of having imposed a blackout on the expression or investigation of queer affect. After all, gay life has long been saturated with affect, soaked in tears and suffused with rage. Now that HIV/AIDS activism, though not HIV/AIDS itself, has been receding from the forefront of gay male life in the developed world, now that the political requirements of HIV/AIDS activism are changing, now that grief and anger are starting to lose their monopoly on the range of queer affects that can be openly expressed, and now that queer culture is re-inventing continuities between contemporary lesbian and gay existence and earlier, pre-Stonewall forms of sexual outlawry, it seems increasingly possible to inquire into aspects or dimensions of the inner life of homosexuality that not so long ago seemed politically dubious, not to say unpalatable, and in any case off limits.[7] One result, which the essays collected in the present volume seem to promise, is the possibility of a new queer history of affect.

For example, George Rousseau, in the leading essay of this collection, calls for a queer history of depression and illness.[8] To be sure, he evinces some embarrassment about bringing those topics into the spotlight of queer history, and he is worried (not without cause) about the possible outcome, which may be to repathologize male homosexuality. By way of extenuation, he presents these queer affects as extending beyond the merely personal: they represent, rather, the impact on individual psychic life of the pathogenic consequences of sexual oppression. That makes the study of them politically defensible. All the same, the result (and it is an entirely welcome one, to my mind) is to rehabilitate depression and illness as topics that ought to feature importantly in our emerging histories of (homo)sexuality.

Rousseau also calls for more attention to the queer history of "discipleship" and friendship. In this he is joined by two other contributors to this volume, George Haggerty and the late Alan Bray, who focus their scholarly efforts on recovering the history of male love. For Bray, this project has to do with recapturing the plurality of possibilities for different kinds of ethical relationship among men, including kinship, association, and formalized affinity – those now hard-to-categorize forms of relationality among men of which Foucault so evocatively spoke. Unlike Foucault, however, Bray concludes that these forms of male relatedness were not "outside of institutionalized social relations," at least not in the pre-modern past, and he implies that they may and perhaps should come to be formalized once again in the postmodern future. Now that "the permafrost of modernity is at last beginning to melt," as Bray says in a strikingly resonant phrase, our historical vision may be able to reveal the outlines of various webs of relationality – voluntary kinship, interlocking networks of obligation, forms of ethical commitment – which have been obscured by the intervening rise of a secular civil society but which may be about to take on, with the decline of that society, a new salience and a new importance for postmodern human subjects.

George Haggerty goes further: "Love," he says, "has often been ignored in histories of sexuality, in part because it is the most elusive of the four-letter words and in part because it has not been understood as central to the question of sexuality itself." And yet, Haggerty insists, "love does more to establish a new kind of sexual subjectivity than histories of sexuality have previously led us to believe." Here, once again, we see the determination to rescue a history of *subjectivity* from existing histories of *sexuality*. Haggerty's method is to focus on "intense loving relations that form the basis of a male-male intimacy" in eighteenth-century England. His breathtakingly simple but brilliant move, here as in his book *Men in Love*, is to ask what the history of male (homo)sexuality would look like if it were written from the perspective not of sex between men but of love between men. After all, as he says, "this is the history of sexuality too." I would strongly agree – even if I don't accept the critique of my own work that occasions some of Haggerty's arguments.[9]

Of course, I wouldn't like to see the history of sexuality abandon sex (nor does Haggerty propose such a thing), just as I would not want gay male studies to find in ethics, friendship, loyalty, "sworn brotherhood," voluntary kinship, fraternal bonding, intimacy, emotional closeness, family ties, the history of subjectivity, and the vicissitudes of queer affect a new alibi for downgrading or trivializing the historical study of sex and sexuality.[10] But I think that our understanding of sexuality will benefit significantly if we expand it to include within its purview the range of affective possibilities that Haggerty's and Bray's work discloses.

Not all the contributors to this volume are as explicit as Rousseau, Haggerty, and Bray in calling for a new queer history of affect. But all of the essays collected here betray a strong interest in such a history. In his own contribution, Alan Stewart analyzes the affective pull of a history of homosexuality that focuses on the history of famous homosexuals, attempting to explain the intense "popular interest in assigning sexual identities to historical figures." As he says at one point, "My question here is why it is that we still find 'homosexuals in history'? Or, more to the point: *how* do we find homosexuals in history?" Although Stewart's answer to that question is quite different from Randolph Trumbach's, the latter's attempt to differentiate historically and geographically the changing sexual systems of Europe is equally engaged with questions of human subjectivity – indeed, it is designed to produce a new map of the historical transformations in human subjectivity.

Similarly, Mario DiGangi sees different logics of affect from ours at work in the English Renaissance, and his reflections on discontinuities between past and present spring directly from his interpretative effort to discriminate premodern and modern forms of subjectivity. Nicholas Radel does what he can to recover some sense of the agency, voices, and desires of those who were branded with the identity of sodomite in England during the sixteenth and seventeenth centuries: his central question – "can the sodomite speak?" – dramatizes the persistent concern with subjectivity that runs throughout this entire volume. Finally, Jody Greene takes the sexual and emotional temperature of English neo-classicism, asking what kinds of affective relations were established, and what kinds of emotional exchanges were transacted, among male poets, translators, and critics by means of their appropriations of the figure and words of the Greek lyric poet Sappho.

The cumulative effect of these contributions is most welcome. The result, after all, is to enhance our sense of what we need to do, if we are ever to give a historically specific answer to Foucault's question, "What is it like for men to be among men … ?"

Notes

1. "Comment est-il possible pour les hommes d'être ensemble ? de vivre ensemble, de partager leur temps, leur repas, leur chambre, leurs loisirs, leur chagrins, leur savoir, leurs confidences ? Qu'est-ce que c'est que ça, être entre hommes, « à nu », hors de relations institutionnelles, de famille, de profession, de camaraderie obligée?": Jean Le Bitoux et al., "De l'amitié comme mode de vie. Un entretien avec un lecteur quinquagénaire," *Le gai pied*, 25 (April 1981), 38–9 (at 38); my translation. The French text has been reprinted in Michel Foucault, *Dits et écrits, 1954–1988*, ed. Daniel Defert and François Ewald (Paris: Gallimard, 1994), IV, pp. 163–7. An English translation by John Johnston can be found in Sylvère Lotringer, ed., *Foucault Live: Collected Interviews, 1961–1984* (New York: Semiotext(e), 1996), pp. 308–12, amended in Michel Foucault, *Ethics: Subjectivity and Truth*, ed. Paul Rabinow, *Essential Works of Foucault 1954–1984*, Vol. I (New York: Free Press, 1997), pp. 135–40. The quoted passage also receives prominent attention from the editors of this volume in their obituary for Alan Bray.

2. See Arnold I. Davidson, "Ethics as Ascetics: Foucault, the History of Ethics, and Ancient Thought," in Jan Goldstein, ed., *Foucault and the Writing of History* (Oxford: Basil Blackwell, 1994), pp. 63–80, 266–71. See also Didier Eribon, *Réflexions sur la question gay* (Paris: Fayard, 1999), pp. 372–442, translated by Michael Lucey as "Michel Foucault's Histories of Sexuality," *GLQ: A Journal of Lesbian and Gay Studies*, 7.1 (2001), 31–86.

3. Judith M. Bennett, "'Lesbian-Like' and the Social History of Lesbianisms," *Journal of the History of Sexuality* 9.1–2 (2000), 1–24. See Carroll Smith-Rosenberg, "The Female World of Love and Ritual: Relations between Women in Nineteenth-Century America," *Signs*, 1 (1975/76), 1–29, rpt. in Nancy F. Cott and Elizabeth H. Pleck, eds., *A Heritage of Her Own: Toward a New Social History of American Women* (New York: Simon & Schuster, 1979), pp. 311–42; Lillian Faderman, *Surpassing the Love of Men: Romantic Friendship and Love Between Women from the Renaissance to the Present* (New York: William Morrow, 1981).

4. Quoted by Davidson, "Ethics as Ascetics", p. 63.

5. "Homosexuality's Closet," *Michigan Quarterly Review*, 41.1 (Winter 2002), 21–54. This essay recapitulates the earlier and more eloquent argument to the same effect by D.A. Miller, *Place for Us [Essay on the Broadway Musical]* (Cambridge, MA: Harvard University Press, 1998).

6. For an early, brilliant critique of this gay tendency to distinguish between good and bad emotions, see Lee Edelman, "The Mirror and the Tank: 'AIDS,' Subjectivity, and the Rhetoric of Activism," *Homographesis: Essays in Gay Literary and Cultural Theory* (New York: Routledge, 1994), pp. 93–117, 256–60.

7. See, for example, Douglas Crimp, "Mario Montez, For Shame," in Stephen M. Barber and David L. Clark, eds, *Regarding Sedgwick: Essays on Queer Culture and Critical Theory* (New York: Routledge, 2002), pp. 57–70, who calls his project "Queer before Gay"; it was anticipated in certain respects, as Crimp himself acknowledges, by Eve Kosofsky Sedgwick, "Queer Performativity: Henry James's *The Art of the Novel*," *GLQ: A Journal of Lesbian and Gay Studies*, 1.1 (1993), 1–16.

8. "What then is my claim? I am saying, basically and in our coinage, that the triad of friendship, depression, and illness has been overlooked in the history of homosexuality" (p. 40 in this volume).

9. Since Haggerty has devoted much of his essay in this volume to contesting a highly speculative point I made in "How to Do the History of Male Homosexuality" (*GLQ: A Journal of Lesbian and Gay Studies*, 6.1 [2000], 87–124), I suppose I should say something here by way of response. First of all, since I always write in the hope of being corrected, and since I would not want to mislead other scholars, I welcome Haggerty's effort to remove my misapprehensions and to undo any false generalizations I may have made about the possibilities for male love in eighteenth-century England. His demonstration that writers of the period were able to represent same-sex relations among men in ways that sometimes combined notions of sexual activity or penetration with notions of love and friendship, and his insistence (following Randolph Trumbach) that neither sexual penetration nor male same-sex love was incompatible with notions of effeminacy, seem valuable and important to me. Without attempting to challenge his claims, which I am not competent to do, I would simply like to clarify my own

argument about the tradition of male friendship and love, which I think Haggerty has not understood and which does not seem to me to have been affected by his vigorous rejoinder.

According to Haggerty, I make "rigid distinctions" between sexual love and friendship, "[reifying] male-male relations and [making] it impossible for men who see themselves as equal to express their love for one another." I hope I have done no such thing; what I intended to do was to pluralize the history of homosexuality, to put in place a multiplicity of both homo-sexualities and histories so as to allow historians greater leeway and subtlety in differentiating among pre-homosexual versions of homosexuality and thereby to make it easier for them *not to have to conflate* love and friendship with sodomy, passivity, effeminacy, or homosexuality. I did not assert that these things never coincided before the modern period. (Thus Mario DiGangi, in his contribution to this volume [Chapter 6, note 26], observes that the nomenclature applied to the various discursive traditions I delin-eate overlaps considerably in Renaissance English texts; far from seeing that overlap as erasing the distinctiveness of the different traditions, DiGangi finds that "this discursive overdetermination helps to corroborate Halperin's theory of the synchronous existence of different pre-homosexual models in pre-modern Europe." In other words, the discursive traditions can be combined in their application to individuals without losing their discursive distinctiveness.)

In addition to indicating that my hypothesis was tentative, provisional, and heuristic, I emphasized at the outset of my argument that the different traditions or figures of pre-homosexual discourse I had identified were both separate and interrelated. I wanted those models to be flexible, not rigid; I tried to avoid reifying them. In the case of the tradition of male love or friendship, my thinking was based in no small part on the superb essay by Alan Bray and Michel Rey, "The Body of the Friend: Continuity and Change in Masculine Friendship in the Seventeenth Century," in Tim Hitchcock and Michèle Cohen, eds., *English Masculinities 1660–1800* (London: Addison Wesley Longman, 1999), pp. 65–84. (That essay wasn't cited in my article, because the latter had gone to press before the former was published, but Alan Bray had presented an earlier version of it to a study group of which I was a member, and he allowed me to draw on it.) Bray and Rey persuaded me that it would be wrong to sexualize what might look to us like expres-sions of physical love among friends before the eighteenth century and that it was during the eighteenth century that the English in particular became very uncomfortable with any physical expression of friendly feeling between males; see, on this, the earlier remarks of Lee Edelman, "The Sodomite's Tongue and the Bourgeois Body in Eighteenth-Century England," *Homographesis*, 121–8, 260–1. Haggerty's quarrel, if he really wants to have one, ought properly to be with Rey and Bray, not with me.

Furthermore, although Haggerty convincingly argues that *some* relations between men in the eighteenth century actually combined sex, friendship, and love, Alan Bray's contribution to this volume presents irrefutable evi-dence that the discursive traditions of friendship and sodomy still managed to remain hermetically separate even in eighteenth-century England: that much is plain from Bray's description of the monument marking the joint burial of Granville Piper and Richard Wise (d. 1726) in the church of St Mary Magdalene in Launceston. The fact that same-sex pairs of friends, whether male or female, had been buried together and memorialized together in English churches (both in England and in Rome) from the four-teenth century right up through to the nineteenth indicates the perennial ease with which their contemporaries were able to draw the distinction between love or friendship, on the one hand, and sodomy, on the other. For if the funerary monuments Bray describes had conveyed even the faintest suggestion that the *connubium* of friends celebrated in them had consisted in a sodomitical union, we would not find those monuments enshrined in Christian churches. I do not infer from this alone that Piper and Wise never had sex (though Bray makes a very strong claim to that effect about John Henry Newman and Ambrose St John); in most cases, I assume, the evidence does not allow us to draw any firm inferences one way or the other. But I do deduce that the *rhetoric* of friendship or love employed in those monuments succeeded in sealing off the relationships represented in them from any suggestion of being sodomitical. And that was precisely my reason for wishing to foreground the multiplicity of differ-ent discursive traditions, or models, or figures of sex and gender practices that are now subsumed by the modern paradigm of homosexuality and that now appear as among its manifold aspects.

In the revised version of "How to Do the History of Male Homosexuality," which appears in my book, *How to Do the History of Homosexuality* (Chicago: University of Chicago Press, 2002), pp. 104–37, 185–95 I qualify even further the already tentative hypotheses that Haggerty objects to, and I do so partly in order to meet some of his objec-tions (unfortunately I was not able to take account of the critique under discussion here because Haggerty did not share it with me). In particular, I allow for the possibility that the *rhetoric* of the friendship tradition could be used by dramatic characters as a cover for what the dramatists and their audiences alike might well have understood as a sexual relationship. Citing as an example Marlowe's Edward II, who says to Gaveston "Why shouldst thou kneel? knowest thou not who I am? / Thy friend, thy self, another Gaveston!" (1.1.141–42), I concede that "Dryden's Antony might be invok-ing this very precedent" (p. 121). Of course, if I am now correct in suppos-ing (following Haggerty) that Edward's or Antony's language would have been interpreted to function as a transparent cover for a sexual relationship, it would still be necessary to posit in the first place that there was a certain separation between the rhetoric of friendship and the rhetoric of sodomy, since otherwise the former could not be used to protect and dignify the latter.

In short, I'm happy to admit that the hypotheses in that article of mine are wrong: in fact, they're so general, and so historically ungrounded, that they're bound to be wrong, or at least misleading and imprecise, within the context of many different historical periods and geographic locations. And I would be delighted if others would refine my approach and apply it more concretely and more intelligently than I do. Moreover, if I held the posi-tions that Haggerty ascribes to me, his counter-argument would be devastatingly effective. As it is, I don't *think* his objections, however powerful in themselves, are actually objections to the points I was trying to make.

10. I wish to thank Elizabeth Lapovsky Kennedy for prompting me to make such a declaration. She responded sharply to my remarks during the final plenary session of "The Future of the Queer Past: a Transnational History Conference" at the University of Chicago on 17 September 2000, where Alan Bray had given an earlier version of the lecture included in this volume, and I had commented on it somewhat along the lines of my remarks here. Kennedy warned me, in effect, against succumbing to a gay male version of the cultural feminism against which historians of lesbian sexuality have had to struggle in order to prevent the sexual specificity of lesbianism from being reduced to such things as woman-identification, politically supportive alliances among women, forms of conjugality, emotional intimacy, and networks of association. I never thought I would have needed to be warned against making such a move, but I gratefully take the point.

1

"Homoplatonic, Homodepressed, Homomorbid:" Some Further Genealogies of Same-Sex Attraction in Western Civilization

George Rousseau

Cultural contexts for neologisms: Hermaphrodites and third sexes

The coining of neologisms, especially when they are polysyllabic and appear pathological to the eye, is a fraught business; all the more so when the new words seem to derive from disciplines or subject fields (philosophical, medical, historical, aesthetic). Hence my new words – homoplatonic, homodepressed, homomorbid – exist not merely in relation to the periods and intellectual movements embodying them (Renaissance, Enlightenment, Romanticism, Modernism), but with the goal of recognizing what actually occurred in history: that is, the neologisms are acknowledgments of responsibility so that the world will never forget what transpired in the suffering and injustice done to homosexuals; the neologisms are windows to memory – especially memory of the maladies of persons attracted to their own sex. We coiners (myself included, of course) do so additionally for heuristic purposes: the dream of opening up the borders between diversely perceived sexualities – categories other than "straight" and "bi" and "gay" that enable sexuality's remarkable fluidity. Otherwise, responsibility is subverted and sexual history, and medical history, become too hard to explain as well as difficult to write. We coin these expressions fully aware that the neologisms may sound as forbidding as the old generic words: if "homosexual" were not, for example, such a charged word in English, conjuring images of disease and biological pathology, it might have proved much less offensive in the last century. How much sweeter to be – the blissfully old-fashioned – gay.[1]

The critical epistemological issue is whether cultural history can be written without any labels and classifications that are historically and culturally framed. That is, whether it can be meaningfully claimed that biographical subject A was individual in the following ways without resorting to the use of any labels or classifications. As soon as the latter enter, all sorts of questions about them arise, including their origins, contexts, social milieu, political agendas, and so forth. An example of these labels and classifications occurs in the genesis of the nostalgia diagnosis. In the year of the Glorious Revolution, 1688, an obscure Alsatian military doctor, Dr Johannes Hofer, coined the neologism "nostalgia:" from *nostos*, the Greek root for home, and *algia*, the pain or malady of endurance. In a blink a new illness based on yearning for the home, homesickness, was born.[2] Hofer did this, in part, for a pedagogical purpose: to help others to "see" better; see, that is, within the classical standard scientific picture of knowledge. Homesickness had existed long before 1688: Greek shepherds piped about it, as did Renaissance pastoralists, but medical "nostalgia" – the diagnosis, that is – was unknown because the word did not exist. But the new word was defective and over three centuries has caused more confusion than it ever intended. By the period of the French Revolution – a mere hundred years after the coinage – nostalgia had accreted many synonyms (for example not merely variants of homesickness such as love of the mother country but metonymies and euphemisms for patriotism and national dedication). And by 1918, at the end of the Great War, the classification Hofer originally coined to describe homesickness was being christened, and confused with, the new "war neurosis."[3] Hofer's coinage was limited to the sick soldiers he examined; he found no name for their constellation of syndromes in medical literature. Within two generations – by the mid-eighteenth century – nostalgia took off as a new medical diagnosis of *military illness*, and, within a century, was extended far beyond military malady into the realms of philosophical aesthetics and, still more broadly, into the frames of mind in which people could popularly describe themselves as being.[4] Nostalgia for the past became a mode of consciousness among broad types of Romantic thinkers – the German nature philosophers, the Wordsworths and Coleridges, post-revolutionary utopians – craving terrestrial and paradisiacal homes. Hence what started as a medical term in Alsace culminated in an aesthetic ideology.

Equally spectacular in these coinages, whose relevance for homosexual knowledge will soon become evident, was the rise of the nerves in the popular imagination. The anatomical nerves, fibers, and animal spirits, which heralded a post-Cartesian epistemology of body and mind, by the eighteenth century had given rise to a new identity and subjectivity called "nervous."[5] This was not merely the anatomical discoveries of "nerves" and their relation to the brain, as in Thomas Willis's touted discoveries in the seventeenth century, but an infiltration of nervous anatomy into Lockean epistemology and Humean skepticism about selfhood. Within one generation (1690–1730) "nervous diseases' became the most fashionable of all British maladies, an impossible attainment without the new category; and human subjectivity was newly reconceptualized according to the metaphoric lines of all things "nervous." Dr. James McKittrick Adair, a prominent Scottish physician flourishing at mid-century who was a pivotal figure for relating nervous personality types to social rank and class, explained how the neologism "nervous" had spread like wild fire, dating the rampage exactly, if cheekily, to 1764:

> Upwards of thirty years ago, a treatise of nervous diseases was published by my quondam learned and ingenious preceptor DR [ROBERT] WHYTT, professor of physick, at Edinburgh. Before the publication of this book, people of fashion had not the least idea that they had nerves; but a fashionable apothecary of my acquaintance, having cast his eye over the book, and having been often puzzled by the inquiries of his patients concerning the nature and causes of their complaints, derived from thence a hint, by which he readily cut the Gordian knot – "Madam, you are nervous"; the solution was quite satisfactory, the NEW term [nervous] became quite fashionable, and spleen, vapours, and hyp, were ALL forgotten.[6]

I cannot expect my triple alliance of neologisms to catch on in this firebrand way or become socially fashionable. I will be satisfied if the assessors of these neologisms, and the energy underpinning them, have compassion on the intellectual frustration I have experienced in trying to do my historical work without them. It must also be acknowledged from the outset that the main agenda is to undermine pathological typology and the ability of cultures and individuals to characterize homosexuality as some sort of alien, aberrant condition far inferior to heterosexual superiority. This agenda should not be incompatible with the historian's dream of accurately capturing and describing aspects of the past. The neologisms work to permit a more adequate, and certainly more complete, social history of same-sex relations than we have had so far. They permit us to see (what we would call) homosexuality as something far more complex than a narrowly medical or pathological condition. The agenda locates the historian's own current perspective and moral affiliation and even helps to understand why this project has been undertaken. But the combination of historical enterprise and agenda does not prevent him from accepting limitation and acknowledging defect – in this case the recognition that an ideal reconstruction of this material would have been far more Darwinian than I have been able to demonstrate here. As Ernst Mayr and other Darwinian exponents have explained, Darwinism undermines all fixed, typological thought of the type I invoke below, and replaces it with population thinking focused on individual variation and uniqueness.[7] Hence my categories and their neologisms – homoplatonic, homomorbid, etc. – ultimately seem to work *against* my agenda by reinscribing these stereotypes. What is to be done in this predicament?

The fundamental epistemological issue here is whether it is practicable to think that we can exist without classifying human beings according to sexual types *altogether*. Surely the matter is one of degree. I am suggesting that, although we cannot do that, equally we cannot dispense with the classification altogether as an irrelevancy, hence the issue of degree. A middle zone exists in which we aim to explain people as individuals rather than as members (for example) of racial, sexual, political, or other types. Moreover, we aim for this middle state based on individual differentiation aware that we largely fail, just as we know that most of the time we fail to be rational and logical creatures. The historian, however – especially the historian of sexualities – also aspires to explain people as individuals rather than classify them merely as representatives of groups or types; but soon learns that the group exerts its pressures everywhere – "no man is an island." What is he to do at this seeming impasse between history (what actually happened to people) and Darwinian necessity (forever working against the typological stereotypes these people in history fixed)? Surely Darwinians can accept the frailties of the past and empathize with the historian's dilemma in wishing, on the one hand, to describe them as fully as possible, while aspiring on the other to recognizing individual uniqueness apart from the stereotype. The fact that I am clearly unable to achieve such radical democratization does not invalidate, it seems to me, my ideal politico-moral goal of dispensing with the classification of human beings according to choice of sexual object.

My neologisms – homoplatonic, homodepression, homomorbid – provide properties sufficient to distinguish these entities from others outside the class. In this provision they seem to detract from themselves by delimiting the class itself; that is, they fix each class (homoplatonic) and render it static and thereby capable of further stereotyping. But I *also* claim that heteronormative assumptions omit the degree to which their subjects partake of these very same attributes.[8] That is, the numbers of allegedly heterosexual historical figures who were also implicated in these arrangements ranging from friendship and education to depression and illness. Herein therefore lie the more fluid state of sexuality and the undermining of homosexuality's pathology that constitute the basic agenda. Most heteronormative historians and biographers are loath to concede that their subjects (their figures) were "pathological" precisely because they shared attributes of their lives in homoplatonic or homodepressed conditions. These heteronormative historians and biographers may concede, for example, that their figure's all-male tutorial arrangements (one thinks of Thomas Hobbes, John Locke, many other Oxbridge scholars) partook of the attributes of homoplatonism, or that their subject's depression originated in sexual deprivation almost identical to the variety suffered in homosexual frustration. But they are loath to take the extra step to acknowledge what small distance lies between heteroplatonic and homoplatonic varieties, or between heterodepressed and homodepressed maladies.[9] As I will suggest below, the distance between a homodepressed Gray (who probably was homosexual) and a heterodepressed William Collins (who probably was heterosexual) is much less than it would seem to be. And by rendering these gaps smaller we reduce the distance between competing sexualities and render sexuality itself more fluid.

Now the abandonment of my neologisms would not advance my agenda *provided* – a crucial proviso – it is made perfectly clear that the neologisms exist to enable better understanding of the protagonists, poets such as Thomas Gray, Mark Akenside, and Collins, each with his customized biography; that is, the neologisms in the service of recapturing the individual. If we can understand that the distance – as just explained – between a homodepressed Gray and a heterodepressed Collins was much less than has been thought, we may comprehend both figures more fully.[10] We may also understand, thus, that sexual fluidity in history has been grossly underestimated by heteronormative cultural scholars and historians of sexualities. What are we to make, for example, of menstruating males and cross-dressed macho-male soldiers in history?[11] Conversely, what do we make of flagellating but otherwise prissy "femme" women and other females persuaded they had penises,[12] or of heterosexual men endowed by nature with large lactating breasts, and homosexual men who dream of making love to males possessed of both penises *and* breasts?[13] Or adult women with large external sexual organs? The examples proliferate into the dozens, as any competent psychoanalyst who has listened to the dreams and fantasies of her or his patients can confirm.

Furthermore, the continuities I have teased out of the early (pre-1800) modern world segue into our own postmodern one and struggle without them; at least they are harder to explain without noticing them. Let us consider some examples that necessarily straddle the broad chronology 1500–1900, symmetrically framed on both sides by the crucial eighteenth-century Enlightenment. It is not true, for instance, that a "sodomitical species" suddenly sprang full blown in the aftermath of Darwin's *Origin of Species* in 1859. A century earlier, the Augustan bluestocking and radical intellectual Lady Mary Wortley Montagu had wittily quipped about Lord Hervey's being a member of a "third sex," and even if she intended nothing phylogenetically serious, let alone systematic, she nevertheless harbored an inkling about another type of human creature.[14] Yet Wilmarth S. Lewis, the potentate baron of Walpole manuscripts at Farmington, in Connecticut, suppressed her comment in his edition. He did this because it might begin to sully Horace Walpole's then entrenched heterosexual profile. Hence the categorical and the political, in my analysis, converge here. Earlier than Lady Mary, however, the seventeenth-century legal scholar Paolo Zacchias – author of the some of the earliest forensic works dealing with the jurisprudence of sodomy – also speculated about the possibility of another "species" when aiming to prove that sodomy, or penetration of the anus, had occurred. What did not exist either in the mindset of Zacchias or Montagu, separated by a century, was *coherent* scientization or medicalization of the homosexual. This arose after the 1860s: in the decades of Benkerts and Westphal and Ulrichs, and other early sexologists. And it is as myopic to omit the continuities before and after as to think we can perform deep-layer analysis (in anthropologist Clifford Geertz's sense of "thick analysis") without resorting to labels and categories to help us.[15]

Now the pre-1840 ontological status of this "third sex" is mysterious, haphazard, and fragmentary. Certainly no one taking the long view could compile a coherent view of its existence before 1600. Some embodiments of it had been made in the image of the hermaphrodite, which was itself a sub-species of the monster. Monsters had been conceptualized from time immemorial, and ordinarily existed in a juridical, as well as magical, profile: that is, in relation to sets of laws which they violated, even if their transgressions were universally committed against the "laws of nature." Throughout early-modern history – the

Middle Ages, early Renaissance, even the late Renaissance – cultures had privileged one monstrous type over another, as Lorraine Daston and Katherine Park demonstrated in *Wonders and the Order of Nature*,[16] and Foucault noticed that the early classical age superimposed the hermaphrodite on to the imprint of earlier monstrosities to provide proof of pathology.[17] Zacchias explains these superimpositions in his *Quaestiones Medico-Legales*, published in Leiden in 1655, which was revised and reprinted in the early eighteenth century. Nevertheless, no matter how hermaphrodites were then imagined, mentally internalized, or symbolically pictured, it was always as an abnormal, disordered, pathological creature, combining two elements that did not belong together. The hermaphrodite, the precursor of the "third sex," was already incommensurate. By 1612 Jacques Duval, a professor of medicine in the University of Montpellier, classified women with huge clitorises, "as thick as a virile member," as hermaphroditical monsters in need of restoration to conventional health.[18] Zacchias also dwelled on the hermaphrodite's anatomical deviance, suggesting that hermaphroditical bodies – internal and external, intruding and extruding – were mischievously disjointed. Deviant in this or that anatomical way (the argument went), they pursued aberrant acts. Any number of cases had proved the connection long before Herculine Barbin's in mid-nineteenth-century Paris.

Over time the monstrous hermaphrodite evolved into a different, more anatomically and psychologically complex, type of creature. The juridico-natural cupola of Zacchias' mid-seventeenth-century configurations emerged in the eighteenth century as a new species precisely because of its sexual behavior. That is, the hermaphrodite was a transgressive monster and hence another "species"; not merely on anatomico-somatic grounds but also, and now more crucially, because of his behavior. Given the intimate yoking of morality to behavior in high Enlightenment philosophical thought (both British and Continental), it is not surprising that the sodomite's new crime (new, that is, in the world after Zacchias) should not be merely his imperfect soma (body being so out of joint with soul), but also his treasonable behavior in committing sodomitical actions. This background from 1650–1750, from Zacchias to Lady Mary, this new classical sense of "species" derivative from the discourse of monstrosity, informed Foucault's magisterial if controversial claim near the beginning of *The History of Sexuality, Volume One*. And Foucault extended the chronology from 1750 forward to the emergence of the "third sex" in the Darwinian world: "Homosexuality appeared as one of the forms of sexuality when it was transposed from the practice of sodomy onto a kind of interior androgyny, a hermaphrodism of the soul. The sodomite had been a temporary aberration; the homosexual was now a species."[19]

The "third sex" (not yet homosexual in our sense) was now – sometime after c.1750 and before c.1860 – a "species." But "when" did the "aberration" evolve into the "species?" When was when? These are not questions which can be answered with chronological laser-precision because classifications and the types on which they are based do not occur overnight. Hence my need for neologisms (crude as they are) and their related categories to help explain the interstices between these multiple transformations. The historian of sexuality knows that both aberration (the monstrous) and newly perceived species (the hermaphrodite) had been available religiously, legalistically, and discursively long before Zacchias speculated juridically about fallen species in need of amelioration.

Historically, this no-man's land lay approximately in the first half of the nineteenth century. This was the troubled era Foucault seems to have borne in mind when positing his genealogical birth of the new species. Before c.1750 the "third sex" was still imbricated in a demonic-religious axis, as the law cases and police records of the age demonstrate.[20] After c.1860 many types of post-Darwinian species (urnings, Uranians, Dorians) were said to have been evolving in the effort to prove that a "third sex" – always fundamentally male despite hermaphroditic parts – exists. But it was conceptualized as inferior, weak, rarely as a competitor to normative heterosexual types. The historical epoch encompassing c.1750–1840 (this intentionally to remove the problematic Darwin) in Western Europe is a strange, post-Walpolian, pre-Darwinian country, coinciding with the biographical life spans of such figures as Matthew Lewis, William Beckford, Lord Byron, and Samuel Taylor Coleridge (similar figures could be named, of course, in France and Germany: Astolfe de Custine and Johann Friedel, the radical author and Jacobin social critic, for example, although there are many others, including those gathered around the great composer Franz Schubert in Vienna). Yet the astonishing fact of biographical and literary history is that a trinity of heightened friendship, depression, and illness reigned in the lives of virtually all these figures (Gray as well as Schubert). These had already been found earlier, for example in the magisterial friendships of the Walpolian group playfully called the "Quadruple Alliance" (eventually paired off into imaginary couples of two – Walpole, Gray, Richard West, Thomas Ashton – and later imitated by Byron and his school chums); in the pervasive maladies of almost all creative spirits from Beckford and Henry Fuseli in that age when genius itself had to be expressed as malady incarnated; and especially as *mental* malady when the sick ailed for reasons they knew not and because they could not point to any place in their body. Hence a cluster of three defining attributes which were not inherent in the era's Geist, no matter how fashionable these practices and behaviors may have become, but as lived experiences of flesh-and-blood people.[21]

These strands of thought must be disentangled in relation to the neologisms. The point is *not* that the transformative period 1750–1840 has been understudied within the larger curve of sexuality. All sorts of good work exist.[22] It is rather that the era, having been viewed as less transformative than the previous one (1660–1750) and the subsequent one (1860–1900), has lain in some neglect *vis-à-vis* these three components: friendship, illness, depression. Comb the historiography and you discover much less about these topics than you think. For depression almost nothing exists – hence the likelihood that the categories themselves have been perceived as defective, too difficult to explain, or lacking in breadth and relevance. My goal in pursuing the constellation of friendship, depression, and illness therefore is both historical and clarificatory of the concepts themselves: that is, what depression is within a historical era and whether we can generate a subdivision called "homodepression" that substantively amounts to more than depression with a prefix. Likewise for categories such as platonic and morbid. The main concern is to contribute to the history of homosexuality from the Greeks onward, as in Foucault's unfinished projects. For whatever else the pre-1860 homosexual was ontologically and epistemologically – whether monstrous in one incarnation or biologically evolving in another – he was also (I intentionally generalize here from the male condition rather than the female, which has had a different trajectory) deviant and pathological. And throughout this early modern period, from approximately 1600 forward, it appeared to the rest of society that his friendships, depressions, and illnesses were in some fundamental sense pathological and deviant. Some, today, would claim they still are.

Homoplatonism

Homoplatonism is an inclusive term I coined two decades ago to describe a complex set of arrangements primarily evident in same-sex discipleship and tutelage, and the friendships and other licit and illicit relations arising from these arrangements and their cultural practices.

Homoplatonic orientation was an approach to experience that covered a broad spectrum of human arrangements and – when reflecting on those arrangements – disciplinary relationships. Discipleship remains the most difficult concept among these filiations because its cultural forms touch on everything significant to the development of males ranked according to class or guild or profession. Yet discipleship is also fundamental to education, patronage, mentorship, preferment, diplomacy, and many other varieties of the early modern work-place and its ethical codes. History, in whatever form or national approach, is unthinkable without discipleship; yet, the category itself has no substantial profile despite a significant discursive past because its status has been so fraught. Discipleship could be demonstrated to be problematic in Darwin's world; it became almost impossible to discuss after Freud's sexual revolution, let us say, or during the Third Reich or in McCarthy's America.

The historicizing of homoplatonism renders a useful heuristic category capable of explaining arrangements too difficult, or obscure, through the lenses of other terms. It subscribes to local, that is, rather than transhistorical views of cultures and societies. Homoplatonism differs from male-female "platonic love" in several crucial categories, as can be gleaned in the imitative Clio and Strephon epistolary correspondence.[23] Homoplatonism may antedate its northern European derivative varieties; yet is still broader than Catholic or Protestant versions. Homoplatonism invites comparative forms of discipleship in the Platonic world, as well as later Western European commercial and industrial cultures. Within the domain of same-sex relationships, we lose sight of early homoplatonism if we generalize from only England or France. Forbidden Florentine friendships during the Renaissance had defined themselves, in part, on an intense discipleship that flourished in secret, erotic bonds unimaginable by women.[24] So too all-male friendship in other early microcosmic cultures under different national settings: courts, academies, guilds, colleges, monasteries, the military. Yet today discipleship is not retained as a category: stable, unstable, or otherwise. We have neither a history of discipleship nor – in the Foucaldian sense – an archaeology of its arrangements.[25] When the late Thomas Gould, Dodds Professor of Classical Philosophy at Yale University, proposed a blueprint for it by disentangling the origins and genealogy of Platonic love, his work fell flat off the press. It may be that the neglect was owing to unattractive presentation but this is unlikely. *Platonic Love* is a tightly argued philosophical study written by a world-class Plato scholar.[26] On publication it was read by Platonists and largely ignored by others.[27]

Later, in the 1970s and 1980s, historians of sexuality and friendship failed to retrieve it. Gould – if I may momentarily speak autobiographically – was my teacher of Greek at Amherst College before he moved to Yale, and it was from his book, which I read on publication while a graduate student of Classics at Princeton, that I developed the concept "homoplatonic" many years later. Yet even then, in 1963–4, it struck me that anyone studying the classics – Juvenal, Martial, Ovid, and especially Plato – would be seen as interested in same-sex attachments. I ought to have realized, but did not, that these "Platonic attachments" were especially vulnerable to labeling and could be mistaken for homosexuality, for Plato had developed them at length in his *Phaedrus*. But at that time I still entertained a genderless notion of these "Platonic attachments" that did not develop conceptually and ripen, as it were, for my work until much later.

I still remember the excitement of my first reading of Gould, before the appearance of any of Foucault's major works. Gould sought to unpack a troubled category: the cultural construction of the disciple (the ancient Greek μαθητης – *mathétés*) and the condition of discipleship. The condition became unwieldy after the Industrial Revolution, Gould noticed, because Victorian Platonism, however homoerotic, was something else; altogether different from its earlier versions. Earlier discipleship inscribed the older man and younger follower, legitimized trust, prescribed surrender, parental approbation, and encouraged remote travels. Here in the figure of the *mathétés* – the instructor or mentor – was a fundamental aspect of much later homosexuality; institutionalized attachment thriving on relations between older and younger men in the post-Greek world; barely resembling those relations of the *erastes* and *eromenos*, yet whose dynamics and codes remained secret. Versions of its memory endured into modern times. For example, George Haggerty has offered a reading of Thomas Gray's "Sonnet on the Death of Richard West" which acknowledges my concept of homoplatonism to illustrate that Gray's "elegiac loss" in the poem "is actual physical longing and frustrated physical desire."[28] Gray was steeped in classical literature and philosophy, especially its amatory and erotic differences from the commercial hustle and bustle of mid-Georgian England.

But what has become of homoplatonism? As a term or concept it does not exist. Even as a concept it seems to have been subsumed into the broad realms of homoerotic and homosexual desire.[29] Only its versions of friendship have retained some of their originally alien (alien to us today, that is) nature and the strange intensity of its affect. We cultivate friendship without any of the moral or ethical edge so crucial in its Grecian (Plato in the *Republic* and *Lysias*) or Roman (Cicero in *De Amicitia*) versions. A century ago German sexologist Otto Weininger commented that friendship was the marking characteristic of inversion: "A person who retains from early onwards a marked tendency to 'friendship' with a person of his own sex must have a strong taint of the other sex in him."[30] Hence the proof of difference: the idea had been developing ever since the Renaissance. An invert, or deviant (French and German used other terms, some polite, others not), was consequently someone in possession of a superabundance of the *opposite* sex. Proof for Weininger lay specifically in the degree of *craving* for this friendship with the same-sex person, and despite his having no neologism at hand Weininger seems to have been groping for one. Moreover, his all-male friendship refers not so much to (what we call) homosexual desire but to the sexual *frisson* present in *all* friendships, a position held throughout Western traditions more or less continuously since Platonic times. Homoplatonism permits these sexual tensions to be acknowledged by differentiating levels of intensity without genital undulation (here the metaphor of oscillation is more apt than I have space to elucidate). It endorses their creativity and the way they enhance masculinity and foster the artistic temperament. By Gray's period one could even say that homoplatonism permitted the poet to define himself against the grain of the rest of his culture. And whatever else homoplatonism was, it was based on same-sex desire: this was its supremely energizing element.

The homoplatonic imperative also magnified the tutor, or governor, who already existed in a mature form in the Platonic academy as the *paidágogos*. His educative role in Ancient Greece was brilliantly recreated after the Second World War by Harvard classicist Werner Jaeger in *Paidea* (1948).[31] The *paidágogos* deployed systems of sexuality as intermediary between the family and the state, and in this task ran parallel to the *paidaphiléo* who was fond of boys; a role continuing into the Middle Ages,[32] which endured into early Christianity as a quasi-clerical type well after the Renaissance.[33] This is the pedagogical tutor Foucault fleetingly mentions in his chapter on "The Deployment of Sexuality" in *The History of Sexuality, Volume One*, referring in a brief note to the eighteenth-century German playwright Jakob Michael Lenz (1751–92), the friend of Goethe and sentimental Wertherian gaper who was celibate, clerical, obsessed by soldiers and "forest brothers" (the *waldbrüden* about whom he wrote a play), as well as a comedy entitled *The Tutor* (1772) that satirizes essential strands of homoplatonism. Demented in his own *storm und drang* Lenz suffered a breakdown in 1777–8 at the age of 26. He placed himself in the care of a country pastor, Johannes Oberlin, who treated his patient by calming his delusions and quelling his hallucinations. But Lenz threw himself out of an upstairs window, which stirred Oberlin to commit him to the mental asylum in Strasbourg. Here Lenz existed in alternating states of catatonic excitement punctuated by periodic withdrawal – identified by Kraepelin in the 1880s as the signs of classic schizophrenia – but eventually discharged himself. Lenz then wandered the length of Europe from Germany to Russia in a type of fugue state of mind (the illness of wanderers) until his death almost four years later in 1792: an enlightened but nevertheless maniacal *vagrantus*, he was found dead one night on a Moscow street, like Thomas Chatterton in England or Johann Joachim Winckelmann in Italy; perhaps a suicide or murdered by some Russian Arcangeli. To this day his death, like his insanity, remains shrouded in mystery, his sexuality anything but normatively heterosexual.[34]

The tutor was often ordained, statistically celibate, educated, economically in the perpetual search of sinecures in a social system in which the country house offered him a more secure living than schools, and where universities were closed to him. The tutor was typically employed by a landed family to educate their son(s) into "gentlemen." This was the world of Hobbes' tutors and Locke's (Anthony Shaftesbury was the exception); of Beckford's tutors too, the Robert Drysdales and John Lettices, both clerics who practiced a type of modified homoplatonism. Some of its social arrangements spilled over into the female world, as parodied and described by Sarah Fielding in *The Governess* (1759). Tutors, however, could and often did marry, and – in rich families with large houses – were given accommodation for their wives and children; yet most tutors remained celibate, whether as the result of economic circumstance, temperament, dedication to mistresses, or uninterrupted learning. When the Grand Tour became fashionable, the tutor (sometimes called the "governour") accompanied his tutees, or wards, often remaining with them for months, sometimes years, on the Continent.[35] The tutor was in charge: he plotted the tutee's movements, corresponded with the family, dispersed finances, ate and slept with the boys, spending days and nights in the same room with them. No Freudian psychohistory is necessary to disentangle the intimate attachments and tensions embedded in these older man-younger man arrangements. The condition was an existential hotbed for intense friendship that could not have developed on native soil in homes presided over by strict fathers and uncles, or mothers and aunts.

One such traveling group in the mid-eighteenth century was led by tutor Andrew Baxter (a minor Scottish philosopher from Glasgow whose works Coleridge immersed himself in, and came under the influence of), and his charges, John Hay and the young Lord Blantyre and several others.[36] Baxter's group traveled to Holland where in Leiden they linked up with poet-physician Mark Akenside and his patron-friend Jeremiah Dyson, as well as the young John Wilkes of political reform fame, and the aristocratic, if then tearfully sentimental, young Paul Henri, Baron D'Holbach, later to become the celebrated *philosophe*. Here they formed themselves into a small all-male university club whose members wrote gushing letters to each other for years after congregating in Leiden. Early in the 1980s I reconstructed the club from archival sources in England and Holland, tentatively conjecturing (my conclusion was framed entirely as speculation) that its arrangements were "homosocial" rather than "homoplatonic" – that is, one degree *beyond* homoplatonic in a spectrum of same-sex friendships ranging from the purely platonic based on mutual interest devoid of romantic attachment, through the palpably homoerotic, to the genitally explicit homosexual. There was no evidence of genital physical contact, although the "embraces" in the letters suggested an abundance of touch. My conjecture would have been mauled less if I had ceased at the homoplatonic edge, apparently a less fraught category for heteronormative male scholars persuaded of their proprietorship over historical figures.[37] My "homoerotic" speculation touched a nerve: *en masse* they pounced on the reconstruction, claiming that I had miscopied this word or misquoted from that manuscript source. The larger political agenda was to quash any speculation about the sexual fluidity of their subjects. There is no more guaranteed route to being attacked in print than to challenge entrenched views about the sexuality of established, even canonical, male figures.[38]

A second crucial aspect of homoplatonism is friendship: friendship in clubs, societies, fraternities, universities, schools, the military, at sea, as well as its representations of same-sex relations in the fiction of adolescence. Male friendship in early modern history has been, of course, less tabooed than discipleship. For all-male friendship is less vulnerable, can dare to be less covert, may even be publicly declared rather more openly than the murderously treacherous discipleship. One thinks of the famous discipleships in history that evolved into rival

Oedipal enmities; not merely the Freuds and Jungs, or anti-Lacanians against the Father, but also less well-known figures of the early modern world. Our histories of friendship, not so different from the interdicted accounts of discipleship, have rarely been brave enough to tell the truth because the models they assume are also normatively heterosexist.[39] Only feminists have broken this barrier, perhaps because the stakes for women in history, until recently, have been lower. "Homoplatonism" then is an admittedly imperfect category: a zone aiming to bring these convergences to the surface and explicitly conjoin overlaps of discipleship and friendship (into whose nexus we today would include most versions of mentorship in the work-place). The concept seeks to clear space to retrieve something now lost in the sphere between discipleship and friendship. And the overlaps have produced impediments for any sustained history of friendship. "Homoplatonic" – the category and word – fills some of the spaces without the perception of working on an interdicted border. Some biographical friendships have been well described, as have pairs of friendships in discrete historical periods: each of us can produce favorite examples.[40] But the old conceptions eschewed any mention of erotic fluidity or double-interest: the tutor who loves his wife and dutifully provides for his children, but who *also* reserves his mental energy and romantic ardor for the male students with whom he has passionate friendships conducted at a high temperature of emotional attachment; or the student, or traveler (like Gray and Walpole and their entourage in Italy, or Akenside and Dyson traveling together in Holland), who can alter his persona once he has crossed the Alps. "Homoplatonism," however admittedly imperfect, does not narrow the space between homoerotic and homosocial, or seek to create a bridge between them; rather, through dual energies of discipleship and friendship it acknowledges the vital presence of discursive subjectivity (letters, diaries, poetry, Gothic fictions *à la* Matthew "Monk" Lewis, and so on.). A plenitude of languages taught and learned; languages found in books and the quasi-secret code-dialects used among those, like Gray and Walpole, who had formed charged, emotional attachments. If homoplatonism taps into anything vital, it suggests that historical same-sex collaborations and adolescent friendships were constructed around the bodies of texts no less than physical bodies. "Homoplatonism" privileges language both in discipleship and friendship because it assumes that language, especially conversation, gets coded to kindle desire. A homoplatonic Byron in adolescence explains the omitted side of Byron in Greek love, the feature invested in discipleship.[41]

Homodepression

Psychological depression has become a household concept in our era because Western culture needed some signpost to denote its anxiety over a new threshold of stress. The word itself expanded its horizons in the nineteenth century, but was still restricted to specialized medical spheres. Since the 1970s it has perfectly captured the human predicament most emblematic of, if also problematic for, our health-care practitioners and work-place managers: how to survive it. The antidepressant era, as a contemporary has labeled our age, is our malady par excellence:[42] the supreme condition of the postmodern, which, eventually, its historians (in the plural in so far as there are many depressions which will require many histories) will annotate.[43] Postmodern alienation is unthinkable without its attendant, broad-winged depression. But depression, like its distant cousins discipleship and friendship, has thus far bred inchoate, fragmentary genealogies of its diverse pasts.

In the centuries before Freud, it was construed by theorists as melancholia, black bile, hysteria, vapours, spleen, low spirits, a vast range of male erotomanias and female monomanias, as well as the nervous maladies, neurasthenias, and lunacies configured by such early doctors as Thomas Willis and George Cheyne, down through William Battie and Philippe Pinel to Jean Martin Charcot and the Paris psychiatrists of the Third Republic. Since Freud and Melanie Klein depression has incorporated the "low spirits" of SAD, rampant work-place stress, and a broad range of neurochemical disorders and genetic defects, which now epidemically ravage postmodern societies. But depression's cultural contexts have been far too narrow nor has it been historicized. Same-sex depression I call "homodepressed" because I want a category *confined* to same-sex arrangements for the purposes of further elucidation; one which clears space, bears respectability, and merits research, no less than female maladies or children's illnesses in history, and because (it has seemed to me as a student of illness in history) same-sex depressions – homodepressions – have been different. We need a category of depression where the "lowness" has arisen primarily as the result of a same-sex predicament and its social interdictions. The basic assumption in "homodepression" is that alienated and disaffected minds make their bodies sick. Not all same-sex lovers, of course, were afflicted by homodepression and it is folly to deny, to the contrary, that some same-sex arrangements were manifestly *empowered* and vitally *energized* by their difference.[44] That is, the opposite of my homodepression has often been the biographical fact: a psychology of jouissance rather than misery among lovers. Their sexual difference, social obliquity, even moral-religious transgression energized these lovers, as individuals and as a unit, and often gave meaning to what otherwise could have been emotionally inchoate lives. The history of music (Benjamin Britten and Peter Pears) and painting (Mapplethorpe and his lovers) brims with such exhilarating creatures. But the past is a diverse country permeated with figures whose bodies and minds withered and dessicated as a consequence of their sexual attraction. This is what the heteronormatists have been unwilling to concede. Not all same-sex sorrow was turned to triumph. We have as yet no comprehensive, synthetic post-Renaissance histories of depression; even if they existed it would be patent what a toll same-sex attraction has taken on human mental health over the centuries. Unrelenting despair caused by an attraction that could not be named, and in most cases remaining unconscious even to the lovers themselves. It is a desolate record to retrieve and commemorate, but its voices lie in state waiting to be heard and deserving of remembrance. Same-sex depressions have been historically understudied: neglected from the 1620s milieu of the *Anatomy of Melancholy*, through the rise of Gray's aggravated morbid "leucocholy" and Lord Hervey's very strangely psychosomatic "Account of My Own Constitution and Illness..."[45]

We need a category sufficiently *broad* to deal with the forms of dejection experienced by those whose same-sex aspirations failed and invaded their health. The condition long antedated Oscar Wilde's "love that hath no name" to turn sick on itself. Homodepression unmasks a range of possibilities to account for same-sex suffering *without* permitting this historical retrieval to inscribe the homosexual as pathological deviant, or suppress the many "healthy" homosexuals in history (Gray clearly was not one) – a suffering retentive of its socio-economic realities without suppressing the often fatal (and sometimes comic) blow of gender. The emphasis in our historical retrieval must shift, in part, from broad disease classification (depression) to the actual experience of sexually based dejection itself (hence the narrower but more specific homodepression); from a heteronormative assumption that anguish in history, including the vast range of mental illness, is gender-free or at least that it has not been worth retrieving and commemorating. Under certain conditions germs and viruses may be immune to gender-trouble (Judith Butler's wonderful construction that continues to resound in the early twenty-first century): in maladies such as influenza and heart disease. But even in cholera and tuberculosis gender historically played a major role, especially in the way women were demonized by its early theorists, not to resurrect the much more obviously gender-bound group of melancolias and depressions in which the disappointments over same-sex love weakened the biographical figure to the point of despair and suicide. By suggesting that such a category as homodepression can be useful for erecting the possibility of same-sex lover-based depression, every effort must be made to resist reinscribing the newly found homodepressive as a pathological figure comparable to the old homosexual; from ascribing stigma merely as the result of pathology. The culprit is our lack of toleration for the Other: that old enemy, difference and dissimilarity. For the *raison d'etre* of the new category – homodepression – is restoration of the voices of the afflicted; just as the last generation of historians of medicine retrieved the patient as a legitimate category of inquiry without stigmatizing him, and whereas previous medicine had consisted almost exclusively of doctors and maladies, as if patients were inconsequential. We have moved on from the Freudian days when homosexuals could *only* be sick: deviants to be converted in psychotherapy to traditional morality. Furthermore, the history of medicine has made giant strides in the last two generations, explaining huge chunks of the past that lay neglected in this particular domain. By tapping into the maladies of the pre-Prousts of the early modern world – figures from Alexander Pope and Gray to William Cowper and Byron – we do not hurl opprobrium, any more so than when we discuss the needs of our disabled and deformed. The curious among us want to discover how the "homodepressed" became patients before our coinages: what were the mechanisms and processes? What the conditions and settings interlinking sex and patienthood? Most of their biographers have underestimated the toll taken by homodepression, until recently, even for Marcel Proust, literature's most famous homosexual patient.[46]

The range of homodepression's maladies has no name, so far no subcategory of explanation. Homodepression, despite its self-evident constraints, jolts us to explore and excavate new possibilities for our figures. Think merely of the toll it took on the great poet Pope, whose maladies were as predictable as his sexuality was unfixed: everywhere an unhinged and ambiguous masculinity, empowering his creativity while sorely diminishing his health. Homodepression was the male nightshade of female neurasthenia in the world from Mary Wollstonecraft and Charlotte Smith to the troubled women Elaine Showalter retrieved in *The Female Malady*.[47] Homodepression seeks to establish (among other pressing concerns) which doctors in history rendered their male patients physically and mentally worse than they were before. It does so no less fervidly than our feminists who have identified and exposed the deleterious panaceas of physicians who harmed women over many centuries: doctors such as the American Silas Weir Mitchell (1829–1914) of "Yellow Wallpaper" notoriety who isolated his depressed women such as Charlotte Perkins Gilman, and sent them to bed for years, while telling them never again to read a book or take a pencil in hand. Who were the Mitchells ministering to the homodepressed? – not merely treating them injuriously in the eras of Gray and Byron but more recently as medicine has continued to claim it is "enlightened"?

Homodepression thus constitutes a domain of continuity over generations. In one sense it is the lowness, especially the attendant physical disability that results from the sufferer's status as a same-sex lover; a response to real-life conditions and historical entanglements that disable high-level performance. On the other hand, homodepression energizes, enthralls, and enhances genius and creativity, as it did for most of the writers we have been discussing here.[48] Everywhere its oppositions are paramount, working to enable as well as disable. In action it transforms the healthy person and renders him – or her – a patient. But homodepression was not the only illness which same-sex love bore in the early modern world. Like Hamlet's oblique variety of madness or "north-northwest" melancholy, homodepression had a particularity whose morbidity we are just beginning to understand. This is why, in part, Gray's new profile as a morbid patient, as well as creative artist, is so enthralling. We disempower our historical figures – whether Grays or Winckelmanns – by labeling or describing them as "homosexuals" when it is their particular *variety* of alienation, or melancholy, we seek. Yet homodepression has been among the least-well-understood maladies of homosexuals in history because we have so few scientific categories for ailments based on, or derivative from, life's *condition*, especially the impossibility of the discovery of love.[49]

Even preliminary lists of same-sex depressives are long: the Bacon brothers (Anthony and Francis), James I, Desiderius Erasmus with his lifetime of poor health, James Howell, Franz Schubert, Ludwig II, the Marquis Astolphe Custine (already mentioned, who triumphed over his homodepression by nurturing his love for Edward Saint-Barbe and by the creation of one of Paris' most cultured salons),[50] Peter Ilich Tchaikovsky, Proust, Aubrey Beardsley (who seemed to have a natural affinity for attracting every disease he could to himself), Gray (who, in the words of one critic, "came near to becoming a professional hypochondriac"); William Beckford (who was always something of a valetudinarian, despite a robust constitution, and whose letters often start with musings about Gray's lot, especially his passion for collecting natural history and his landscapes); Lytton Strachey (an ingrained hypochondriac as well as depressive); Paul Verlaine (who lived in hospital for the last decade of his short life, wrote a book on the subject, *Mes Hôpitaux "Souvenir D'Hôpital,"* and who was, in turn, written about by his doctors, as in Dr Benassis' *"Essai De Clinique Litteraire: Paul Verlaine"*); Arthur Rimbaud (whose short life was punctuated by prolonged illness in his final years, cancer, and the amputation of a leg); Somerset Maugham (who despite surviving into great old age turned his hypochondria into an aesthetic); Nijinsky (whose mental breakdown after the affair with Diaghilev, and subsequent manic depression, is now well documented); Roland Barthes (whose life-long pulmonary consumption amounted to more than tuberculosis and took a psychological toll on his social relations); Horace Walpole (whose physical frailties were always more than merely gouty); poet W.H. Auden's complications in surgery; Tennessee Williams and Truman Capote (both steeped in chronic alcoholism which was as self-destructive as the self-revenge for a life-long obsession with their unfulfilled sexuality); Hart Crane (whose adolescent hypochondria landed him in breakdown and suicide); Andre Gide (who – like Hart Crane – suffered from severe childhood hypochondria despite having been wrongly diagnosed as merely tubercular); Henry James (who almost miraculously discovered that he could write himself out of depression); Walt Whitman (whose great breakdown and transformation was caused by revelations sustained while nursing soldiers in the American civil war and the exhaustion the activity took on his constitution); Jean Cocteau (who failed in his attempts to break his addiction to drugs – he wrote about these experiences in his autobiographical memoir *Opium*); the Greek poet Constantine Cafavy (who developed from an aesthetic hedonist into a middle-aged depressive recluse by transforming his sexual guilt into minor psycho-physical maladies); the Franco-Jewish poet Max Jacob (1874–1944 – contemporary of Proust and Guillaume Apollinaire, whose thwarted sexuality drove him to suffer severe "manias" suggestive of psychotic paranoia). Many on the list cultivated a clinical hypochondriasis as shield for, and mask of, their tortured sexuality. The varieties of hypochondria among the homodepressed leap out of their pages, both for women and men: overlooked syndromes difficult to diagnose and definitively prove.

Even their best biographers routinely overlook their common grounds: lowness caused by their life situation rather than specific biographical tensions or – alternatively – socio-economic conditions disturbing them. No competent epidemiologist today would be so blithe about other groups. These same-sex patients often were socially or economically deprived; typically, there were causes exceeding these as the brick and mortar of their malady. Consult, for example, the biographies of Horace Walpole. Every day in his life has been accounted for, every fact annotated, every name glossed, every date verified. But his biographers omit his strange state of health and psychological orientation to the world; his particular blend of asceticism, aestheticism, cloistered Gothicism, bitchiness, and hypochondria in an "Era of the Gut" when "Extreme Hypochondriasis" afflicted many literary men, not merely those with driven same-sex attractions.[51] There is insufficient space here to put together all the pieces, but Walpole's idiosyncratic homodepression at least infiltrates his defence system in monkish, if raffish, retreat. It pierces through to the essence of his character, while retaining his connoisseur cult of the sublime that functioned to assuage his psyche, and the retreat into Gothic fictions that energized his depressive states. And the diagnosis of homodepression retains his campy bitchiness, which was more spiteful than anything the era of Pope had seen. It may be just another category – a label too – but penetrates to a high threshold of personality analysis. The question "was Walpole homosexual?" is incapable of adequate reply when framed in such modern terms and with such a political edge. But if, having adequately constructed the parameters of homodepression, you ask "was Walpole homodepressed?" a reply may be perfectly demonstrable provided you do not despise psychobiography and psychoanalysis, which many Walpolians – of course – do.[52]

Homomorbidity

> "From what passion did such a pain arise? Would the man-God be distressed, that is, haunted by death, *because* he is sexual, prey to sexual passion?"
> (Julia Kristeva, *Black Sun: Depression and Melancholia,* p. 112).

Walpole's adolescent friend Gray typifies the third neologism par excellence. Even in his own time Gray's essential ego formation (personality structure) was said to have been "morbid." But the word has had a charged lexical history. Whatever it denotes today, or wherever one stands on the great divide of Gray's sexuality, there can be no doubt that he was "a morbid type" suffering from serious hypochondria of the heart. It is the single recurring phrase used to describe himself in his own works, especially his letters, and in appraisals made about him by those who knew him best. After "Favonius" (Richard West) died in June 1742 aged 26, Gray lived on for almost another thirty years *sans* best friend and lover: West had been that, and more, to him even if Gray's physical yearning was never consummated. Only at the end of Gray's life, when a charismatic young Swiss mathematician appeared on the London scene, did Gray again feel anything remotely proximate to the former ardor for West, although by now he was no longer capable of indulging such erotic passion or quenching his thirst at the same temperature.

Yet suppose you want to distinguish among the types of morbidity, even in Gray's case; refine its repertoire, sort out its varieties. "Homomorbid" provides a new slant to Gray's difficulties, especially if you want to factor in his deeply thwarted homosocial desire. "Morbid" was fundamentally an anatomical concept, as Matthew Baillie explained in *The Morbid Anatomy of Some of the Most Important Parts of the Human Body* (London, 1797). In that domain it had developed over centuries and remained there until it began to shift in the eighteenth century. Anatomy was either morbid or the reverse: healthy. Other forms of morbidity were *secondary* to the corpus (of animals, humans, all living creatures); when corporeal anatomy became pathological, or diseased, the body could wither and die. Hence morbidity was a prelude to the pathological state leading to disease, dying and death. This was still the meaning it held in the nomenclature of Gray's epoch, although it had started to extend its sway into the psychological domain.[53] Hence Samuel Johnson's sole definition of "morbid" in the dictionary as "Diseased; in a state contrary to health," with one citation from Dr. Arbuthnot's *Essay ... Concerning the Nature of Aliments... According to the Different Constitutions of Human Bodies.*[54]

Moreover, healthy bodies were tonic, ill bodies morbid; the more deranged the *corpora fabrica*, the more morbid its gross anatomy. Morbidity marked a turning-point on whose axis the doctor's diagnosis was ultimately made about healthy or pathological and the degree of severity. Gray may not have been "homosexual" in our contemporary sense (he certainly could not have intuited the new confidence about homosexuality's empowerment and the challenge it holds to conventional morality), but he was a "patient" in all sorts of ways and construed as such in his own time, even by himself, as his pathographic notebooks show. He was a psychological depressive; hence the need for the word "homomorbid" as applicable to someone of his sexual cast of mind whose physical cravings were continuously thwarted. Robert Mack's biography in matters depressive has hit the nail on the head:

> From this point on in his life, Gray's physical health began often subtly and more consistently to reflect his inner state of mind. In his correspondence, a seemingly inconsolable sense of melancholy is never far from the surface. He began now routinely to suffer from bouts of near-debilitating mental depression – enduring episodes worse, even, than anything he had experienced as a young man. These attacks – described by the poet himself as a sudden "sinking" sensation in his chest and abdomen, or by a feeling of pain and tightness around his heart – followed hard upon the slightest physical exertion. In the years to come, Gray would begin keeping a record in his diaries and pocket notebooks of the onset of these physical symptoms, carefully marking down any return of identifiable ailments, such as rheumatism, or any attack of the gout.[55]

The "tightness" in his chest was congealed blood that stagnated (in the medical model of his time) because the normal flow of animal spirits had stopped – severe depression could do that. The symptom had been known for centuries, especially as part of the price scholars paid for their wisdom. Literary historians have excavated the psychological malady from these symptoms and labeled them "literary loneliness," lumping together Gray, Collins, Cowper *et al.* (sometimes Christopher Smart) as if they shared their depressive states, but there is more to it than this.[56] Did Collins' blood not also congeal, manic-depressive that he was? Too little is known about his psychosexual development to pronounce in any depth on it, but one thing is clear: whatever Collins' biographical relation had been to sex, love and chastity, the breakdowns that ruined his poetic career and limited it to just one decade (from 18 to 28, after which time he retired into psychosis in Chichester and never again wrote) did not arise from conditions so very different from Gray's. Both men were sexual cripples even if Collins, unlike Gray, may also have been (in our modern sense) schizophrenic. And both were pathologically guilty about the erotic prospects before them, especially as these threatened their mental creative energy. Collins'

guilt over the loss of chastity (if it was loss) was somewhat more religiously constructed than Gray's – which formed itself from social
rather than clerical prohibition – but the resulting depression in both
men primarily arose from their pathetic inability to love and to love
sexually. Hence the reduced gap, referred to earlier, between heterode-
pression and homodepression, for there certainly has never been any
sense of a homosexual Collins.

Gray's symptoms exceeded ordinary melancholy, from which, of
course, he also suffered. Robert Mack demonstrates what toll these
depressive illnesses took on Gray's academic pursuits as well as his personal life; he chronicles Gray's arthritis, gout, rheumatism, repetitive
flu syndrome, chronically weak constitution, rectal surgery, and the
uremia that killed him. Gray's depression began before West's death
but his "homomorbidity" was more inclusive and expansive and
extended to the weird way he let himself go at the end, with Charles
Victor de Bonstetten. Adequate analysis of it requires the genesis, or
genealogy, of a new category.

I dwell on Gray because he was such a representative "homodepressive," steeped in "homomorbidity." In one sense he lacked knowledge of
the erotic desire within him and took his identity from external sources;
in another, he could write poignant love poetry describing its toll. But he
could not look at himself from afar, as it were, and see himself for the
lover he was: so far had he gone beyond the Platonism in which he was
steeped. Mental suffering racked his adult life to the point that retreat and
solitude alone assuaged him – the well-documented burial in his books
and his escape through natural history, antiquities, imaginary travel:
these, rather than people, offered respite from the anguish. Towards the
end of his life Gray was a patient in manifold ways: his uncharacteristically charged response to Bonstetten was the rekindled desire of depressive morbidity run amok. He was almost three times Bonstetten's age, and
fussing over the youth as if they could have had a future together. His
grief at Bonstetten's departure and the psychic conflict over whether to
visit him in Switzerland was massive in proportion to the reality. Gray's
death – said to be from gout in yet another partial diagnosis – occurred
remarkably close to the termination of his friendship with the young
man. How are we to be sure that we have understood this "morbid" life?
A category proximate to "homomorbid" assists because it is richer than
Gray's own version of "morbid" and encompasses his sexuality.

"Morbid" continued to be construed anatomically at the end of the
eighteenth century. However, with the rise of medical madness and the
insanity diagnosis (from Dr. Battie and William Haslam in England to

early psychiatrists Pinel and Esquirol in Paris), "morbid" was increasingly used to denote mental difference. Hence Samuel Johnson's "state contrary to health" shifted from the somatic to the mental, gradually transferred from body to mind. Perform a survey of medical works from 1770 to 1830 and you see how "morbid" is gradually eroding from an anatomical base to take account of the new "morbidity of the mind": psychiatry.[57] Parallel with the change came a new application of morbidity as a fundamental building block of the developing concept of sexual inversion. That is why we pursue it so assiduously here: an intimate link developed between a figure's homodepression and homomorbidity, the first preparing the soil for the growth of the second. The lower his spirits and the more chronically depressed, the greater the likelihood of sexual difference, or even mortal illness. Eventually the deviant, or invert, despite his inchoate status as an undefined "species" in those pre-Darwinian days, was still being medicalized. Two generations after Gray's death (i.e. the generations 1770–1830), the old-style sodomite (in Randolph Trumbach's sense) evolved into a "homomorbid" creature displaying medical pathology. He was not, of course, called that; hence the need for the category in the reconstruction. One generation forward – specifically in 1862 – the homosexual, or "urning," will be named but was not then suddenly medicalized: Karl Maria Benkerts provided the label, not the legwork that required generations for crystallization. This difference between the coinage of a label and deep-layer rationale underpinning it, is the theme of this essay. The same can be said for my neologisms: they were named at specific dates but did not spring up then. In fact the "homomorbid" species, or type, had been evolving in a gradual state of medicalization – the gathering homosexual diagnosis – from the eighteenth century onward.[58]

One other pre-1860 context for the rise of "homomorbidity" is germane. Recent scholarship lends an impression that a science of sex – sexology – was a post-Darwinian development, commencing after *The Origin of Species* in the crucial decade of the 1860s and culminating in the great pronouncements of Richard von Krafft-Ebing (1880s) and Havelock Ellis (1890s). A strong case has been made for it. However, such genealogy – especially in Foucault's sense of the formation of a discourse and the mindsets accompanying it, as well as the epistemic modes in which the discourse eventually breaks with its former life – omits the "three-sex" stage of the world of Gray, Akenside, and Byron and their scientific contemporaries. A version of sexology, even if primitive by the later standards, thrived in

Napoleon's Third Republic and in the England of Victoria's ascension.[59] The 1830s are permeated with scientific or pseudo-scientific works correlating body types to explicit sexual practices: the decade, for example, of Isidore Geoffroy Saint-Hilaire's seminal writings (not to be confused with his namesake Etienne, who also wrote on anatomical deviation) about the juridical aspects of hermaphrodites and whose theories extended to notions of morbidity and pathology in the realm of human emotion.[60] His teratological theories swept Paris and London and, once popularized within the realms of moral deviance and bodily monstrosity, were the talk of the salons, as is known from the memoirs of Georges Sand. Crucial to this welter of discussion about human anatomical monstrosity was the perception of normal penis size: at birth, during puberty, in adulthood and senescence, in both genders and in different nations, and especially among hermaphrodites and women with abnormally developed clitorises. By the time Heinrich Kaan published his *Psychopathia Sexualis* in 1844 in Germany, sexology was a developing discourse: this was two generations before Krafft-Ebing's similarly titled work of 1886.[61] The further development of forensic medicine (starting with Zacchias, already discussed, in the mid-seventeenth century) filled in the picture of inverts as proto-morbid creatures deformed in *both* mind and body. No one in France in the 1840s and 1850s did more to bring these intriguing matters into the foreground than Ambroise Tardieu (1818–79), the sexological physician whose ideas Foucault discusses in *Herculine Barbin*.[62] Tardieu identified these morbid varieties by building on Geoffroy Saint-Hilaire and correlating their genital, usually anal, markings with psychological traits and patterns of social and antisocial behavior. Throughout this dense jungle of paramedical and pseudoscientific writing published between 1800 and 1870 "morbid" is a recurrent word, in French, English, German, Italian; soon to be dislodged from its anatomico-pathological specificity and enter the popular domain to denote the freaky or funny or – queer. Gender difference lay at the base of all these hypotheses and discussions.

Inspect the vast undergrowth of the next stage of sexological writing in Europe (1860–1900) and the *morbidity concept* intensifies, especially as it amalgamates to the developing "third sex" as signifier of its innate organic structures and mental states. All aspects of third-sex existence – the theory went – were "morbid": anatomy and physiology, as well as its mental and psychological components, not least its versions of love. By 1891 Dr. Emile Laurent, who had read much that Tardieu had written, was claiming that all deviant love was "morbid."[63] Hence morbidity was not restricted to the "third-sex" but was the *sine qua non* for its aberrant status, especially those *mental* states preventing care of the healthy self and conventional social relations.[64] A new discourse of anatomical morbidity applied to inverts had been developing for well over a century, which intensified at the end of the nineteenth century. When German psychopathologist Hermann Loehr finally produced the results of his life's research on William Shakespeare at the *fin-de-siècle*, he did so under the title *The Presentation of Morbid Mental States in Shakespeare's Plays* (Stuttgart, 1898) – so far had the concept been unhitched from gross anatomy in Baillie's nomenclature a century earlier.[65] Loehr's study was not restricted to inverted types or third-sex, homoerotic, Shakespearean characters but amassed varieties of psychological difference ranging from the Medieval *accidie* (*ennui*) and Renaissance melancholy (Hamlet) to the newer insanity and clinical lunacy developed in the Enlightenment. All, Loehr now claimed, were "morbid." Earlier Frederic Chopin, the great composer and pianist, reflected on his own morbidity in an intense moment near the end of his life (1849), when the temperature of his melancholy and patriotism were running high, and called himself a "morbid flea." Chopin's sexuality may have been fluid, in life and in the styles of his musical composition, but he could not be said to have been homosexual.[66] His label aimed to capture the degree to which both body and mind had been afflicted. Later Freud construed Leonardo Da Vinci's inversion as "morbid": his letter to Fliess labeled Leonardo as having been "perhaps the most famous left-handed individual" in history.[67] The 1903 German translation of Merezhkovsky's study of Leonardo (1902) became one of Freud's favorite books and further encouraged him to explore Leonardo's homosexuality. During 1907–8, when Freud was preparing to address the Vienna Psychoanalytical Society about Leonardo, and later in 1910, when he published his study, Freud sustained the concept of the "third-sex" as fundamentally constituted of "morbid types." A decade later, in such texts as the 1919 note accompanying the passage about homosexual development, Freud discarded the "third-sex" concept (to describe both innate and acquired homosexuals), and claimed instead that psychoanalysis was capable of repairing, even converting these "morbid" homosexuals. Morbid *mental* states, especially the morbidity resulting from unresolved Oedipal fixes, pervade Freud's Leonardo essay and remain an important insignia of its inception *circa* 1900.[68]

The assimilation of these medical theories into literature reflects further use of the term. Hence when Edward Carpenter, the liberal popularizer of new attitudes to love and sex, explained to his reading public that there were "two kinds of same-sex love" – healthy and diseased – he invoked the predictable codeword of morbidity, which only selected readers in Thomas Gray's world would have understood. "I have now sketched," Carpenter writes of the evolving "intermediate sex:"

> . . . both the extreme types and the more healthy types of the Intermediate man and woman: types which can be verified from history and literature, though more certainly and satisfactorily perhaps from actual life around us. And unfamiliar though the subject is, it begins to appear that modern thought and science will have to face it. Of the latter and more normal types it may be said that they exist, and have always existed, in considerable abundance, and from that circumstance alone there is a strong probability that they have their place and purpose . . . . there is no indication of *morbidity* [italics mine] about them [i.e. the very nature of existence itself for third-sex members whose homosexuality had been innate rather than acquired], unless the special nature of their love-sentiment be itself accounted *morbid*; and in the alienation of the sexes from each other, of which complaint is so often made to-day, it must be admitted that they do much to fill the gap.[69]

Carpenter suppresses the interstices and bypasses the cultural equivalent of homodepression to make his point about (what we would call) healthy and sick varieties of homosexuals. He works hard to distinguish them. But, nevertheless he embeds the all-important code word "morbid."

There isn't space to list dozens of other usages in the late nineteenth and early twentieth centuries but E.M. Forster's are as representative as any because he was a wordsmith and knew whereof he spoke. *Maurice*, his novel about same-sex love that was posthumously published in 1971 (he died in 1970) with a famous preface enlisting his reasons, uses the word "morbid" to describe the attraction of the male lovers. Lytton Strachey read a manuscript of *Maurice* and quickly wrote to its creator on 12 March 1915, claiming that:

I really think the whole conception of male copulation in the book [*Maurice*] rather diseased – in fact morbid and unnatural. The speechification by which Maurice refuses to lie with Alec on the last night – no! – That is a sort of self-consciousness that would *only* arise when people were *not* being natural. It is surely beastly to think of copulation on such an occasion – shall we copulate? shall we not? ought we to? etc. – All one can think of is that one must embrace.[70]

But embrace "morbidly" or not? This is the question and Strachey, a practitioner, could pierce to its heart. Philip Gardner notes that Strachey's criticisms of Forster's attitude to sexual contact may be contrasted with Strachey's own fresher approach to such matters, as revealed in his short epistolary novel *Ermyntrude and Esmerelda*.[71] It may be so but it overlooks the symptomatic vocabulary of morbidity Strachey predictably invoked.

Conclusions

What then is my claim? I am saying, basically and in our coinage, that the triad of friendship, depression, and illness has been overlooked in the history of homosexuality. The claim must not imply that Greek homosexuals were depressed or Renaissance homosexuals sick, or vice versa. Or that only those who are steeped in friendship can be homosexuals. Least of all that homosexuals today should think of ourselves as depressed or ill. Many of us are, just as many heterosexuals are, but the point is rather that little has been written about these categories in any depth: as routes to understanding how so many homosexuals in the past (like Gray) fell into their morbidity, almost naturally sank into it, became victimized by it, and virtually drowned in it.

Nor do I want to claim that the three categories, reflected in their neologisms, conjoined into one diagnosis; specifically, that eighteenth-century homosexuals, for example, who may have had many friends, were also depressed or became ill; or that *because* they were depressed and ill they latched on to friends out of neediness. There is little, if any, *causal* relation among the three, although there will inevitably have been coincidences, convergences, and overlaps, as when homosexuals in history have craved friendship out of the desperation of religious marginalization and social ostracism. I suspect that the triad – homoplatonic, homomorbid, homodepressed – was biographically discrete without overlaps; that is, in most historical cases one or another applied but not all three and without necessary overlaps. The point is that the three categories remain in need of development and abundant research.

Furthermore, the status of each of the three categories construed individually continues to lack high profile: we have as yet no adequate histories of any of the three, only fragments and anecdotes. Perhaps (although I doubt it) the histories of the neologisms cannot be written. Surely one reason why the history of homosexuality has omitted the triad of convergences, especially as conjoined, is that the categories themselves are difficult to chart in the early modern world. Who has been brave enough to compile a pre-1800, or even pre-1900, history of depression? Eventually these compilations will be made and histories of depression will be assembled, just as histories of smallpox, syphilis, tuberculosis and cholera were. When they are, homodepression will occupy a small, but nonetheless important, niche configured as one of the deviations of depression in relatively late capitalism. Likewise for friendship and illness, immensely different as these categories are and with somewhat different cultural profiles.

Finally, I am contending that historically it is narrow-minded to omit the pre-1860 construction of the homosexual. The late Renaissance anatomists suggested that "sodomites" could be differentiated by the anatomy of the folds in their fundament; a position extended around 1650, as we saw, by Paolo Zacchias and the early modern forensic anatomists. Four centuries later, in September 1960, octogenarian E.M. Forster, no anatomist or legal mind, was still plugging this salient marking difference while *Maurice* was circulating privately among readers when claiming that it is the anus above all which distinguishes "us" from "them": the fact that the "intermediate sex" has gruesomely forced the other two to recall that it has a bum whose anatomy and sexual functions will not disappear:

> We had not realized that what the public really loathes in homosexuality is not the thing itself but having to think about it. If it could be slipped into our midst unnoticed, or legalized overnight by a decree in small print, there would be few protests. Unfortunately it can only be legalized by Parliament, and Members of Parliament are obliged to think or to appear to think.[72]

Forster, the polite post-Edwardian gentleman who practically names the relevant anatomical part, leaves us hovering in no doubt about what they "are obliged to think or appear to think," suggesting that these continuities of friendship and illness in the creativity debates persisted despite major shifts of belief. But this curve of thought differed for women who were – of course – also associated with varieties of physical and mental illness in the swath of chronology surveyed here, especially during the long nineteenth century. This convergence of friendship, illness, and depression eluded queer women until our century, when it (the convergence) has appeared with a fervor unknown in previous eras. Therefore, I have also been suggesting that although it is impossible to establish origins in the Foucauldian sense for these sets of converging characteristics – already present in the ancient world, flourishing in Renaissance Italy, appearing here and there in the Enlightenment in the gathering cults of sensibility and the new Man of Feeling, and especially pervasive in the Romantic period when creativity depended almost isomorphically on convergence of the three – they nevertheless played a role in the formation of the queer male. Can anyone imagine the milieu of Gray, Johann Wolfgang von Goethe, Byron, Schubert, and Custine without them? No biographical profile of these and other similar figures is adequate without the convergence of these characteristics.

As the nineteenth century evolved these converged characteristics came to be associated almost exclusively with the queer man as a type fundamentally distinct from other deviant versions of masculinity. While the varieties of masculinity continued to be medicalized and pathologized, the clue to queerness increasingly lay in two distinct but nevertheless concrete marking spheres: the anatomic one obsessively delimited to the fundament (here, for example, were thought to lie the clues to inversion); and the psychological one amalgamating these converged characteristics of friendship, illness, and depression into a new template of the emerging homosexual male. I have primarily been discussing the latter and my neologisms – homoplatonic, homodepressed, homomorbid – are imaginary linguistic doors to unlock the linkages. If the links were rigorously and microscopically followed up, like animal spirits flowing through the channels of the blood stream throughout the body, it could be shown that prior to c.1900 the emerging homosexual *female* had a rather different profile largely devoid of these three convergences. Stated otherwise and in the language of the time, the psychological arrangements of the pre-1900 female invert were rather different from those of the male. The implication of this difference for the history of gender and sex is something to mull over.

Notes

1. A history of attitudes towards, and receptions of, the word "homosexual" rather than the concept underlying the word from the time of its coinage in 1897 would be a useful record to possess but does not yet exist. Alternatively, the linguistic reception of "queer," as in "queer people," "queer bodies," "queer texts," is a more recent vintage, of course, but would demonstrate, I think, equally pejorative connotations for most of its history despite the epistemological status of "queer" as less sexually grounded than "homosexual" and, moreover, because "queer" now possesses a theoretical edge among academics which "homosexual" never had. Nevertheless, connotations of disablement and quasi-pathological difference permeate both words, as "gay" does not, one reason the American gay movement of the 1960s advocated that "gay" replace all competitors.

2. See George Rousseau, *The Nostalgia Diagnosis: the Forgotten Malady* (forthcoming). I am grateful to philosopher of science Subir Trivedi of the University of Chicago who served as the formal respondent of an earlier version of this chapter when it was delivered as a talk there in October 2001. Dr. Trivedi's philosophical critique has been especially useful for assessing the epistemological and philosophical bases of my enterprise and I am grateful to him for permitting me to quote him below, as well as to Leverhulme Grant F793A during which tenure in 1999–2001 the research included here was conducted.

3. For aspects of the transformation see Anthony Babington, *Shell-Shock: a History of the Changing Attitudes to War Neurosis* (London: Leo Cooper, 1997); J.M.W. Binneveld, *From Shell Shock to Combat Stress* (Amsterdam: University of Amsterdam Press, 1997).

4. The aesthetics of nostalgia crested in the early-nineteenth-century Romantic period in all the arts, including painting and music; for its relation to melancholy and madness and the formation of the Romantic genius as diseased see my discussion below of homomorbidity. For the crucial role of names and labels in my enterprise here I have been influenced by Ludwig Wittgenstein's theory of naming; see Saul A. Kripke, *Naming and Necessity* (Cambridge, MA: Harvard University Press, 1972).

5. See G.S. Rousseau, "Nerves, Spirits and Fibres: Toward the Origins of Sensibility," in R.F. Brissenden (ed.) *Studies in the Eighteenth Century* (Canberra: Australian Natural University Press, 1975), pp. 137–57.

6. James McKittrick Adair, *A Treatise of Fashionable Diseases* (Edinburgh, 1790), 114–5; for the background of fashionable nervous diseases see G.S. Rousseau, "Cultural History in a New Key: Towards a Semiotics of the Nerve," in Joan Pittock and Andrew Weir (eds.) *Interpretation and Cultural History* (Basingstoke: Macmillan Press [now Palgrave Macmillan], 1991), pp. 25–81.

7. See the prolific writings of Ernst Mayr on Darwinism, especially *One Long Argument: Charles Darwin and the Genesis of Modern Evolutionary Thought* (Harmondsworth: Penguin, 1988) and T.F. Glick (ed.), *The Comparative Reception of Darwinism* (Chicago: University of Chicago Press, 1978).

8. The concept "heteronormative" has not received the treatment it deserves because it is so difficult to establish and then decode. It is the brave scholar who can first extricate herself/himself and then take on its practitioners.

The practice assumes, among other things, that biographical figures are heterosexual until proved otherwise. Comparisons of it with the law (i.e. innocent until proved guilty) demonstrate how fraught the concept is in practice. See also n. 37.

9. Julia Kristeva is unfortunately off the mark when she differentiates homosexual depression according to the psychodynamics of same-sex sadomasochism, claiming that "the homosexual shares the same depressive economy: he is a delightful melancholy person when he does not indulge in sadistic passion with another man." See *Black Sun: Depression and Melancholia*, trans. Leon S. Roudiez (New York: Columbia University Press, 1989), p. 29. Those who consult the authoritative biographies of Hobbes and Locke, for example, discover how little is actually said about these matters; little is related to homoplatonism or sexuality, and it is a misnomer, if not a thoroughgoing fiction, to believe that these matters have been discussed fairly and openly.

10. It may well be asked whether this example merely entails new application to specific biographical figures, or generates a new epistemic awareness that reconceptualizes history. My own reply is in the direction of the former; and the rationale is to historicize the history of homosexuality as well as help to define the felt experiences of particular sub-groups.

11. See G. Pomata, "Menstruating Men: Similarity and Difference of the Sexes in Early Modern Medicine," in Finucci Valier and Kevin Brownlee (eds.), *Generation and Degeneration* (Durham: Duke University Press, 2001), pp. 109–52; Beth Kowaleski-Wallace, "Shunning the Bearded Kiss: Castrati and the Definition of Female Sexuality," *Prose Studies XV* (1992): 153–70; Marjorie B. Garber, *Vested Interests: Cross Dressing and Cultural Anxiety* (New York and London: Routledge, 1992).

12. David Hillman and Carla Mazzio (eds.), *The Body in Parts: Fantasies of Corporeality in Early Modern Europe* (London: Routledge, 1997); Gary Taylor, *Castration* (London: Routledge, 2000).

13. Marilyn Yalom, *The Breast* (London: HarperCollins, 1997); and Klaus Theweleit, *Male Fantasies: Women, Floods, Bodies, History*. Vol. I, trans. Stephen Conway (Oxford: Polity, 1989).

14. See W.S. Lewis *et al.*, *The Yale Edition of Horace Walpole's Correspondence* (New Haven CT: Yale University Press, 1937–1983), XVII, 24 and J.R. Dubro, "The Third Sex: Lord Hervey and his Coeterie," *Eighteenth-Century Life* XI (1976): 89–95. Montagu's throwaway quip was actually that there are three sexes – "men, women, and Herveys." Little could she have anticipated that in a century and a half Max Hirschfeld would be promoting the third sex as a scientifically demonstrable type. Her anticipation is not discussed by Lady Mary's most recent biographer; see Isobel Grundy, *Lady Mary Wortley Montagu* (Oxford: OUP, 2001).

15. See Clifford Geertz, *The Interpretation of Cultures* (New York: Basic Books, 1973). In his commentary Subir Trivedi (see n. 2) has observed that my method appears to invoke "the notion of a *Geist*, or spirit of an age, that is generally relevant in the analysis of the period"; that is, eras which differ from each other as much as resemble them. The subsequent analysis, he claims, "partakes of the categories of the *Geist*," especially the newly coined neologisms despite their having different names (i.e. homodepressed), and

then aims to apply them to the experiences of particular sub-groups, in this case clusters of homosexual men in history. Trivedi scores a point but it remains to be shown that there is a defect in the procedure if it assists us to understand the figures and historicize homosexuality more adequately. Why should contemporary classicists not invoke some of the categories of explanation of the ancient Greeks, for example, and Renaissancists of their epoch? Especially given that we cannot invoke *all* their categories of explanation because we cannot possibly experience the world as they did. The method of converging *"Geists"* described by Trivedi becomes defective only if the figures and their milieu become *less* comprehensible than they were, i.e. that they go against the grain of historical understanding. The fundamental issue is whether one subscribes to a transhistorical view of sexuality and desire, which I do *not*. Those who see no need to historicize sexual identity proceed, as Trivedi suggests, transhistorically. For the debate and its issues see Edward Stein (ed.), *Forms of Desire: Sexual Orientation and the Social Constructionist Controversy* (New York and London: Routledge, 1992, rep. ed.). For yet other epistemological hurdles to constructing sexual desire see two works published in 1989: David F. Greenberg, *The Construction of Homosexuality* (Chicago: University Of Chicago Press, 1989) and Michael Ruse, *Homosexuality: a Philosophical Inquiry* (Oxford: Basil Blackwell, 1989).

16. Lorraine Daston and Katherine Park, *Wonders and the Order of Nature, 1150–1750* (New York: Zone Books, 1999). For sodomites as monstrous see the anonymous *Eronania: or the Misusing of the Marriage Bed by Er and Onan Judah's Two Sons: Genesis 38. Or the Hainous [Sic] Crime of Self-Defilement, with All Its Nine Miserable Consequences in Both Sexes, Laid Open to All Those, Who May Ever Have Been Guilty of This Ill Action* (London, 1724).

17. See Foucault's discussion in *Herculine Barbin: Being the Recently Discovered Memoirs of a Nineteenth-Century French Hermaphrodite* Introduced by Michel Foucault and translated by Richard McDougall (Brighton: Harvester, 1980).

18. Quoted in Jeffrey Merrick and Bryant T. Ragan Jr (eds.), *Homosexuality in Modern France: a Documentary Collection* (New York: OUP, 2001) 27; for Zacchias see Paolo Zacchias, *Quaestiones Medico-Legales*, 2nd ed. (Venice, 1751).

19. M. Foucault, *The History of Sexuality: Volume One: an Introduction.*, trans. Robert Hurley, (London: Allen Lane, 1978), p. 43.

20. Jeffrey Merrick, "Commissioner Foucault, Inspector Noël, and the 'Pederasts' of Paris, 1780–3," *Journal of Social History* 32.2 (1998): 287–307; Gert Hekma, "A History of Sexology," in Jan Bremmer (ed.), *From Sappho to De Sade: Moments in History and Sexuality* (London: Routledge, 1989), pp. 173–93.

21. The epistemological point *à la* Trivedi (n. 2) gains clarity by comparing this trinity with analogies in our time. Will historians of the future claim that the rampant depression of our epoch is a *"Geist?"* Or our rise in diagnosed breast cancer? It may be that depression is now more widely diagnosed than it was hitherto but it would be difficult to deny that its depressive symptoms are none the less experienced and cause widespread suffering. When one of us is diagnosed and told that we have entered the ranks of depressives (either as out–patients or, more drastically, in-patients as the result of a psychotic episode) do we reason to ourselves that we are part of the *Geist* of the age suffering a Hegelian malaise? The more philosophical among us may place our illness within a context of widespread stress but even this mental

activity does not diminish the reality of symptoms we feel. Depressive malaise is indeed endemic to our time, as the psychiatric and psychotherapeutic establishment is assuring us, but not because of a prevailing Hegelian *Geist* that extols mental anguish and renders it fashionable but as the result of socio-economic conditions in late capitalism that permit its diagnosis and treatment. There is no doubt, of course, that huge segments of the population of Western countries are stressed out as they have never been before, but neither is this state of affairs the result of a prevailing *Geist*.

22. Even if somewhat less studied for its same-sex arrangements than the pre-1800 period or post-1860. See Richard Dellamora, *Masculine Desire: The Sexual Politics Of Victorian Aestheticism* (London: University of North Carolina Press, 1990).

23. See William Bond, *The Platonic Lovers: Consisting of Original Letters, in Prose And Verse, That Pass'd Between an English Lady, and an English Gentleman in France...* (London, 1732, 3rd ed.).

24. Michael Rocke, *Forbidden Friendships: Homosexuality and Male Culture in Renaissance Florence* (Oxford: OUP, 2000). Stuart Miller's *Men and Friendship* (Boston, 1983) had not historicized his figures.

25. Michael A. Cooper, "Discipl(in)ing the Master, Mastering the Discipl(in)e: Erotonomies of Discipleship in James's Tales of Literary Life," in Joseph A. Boone and Michael Cadden (eds.), *Engendering Men: the Question of Male Feminist Criticism* (London: Routledge, 1990), pp. 66–83, coins the word "erotonomy" to designate the erotic economy of the master/disciple relation, and, while so doing, speculates about the parlous state of homosexual panic within the American academy at large. His exploration is admirable, especially Cooper's own useful neologism, but one wonders whether discipleship is genuinely prominent, or even possible, in the current American academic scene, given that all masters have been discredited or toppled, or whether homosexual panic bred in a principally homophobic academic environment, often abetted by church fundamentalism, is not more culpable. In any case, the observation about a genealogy of discipleship *à la* Foucault, and not merely a literary history, remains.

26. London: Routledge and Kegan, 1963. For the genesis of my coinage ('homoplatonism') see n. 37 below.

27. As its early reviews demonstrate and despite a reissue in 1981; I have never found a reference to it in studies of the history of friendship, nor was it assimilated into gay and lesbian studies. The reason could be due, in part, to the lingering memory of Gould's difficulties with the administration of Amherst College, which was similar to, if less nationally publicized than, American literary critic Newton Arvin's at Smith College two decades earlier or, earlier yet, world-class anthropologist Clyde Kluckhohn's (1905–55) at Harvard University. For Arvin's tragedy see Barry Werth, *The Scarlet Professor: Newton Arvin: a Literary Life Shattered by Scandal* (New York: Anchor Doubleday, 2001). Some day these will be annotated, especially in a biography of Gould.

28. See George Haggerty, *Men in Love: Masculinity and Sexuality in the Eighteenth Century* (New York: Columbia University Press, 1999), p. 121. Haggerty was virtually unique among American academic critics in publicly acknowledging Gray's 'physical longing and frustrated physical desire.' Until the 1990s the position was uniformly attacked and anyone

who proposed it, as I had in 25 years earlier, was mauled. The attacks continue today despite the sensitive studies by Haggerty and Robert Mack, and are extended to other figures of the same epoch: Walpole, Akenside, Beckford, and even Pope. Young scholars who think otherwise are timid in speaking up for fear that their academic careers will be aborted or altogether quashed. See Robert Mack, *Thomas Gray* (New Haven and London: Yale University Press, 2000).

29. A survey of secondary works dealing with same-sex desire since 1980 reveals no examples.

30. O. Weininger, *Sex and Character* (New York: AMS Press, 1975) 40–49.

31. Werner Jaeger, *Paideia: the Ideals of Greek Culture,* trans. from the second German ed. by Gilbert Highet (Oxford: Basil Blackwell, 1939–45, 2 vols.).

32. The index of John Boswell's *Christianity, Social Tolerance, and Homosexuality: Gay People in Western Europe from the Beginning of the Christian Era to the Fourteenth Century* (Chicago: University of Chicago Press, 1980) for "education" and "pedagogy" proves revealing here.

33. See, for example, Bruce R. Smith, *Homosexual Desire in Shakespeare's England: a Cultural Poetics* (Chicago: University of Chicago Press, 1990); clerics, tutors, and schoolmasters are omitted. Alan Bray stressed the signs of friendship then as well; see his "Homosexuality and the Signs of Male Friendship in Early Modern England," *History Workshop Journal* 29 (1990): 1–19.

34. M. Foucault, *History of Sexuality, Volume I,* p. 110. Georg Büchner (1813–37), the German political refugee and author of *Lenz* and *Woyzeck* died young himself at the age of 23. He had been obsessed with Lenz as a looming madman and tragic figure and persuaded Oberlin to surrender his account so Lenz could write the *roman* Büchner called *Lenz.* See G. Büchner, *Lenz and Other Writings,* trans. John Reddick (Harmondsworth: Penguin, 1993) and J.L. Crighton, "The Portrayal of Madness in Georg Büchner's *Lenz* and *Woyzeck* and Some Possible Sources," unpublished PhD thesis, University of Leicester, 1994. Lenz should figure in any study of the homoplatonic Enlightenment.

35. See George C. Brauer, *The Education of a Gentleman: Theories of Gentlemanly Education in England, 1660–1775* (New York: 1959).

36. See G.S. Rousseau, "'In the House of Madame Van der Tasse': Homosocial Desire and a University Club during the Enlightenment," in Kent Gerard and Gert Hekma (eds.), *The Pursuit of Sodomy: Male Homosexuality in Renaissance and Enlightenment Europe* (New York: 1987), pp. 311–48, rep. with an introduction in G.S. Rousseau, *Perilous Enlightenment* (Manchester: University of Manchester Press, 1991), 109–37.

37. Can there be more than a handful of scholars working on any of these minor figures (Baxter, Akenside, Dyson, etc.)? Each stakes out the territory in colonial fashion and ensures that women do not enter the fold. Had there been women, or (in our sense) queer or gay scholars presiding over any of these figures this state of affairs would have been different. Gray's fortunes have recently fared better as the result of sensitive biographers such as Robert Mack (the background of whose recent Yale University Press biography of Thomas Gray, and its reviews upon publication, is another tale that cannot be told here), George Haggerty, Robert Gleckner *et al.* But raise the stakes to Horace Walpole, for whom far more

material exists and who was the center of a public network rising to the highest political echelons, and the temperature of debate is higher. Fortunately, queer and gay scholars have challenged Gray's heteronormative proprietorship here and denounced the homophobic tyranny they seek to hold over sexual freedom in scholarship. For an example of this developing library of counter-attack see Ralph F. Smith and Patricia Jung, *Heterosexism: an Ethical Challenge* (Albany, NY: State University of New York, 1993).

38. The need for a category proximate to "homoplatonism" became evident to me early in the 1970s when it grew increasingly clear that white male biographers of (what we today would call) "queer" figures were not going to surrender their heteronormative and heterosexist biases. Their letters published in reply to my reviews at the time, when I asked questions, for example, about Gray's life and works, especially his love poetry, were trenchant and inflexible. See, for example, Peter Watson-Smyth, "On Gray's *Elegy*," *Spectator*, 31 July 1971. These were followed in the 1980s by attacks for questioning Smollett's motives for writing his early poetic satires (1746–47) which raged against sodomists, and for interrogating Pope's masculinity, which was more complicated than Gray's or Smollett's (even in its transvestite representations in his poem *Eloisa to Abelard*) than heteronormatists had given out. More recently, my frank discussion of Akenside's same-sex friendship with, and financial ties to, Dyson led to near-panic in his contemporary editor, Robin Dix and his sympathizers: see R. Dix, "The Pleasures of Speculation", *British Journal of Eighteenth-Century Studies*. The contributors to R. Dix (ed.), *Mark Akenside: a Reassessment* (Fairlawn, NJ: Associated University Press, 2000) write as if they still lived in a New Critical vacuum devoid of biography, cultural critique, and psychoanalysis. No one reading their essays could believe that Akenside was a flesh-and-blood figure who ever had a life.

39. Whatever its virtues you would not think from reading Christopher Fox, *Locke and the Scriblerians: Identity and Consciousness in Early Eighteenth-Century Britain* (Berkeley: University of California Press, 1988) that the friendships of the Scriblerus Club members had been unraveled. What vested interests lie here to prevent the questions from being put?

40. See John Lehmann, *Three Literary Friendships: Byron and Shelley, Rimbaud and Verlaine, Robert Frost and Edward Thomas* (New York, 1984), or Wayne Koestenbaum, *Double Talk: the Erotics of Male Literary Collaboration* (New York: Routledge, 1989).

41. Referring to Louis Crompton's brave *Byron and Greek Love: Homophobia in 19th-century England* (London: Faber & Faber, 1985), which antedated the surge of recent treatments since then.

42. David Healy, *The Antidepressant Era* (Cambridge, MA.: Harvard University Press, 1997). The "Age of Prozac" and other labels have also been affixed.

43. The attempt to historicize depression has proved challenging; for some of the hurdles, as well as its historiography, see G.S. Rousseau, "Depression's Forgotten Genealogy: Notes Towards a History of Depression," *History of Psychiatry* 11 (Spring 2000): 71–106.

44. The empowerment is deftly intuited without being historicized by Andrew Sullivan in *Virtually Normal: an Argument About Homosexuality* (New York:

Knopf, 1995).

45. Hervey perceives no homomorbidity but relates his somatic body type to his erotics, and his amorous life to his having fallen ill, which comes close to modern perceptions of cause and effect in psychosomatic illness. See also R. Halsband, *Lord Hervey: Eighteenth-Century Courtier* (Oxford: Clarendon Press, 1973).

46. A significant literature about Proust's maladies already exists: see, for example, Bernard Straus, *Maladies of Marcel Proust: Doctors and Disease in His Life and Work* (London: Holmes & Meier, 1980); L. Milton, *Nostalgia: a Psychoanalytic Study of Marcel Proust* (Port Washington, NY: Kennikat Press, 1969). More recently Edmund White has gleaned the toll illness took on Proust in *The Flâneur: a Stroll Through the Paradoxes of Paris* (London: Bloomsbury, 2001), as if to suggest that Proust was the most prominent – in my neologistic sense – of homodepressives. The idea that illness energizes the creativity of such ailing homosexual figures as Tennessee Williams, Aubrey Beardsley, and Hart Crane as a form of empowerment requires more space than can be found here.

47. *The Female Malady: Women, Madness and English Culture, 1830–1980* (London: Virago, 1987). See also her discussion of Dr. Mitchell in "Hysteria, Feminism and Gender," in Sander Gilman, Helen King, Roy Porter, G.S. Rousseau and Elaine Showalter, *Hysteria Beyond Freud* (Princeton, NJ: Princeton University Press, 1993), 297–9. Homodepression also applies to homosexual women despite my omission here.

48. Much work remains to be done in this realm on Monk Lewis, whose students have been rather pusillanimous in making connections between his sexuality and Gothic imagination.

49. The maladies of poverty – especially tuberculosis and malnutrition – seem to be exceptions but they do not uniformly imply depression. By "life's condition" I mean physical impairment or mental anxiety sufficient to abrogate the chance of finding a lasting and fulfilling love. For example, A.L. Rowse, *Homosexuals in History: a Study of Ambivalence in Society, Literature and the Arts* (London: Weidenfeld & Nicolson, 1977) compiled his survey from the Middle Ages to the twentieth century without considering the health of his figures.

50. See G.S. Rousseau and Caroline Warman, "Made from the Stuff of Saints: Chateaubriand's *René* and Custine's Search for Homosexual Identity," *GLQ: a Journal of Lesbian and Gay Studies* 71 (December 2000): 1–29.

51. Samuel Tissot, the Swiss physician, treated them, studied their habits, and wrote about them; see his *Essay on Diseases Incidental to Literary and Sedentary Persons. With Proper Rules for Preventing Their Fatal Consequences. And Instructions for Their Care. Now Translated into English* (London, 1768). Still, it did not occur to him that same-sex desire could be driving some of their malady. See also Anne C. Vila, *Enlightenment and Pathology: Sensibility in the Literature and Medicine of Eighteenth-Century France* (Baltimore: Johns Hopkins University Press, 1998).

52. W.S. Lewis did and wrote a book giving his reasons: *One Man's Education* (New York: Alfred Knopf, 1967). The recognition of such resistance raises a fundamental question about the difference between homodepression and homosexuality. Stated crudely the former has a smaller political agenda: in

an era like ours, when depression is rampant and now routinely viewed as another illness without moral bearings, you cannot fault your neighbor if he, like you, suffers from depression; but you can tar him if his "homosexuality" arouses in you fantasies of lewd and debauched behavior cutting against the grain of your own traditional morality. Here homodepression cannot be compared with AIDS because the former is capable of vast historicization that the latter cannot yet be.

53. Despite examples of "diseased souls" throughout the early modern period, in my limited search I have found none of "morbid souls." Guts and stomachs within bodies were thought to be particularly "morbid" and this morbidity viewed as the source of indigestion; but, as Dr. James Johnson stunningly explained, such "morbid sensibility" was also the source of nervous illness, mental instability, and hypochondria or the condition of fantasizing that one is perpetually sick. By extension such "morbid stomachs" naturally led to sexual hypochondria and the notion that one was longing for members of one's own sex. See James Johnson, *An Essay on Morbid Sensibility of the Stomach and Bowels, As the Proximate Cause, or Characteristic Condition of Indigestion, Nervous Irritability, Mental Despondency, Hypochondriasis, &c. &c.* (London: Thomas and George Underwood, 1827).

54. Published in London in 1734; an influential work among Georgian doctors for making explicit their notion of health.

55. Mack, *Thomas Gray*, pp. 435–6.

56. For example John Sitter, *Literary Loneliness in Mid-Eighteenth-Century England* (Ithaca; NY: Cornell University Press, 1982).

57. This is the complex birth of a new science embracing medicine, philosophy, theology, and the new Romanticism which is currently being examined by historians of psychiatry; for further discussion see Mark S. Micale and Roy Porter (eds.), *Discovering The History of Psychiatry* (New York: OUP, 1994); Stephanie Clark-Brown, "The Birth of Psychiatry in the Age of Romanticism: the Problem of the Psyche in English Medicine and Literature 1790–1840", unpublished PhD thesis, University of Leiden, Holland, 1997; Allen Thiher, "The German Romantics and the Invention of Psychiatry," *Revels in Madness: Insanity in Medicine and Literature* (Ann Arbor, MI: University of Michigan Press, 1999).

58. The history of science progresses in this curious way, a further reason why names and labels, however delimiting, prove crucial to it, as Wittgenstein claimed in his famous essay on naming (see n. 4). It is therefore ironic that illustrious Japanese film director Nagisa Oshima sets his film *Gohatto* (2001), the story of the beautiful young male Kano who arouses the elite samurai Shinsen-gumi militia to fight over him, in the Kyoto of this era during the 1860s. Western ideas about third sexes and same-sex attachments cannot have entered Japan then.

59. For the overview see Lucy Bland and Laura Doan (eds.) *Sexology Uncensored: the Documents of Sexual Science* (Cambridge: Polity Press, 1998), and *Sexology in Culture: Labelling Bodies and Desire* (Cambridge: Polity Press, 1997); Vernon A. Rosario (ed.), *Science and Homosexualities* (New York and London: Routledge, 1997). For the 1830s see the *other* Morel – not degenerationist Morel, but the fiercely conservative moralist Dr Morel de Rubempré, author

of *La Pornologie ou Histoire Nouvelle Universelle et Complète de la Débauche et de la Prostitution Et Autres Dépravations dans Tous les Pays du Monde, Notamment en France Particulièrement dans Paris Depuis les Temps les Plus Anciens Jusqu'à Nos Jours...* (Paris: Terry, 1842).

60. Isidore Geoffroy Saint-Hilaire, *Histoire des Anomalies de L'Organisation.* (Paris: J.B. Baillière, 1832–36). The sexologists of mid-nineteenth-century France routinely referred to his histories of monstrosity, as Foucault notes in *Herculine Barbin* (see n. 17 above), p. 130.

61. Henrich Kaan, *Psychopathia Sexualis* (Leipzig: Leopold Voss, 1844).

62. See his *Étude Médico-Légale sur les Attentats aux Moeurs* (Paris: J.-B. Baillière et fils, 1862, 4th edn.). This work first appeared in the *Annales d'Hygiène Publique et de Médécine Légale*, 2nd series, IX (1858): 137–98 and has never been translated into English. Subsequent editions were illustrated, notably the genital organs; see part 3, "De la Péderastie et de la Sodomie" (1862): 146–224. The seventh edition (1878), 194–296, contains newly added plates; here see especially plate 5 entitled *"exemple des desordres que produit la péderastie passive ou la sodomie"* (the example of anatomical disorders which produce passive pederasty or sodomy). Tardieu, who must be counted among the principal sexologists in the Western tradition, was the son of an engraver. He became a student doctor in 1839, physician in 1843, and in 1851 was appointed chief inspector for "the verification of death" in Paris rising to become its "chef de service." In 1856 he became professor of legal medicine at the Medical Faculty of Paris and, in 1864, its Dean. His medico-legal studies were exemplary in their precision, clarity and for the pertinence of their conclusions. Tardieu also generated the first description of the Battered Child Syndrome, now known as the Tardieu Syndrome. Tardieu taught medicine to Marcel Proust's father.

63. Emile Laurent, *L'Amour Morbide: Étude de Psychologie Pathologique* (Paris: Société d'Editions Scientifiques, 1891).

64. Difference lay in the mind, in the newly developing theories of psychology: mind, or soul, had become perverted in sequence with the body, and the age-old body-mind rift was closed. One could claim, therefore, that nineteenth-century homomorbidity depended on narrow Cartesian mind-body dualism in its search for a biological basis for inversion. After the first wave of sexologists in the 1860s the result of its quest was the opposite: the proposition that inverts were differently evolving bodies concealing sick souls.

65. For Matthew Baillie and morbid anatomy, see p. 33 above.

66. For Chopin's sexual fluidity and the source of the half-witty "morbid flea" see Jeffrey Kallberg, *Chopin at the Boundaries: Sex, History and Musical Genre* (Harvard: Harvard University Press, 1996), p. 40; see especially pp. 258–9 for epistemological commentary on the challenge posed by interrogating unstable sexual categories.

67. James Strachey (ed.), *The Standard Edition of the Works of Sigmund Freud* (London: Hogarth Press, 1953–74, 24 vols.) 14: 145.

68. For "morbidity" in Freud at large see Mark Micale and Roy Porter (eds.) *Discovering the History of Psychiatry* (New York and Oxford: OUP, 1994).

69. Edward Carpenter, *The Intermediate Sex* (London: Allen & Unwin, 1908) 147.

70. Quoted in Philip Gardner, *E.M. Forster: the Critical Heritage* (London and Boston: Routledge & Kegan Paul, 1973) 431.

71. Gardner, *E.M. Forster*, p. 429.
72. E.M. Forster, *Maurice* (London: Edward Arnold, 1971), Terminal Note, section entitled, "Homosexuality," pp. 240–1. The story of the "pregnancy" of *Maurice* is perhaps too well known to be retold: how, in 1913, Forster visited Carpenter and George Merrill who touched his "backside" after which stroke he "immediately began to write *Maurice*":

> George Merrill also touched my backside – gently and just above the buttocks. I believe he touched most people's. The sensation was unusual and I still remember it, as I remember the position of a long vanished tooth. It was as much psychological as physical. It seemed to go straight through the small of my back into my ideas, without involving my thoughts (p. 235).

2
Homosexuals in History:
A.L. Rowse and the Queer Archive

Alan Stewart

"Silly fools! Couldn't they see that I was on their side."
A.L. Rowse on gay criticism of his *Homosexuals in History*[1]

In 1976 Michel Foucault published *La Volonté du Savoir*, the first volume of his multi-volume *Histoire de la Sexualité*, in Paris. Two years later, Robert Hurley's translation, *The History of Sexuality, Volume One, an Introduction*, appeared in the United States and Canada.[2] In Renaissance studies, its influence was particularly decisive. In Foucault's account, the late nineteenth century saw a "new persecution of the peripheral sexualities" entailing what he described as "an *incorporation of perversions* and a new *specification of individuals*" whereby "the nineteenth-century homosexual became a personage, a past, a case history, and a childhood, in addition to being a type of life, a life form, and a morphology, with an indiscreet anatomy and possibly a mysterious physiology." In the Renaissance, by contrast, "[a]s defined by the ancient civil or canonical codes, sodomy was a category of forbidden acts; their perpetrator was nothing more than the juridical subject of them."[3] Inspired by Foucault, among others, Alan Bray most influentially dismissed the notion of the homosexual individual in the Renaissance. Early modern society, he wrote, "was one which lacked the idea of a distinct homosexual minority, although homosexuality was none the less regarded with a readily expressed horror. In principle it was a crime which anyone was capable of, like murder or blasphemy."[4] In Bray's analysis, historians had to stop short of pointing the finger even at a classic homosexual individual such as Edward de Vere, Earl of Oxford, who was caught in sweaty dishabille with a cook's boy. Bray reminds us that the source of this evidence was "accusations"

53

made by Oxford's "erstwhile fellow conspirators" and that on closer reading their meaning lies elsewhere:

> The picture they draw is of a man who was not only a sodomite but also an enemy of society: a traitor and a man given to lawless violence against his enemies. He was also they tell us an habitual liar, an atheist and a blasphemer. The charge of sodomy was not merely added to the list. It symbolised it. If this man was a rebel against nature was it surprising that he was also a rebel against society and the truth (or the Truth) that supported it?[5]

The work of Foucault and Bray has inspired at least two decades of scholarly work and together has become the talisman of an entire new field of studies in the history of sexuality. The homosexual has vanished from the Renaissance.

Yet in the year between the appearance of Foucault's work in French and English editions, another book appeared in London, the impact of which is less well appreciated: A.L. Rowse's *Homosexuals in History*.[6] The work of an astoundingly prolific and popular Oxford historian, the book declared itself to be "decidedly *not* pornography. It is a serious study – or a series of studies – in history and society, literature and the arts." Its focus was "many men of genius or great eminence", through the ages, who according to Rowse were all identifiable as homosexual, a condition that directly influenced their genius. He hoped, he wrote, "that these studies may throw some light on the predisposing conditions to creativeness, in the psychological rewards of ambivalence, the doubled response to life, the sharpening of perception, the tensions that lead to achievement."[7]

Elsewhere in his writings, Rowse developed his thesis of a relationship between homosexuality and creativeness. Reviewing Goldsworthy Lowes Dickinson's posthumously published autobiography, he was angered by Lowes Dickinson's statement that "the homosexual temperament must, I think, be regarded as a misfortune, though it is possible with that temperament, to have a better, more passionate and more noble life than most men of normal temperament achieve."[8] "In that case, why a misfortune?" retorted Rowse:

> ... better than living the life of a clod anyway, if it makes a man more sensitive, more intuitive, more aware, doubling his gifts so that he has both feminine and masculine within himself. Now that the wet blanket of humbug and hypocrisy has recently been

removed, we can appreciate how true this is of so many leading figures in the contemporary arts, of music, ballet, painting, poetry, what not. And why not?[9]

Throwing away the wet blanket, Rowse set his agenda to locate the "homosexuals in history". While clearly believing in some sort of homosexual "essence" that transcended culture and chronology, Rowse argues that:

> The attitude of mind towards this subject shows remarkable variations from period to period, from one country or geographical area to another, and even between social classes and individuals in a given country. The subject is also complicated and confused by a remarkable degree of hypocrisy, the gap between public and private standards, especially in Anglo-Saxon countries, which have undergone Puritan brainwashing. Mediterranean peoples, for example, especially Muslims, think of the predominant English attitude – at least that put forward in public – as just mad. (Its results have been even more repressive, stupid and cruel.)[10]

In the transformation of attitudes towards homosexuality, the Renaissance played a major role, embodying as it does to Rowse "the transition from the medieval to the modern consciousness" (perhaps unsurprisingly, since he admits that "my interests as an historian begin with the Renaissance").[11] *Homosexuals in History* devotes three chapters to the period, dealing with Desiderius Erasmus of Rotterdam, Leonardo da Vinci, Michelangelo, Nicholas Udall, Christopher Marlowe, Henri III of France, Rudolf II, the Spaniard Antonio Perez, Francis Bacon and his elder brother Anthony, and King James VI and I. One big fish slips through Rowse's net – William Shakespeare, whom Rowse is at great pains to keep on the straight and narrow: "Shakespeare himself was even more than normally heterosexual, for an Englishman".[12] In one of his last works, written at the age of 93, Rowse revisited the illicit sexualities, homo and hetero, of Shakespeare's contemporaries in "literary Bohemia", including Robert Greene, Marlowe, the Bacon brothers, his patron the Earl of Southampton, the Earl of Oxford and James I. He concludes:

> all this meant nothing to William Shakespeare: it was not in his line. It was a great advantage to him as a writer to be so responsive to the

other sex, to be deeply sympathetic to feminine nature and understand it intimately (like Tolstoy or Turgenev). He did not have the
cock-eyed view of life, the proportions distorted, as in so many
modern writers, Proust and Gide, Montherlant and Cocteau. He made
no apology for his well-known "sportive blood", as he phrased it.[13]

From the start, Rowse's book came under attack. From the conservative
wing, there were those who were scandalized by his choice of subject
matter; but there was also considerable opposition from gay critics.
Rowse pronounced himself surprised and annoyed: "Silly fools!" he
wrote in a private document, "Couldn't they see that I was on their
side."[14] Even his recent biographer Richard Ollard, generally sympathetic to Rowse's writings (if not to his sexuality), dismisses the book as
a "mixture of gossip, speculation and sometimes improbable self-
identification with figures who, the reader may feel, would be startled
rather than flattered by the compliment."[15] As gay studies and then
queer studies took hold in the academy, Rowse's work faded from view.
Its declining fortunes are clear even from a cursory glance at the
leading works in the burgeoning field of early-modern gay historical
and Renaissance literary-critical studies. *Homosexuals in History* has its
place in the bibliography of Alan Bray's seminal *Homosexuality in
Renaissance England*, remarkably published only five years later. But by
1991, Bruce R. Smith dismissed the book as "highbrow gossip,"[16] and
Gregory W. Bredbeck lampooned Rowse as "the essential essentialist."[17]
Their rejection of Rowse and his methodology was part of a wider
rejection of biographical approaches within both literary criticism and
lesbian, gay and queer studies. The hunt for "homosexuals in history"
seemed to have no place in an academic field heavily influenced by
Foucauldian theories of the social construction of sexuality.

And yet, *Homosexuals in History* remains in print. Popular interest in
assigning sexual identities to historical figures remains intense. Even
the highly self-aware scholars of a collection such as Jonathan
Goldberg's *Queering the Renaissance* find themselves drawn to the life
and works of Rowse's homosexuals: Erasmus, Nicholas Udall, Francis
Bacon. My question here is why is it that we still find "homosexuals in
history"? Or, more to the point: *how* do we find homosexuals in
history?

I take as my case study perhaps the most socially prominent homosexual identified in Rowse's study: King James VI and I. Rowse devotes
an entire chapter of *Homosexuals in History* to "Francis Bacon and the
Court of James I". In Bacon, "an Outsider forever trying to get Inside",

Rowse finds a genius and prophet whose political career, which saw him raised to the post of Lord Chancellor, was destroyed by charges of bribery in 1621.[18] Bacon claimed his innocence, Rowse argues, because he expected to be saved by King James and the King's favourite, his own patron, the Duke of Buckingham. But then there was an unexpected *volte-face*:

> Suddenly his posture of defence caved in abruptly – the historians have not given a satisfactory explanation why. Public opinion at the time thought that a charge of sodomy might well be brought – the kind of anthropological blackmail with which we have been familiarized in our time. The King and Buckingham could not allow *that* sacred issue to come into the open; Bacon had to give way completely, and give up.[19]

The reason that James and Buckingham could not allow "*that* sacred issue" to be revealed, according to Rowse, is that James was also a homosexual. He documents James' alleged passions: as an adolescent for his elder French cousin Esmé Stuart, Lord of Aubigny, and later for a series of young male courtiers: the "fantastically extravagant" James Hay, Robert Carr, later raised to become Earl of Somerset, and then the "extraordinarily handsome" George Villiers, who was to become Duke of Buckingham.[20] Drawing on pop psychology, Rowse traces James' homosexuality to his superbly dysfunctional childhood (in which James was raised to despise his exiled mother, who had murdered his father):

> The poor young fellow needed some outlet for his affections. All his early life he had been starved of love; what became characteristic of James was his insatiable desire to be loved. Towards anyone prepared to love him, he returned unstinted affection; unfortunately the loved one could get anything out of him. It was not easy for him to find the right person, for he was far from glamorous; a woman would have put up with that, but he found only his own sex attractive.[21]

Rowse declared that his work was "the study of concrete fact, the way men actually are and behave: an historian is not impressed by their pretences, the smoke screen they put up, the misconceptions they pathetically cherish".[22] This claim to "concrete fact" might explain why *Homosexuals in History* is written almost without footnotes, a feature for which Rowse became increasingly notorious (in 1996

Jonathan Bate pointed out that *My View of Shakespeare* had only two references, "both to other books by the author himself")[23]. However, the text does mention Rowse's source for several prurient comments about James: Anthony Weldon, a "disappointed courtier" who "'wrote with a pen of gall about James' Court'".[24] Weldon's agenda is all too easy to spot, and other historians have been quick to discount his writings as historical evidence.

Nevertheless, the same historians have pranced around the question of the King's sexuality, noting that James had male favourites on whom he lavished praise, money and titles; some feel that this was only normal in a Renaissance prince, others that it was a sign of a degrading (and unnamed) perversion that fatally compromised his kingship. Recently the historian Michael B. Young has surveyed this critical embarrassment.[25] D. H. Willson, author of the still-standard 1956 biography, wrote that James's "vice was common to many rulers and we need not be too shocked" but that "the completeness of the King's surrender to it indicates a loosening of his moral fibre."[26] Maurice Lee Jr., a leading scholar of Scottish Jacobean history, wrote that "James was one of those people ... who are simply not much interested in physical sex at all."[27] The foremost contemporary James scholar Jenny Wormald suggests that much of the criticism of James was a result of English xenophobia: but do we infer from this that his homosexuality is just an effect of xenophobic criticism?[28] For his part Young has asserted confidently that James "did have sex with his male favourites, and it is nonsense to deny it".[29] To support his claim Young puts to one side clearly hostile documents such as Weldon's (many dating from the Civil War), and instead cites a plethora of documents that accused James of sodomy in his own time. He shows how Scottish Presbyterians associated the King with Sodom; polemicist Thomas Scott wrote that James played with sodomites; and the poem "Warre of the Gods" refers to James "loveinge so 'gainst nature." And these are only the most blatant: Young piles up works by Philip Massinger, Thomas Middleton, William Rowley, Michael Drayton, George Withers, Alexander Leighton, John Reynolds, Thomas Beard, Barnaby Rich, John Everard and others, not to mention anonymous tracts and pamphlets, proving that James was ridiculed and criticized by a consistent set of resonant parallels: Edward II and his favourite Piers Gaveston, Tiberius and Sejanus, Henri III of France and his infamous *mignons*, and the King's own ancestor James III.[30]

Yet a historian in the Bray tradition would argue that in all these documents, there is little clarity as to what is being imputed: early modern allusions to "Sodom" and "sodomites" never map easily onto modern notions of homosexuality (even if we agreed as to the latter); the historical models can point as readily to evil counsel, misgovernment, and inappropriately cross-rank friendship as they can to sexual relations.

In his chapter on James, there is one moment where Rowse detects James' "heart": a highly charged letter to his favourite Somerset, who has withdrawn his affections and is bothering the King about trivial matters:

> I have been needlessly troubled this day with your desperate letters; you may take the right way if you list, and neither grieve me nor yourself. No man's, nor woman's, credit is able to cross you at my hands, if you pay me a part of that you owe me. But how you can give over that inward affection, and yet be a dutiful servant, I cannot understand that distinction. Heaven and earth shall bear me witness that, if you do but half of your duty unto me, you may be with me in the old manner – only by expressing that love to my person and respect to your master that God and man crave of you.

Rowse comments: "in this letter James bares his heart: there was the overwhelming need of the lonely man for affection." In other words, Rowse locates the homosexual "heart" of James in the letter's *rhetoric*; simultaneously, however, he has to admit that that rhetoric also expresses "the dire necessity of a sovereign for service."[31]

In the remainder of this article, I want to suggest another way of locating the homosexual James in history. By this I do not mean to produce evidence of James' self-identification as homosexual, a historical impossibility, nor miraculous DNA evidence of his engagement in "forbidden acts," some semen-stained hose tucked away as a keepsake by one of his favourites. Instead, I propose that we explore the space that produced the letter from Somerset which so appealed to Rowse, a space that we might call a *queer archive*.

My proposition of a queer archive draws on work done both in Renaissance studies and in gay and queer literary studies more generally which has interrogated the sociology of architecture. In her study of Elizabethan miniatures, Patricia Fumerton first drew attention to the importance of the location of these artistic forms, a location in which they not only circulated, but which also gave them their meaning. Miniatures occupied the space of the private room in the Elizabethan aristocratic household; "above all the miniature was a love token," writes Fumerton, "and it is an expression of such private emotions as love that it sought the intimacy of the bedroom."[32] The "intimacy of the bedroom," as the work of Fumerton and Alice Friedman has made clear, was an emergent concept in the early modern period, given rise to by innovations in the architecture of the sixteenth-century country house.[33] I have written elsewhere how these innovations gave rise to the new phenomenon of small rooms appearing all over large houses, sometimes secreted within massive interior walls, in false chimney stacks, in the centre of the house, or in high basements, with little or no natural light. These rooms, known as closets, were used primarily either for devotional purposes, or for study and business. While criticism has often insisted on the closet as a private space, and linked it to the rise of a new individual subjectivity, I argued that the closet was often occupied by more than one person, and that it should instead be seen as a site of transactions – often, because of their inaccessibility to public scrutiny, transactions that were viewed with suspicion.[34]

The closet, although ostensibly a secret, private space, produced its secrecy and privacy through the very *publicity* of that secrecy and privacy. Fumerton argues that the early moderns habitually represented "private experience as inescapably public": the subject lived "in public view but always withheld for itself a 'secret' room, cabinet, case, or other recess locked away (in full view) in one corner of the house." The paradox of being "locked away (in full view)" is central, Fumerton claims, to the early modern perception of public and private. Intimacy was achieved by attaining entrance to the "private" closet, for example by penetrating a long succession of decreasingly "public" chambers. "Such an experience must have registered with a double emphasis: one moved inward, but inwardness could be reached only after running a gauntlet of public outerness .... The overall sense was of privacy exhibited in private life."[35]

Following Fumerton's lead, we can see that not only the room itself and the relationships it contains, but also the textual materials it produces – what we might call its archive – share in the suspicious nature of the closet space. It operates as an "open secret," in D.A. Miller's well-known phrase: even when "we know perfectly well that the secret is known," he argues, "nonetheless we must persist, however ineptly, in guarding it *as secret*."[36] Eve Kosofsky Sedgwick famously developed Miller's ideas in her *Epistemology of the Closet*, noting that the relations of the closet are "the relations of the known and the unknown, the explicit and the inexplicit"; as well as these mappings being "around homo/heterosexual definition," they bear the traces of "mappings of secrecy and disclosure, and of the private and the public."[37] In other words, we are conditioned to see in privacy and secrecy, what is withheld, the signs of the sexual, and more specifically the homosexual. As readers, it is in secret, private texts, withheld from public scrutiny, that we are still willing to find the "homosexual in history."

The texts I want to consider here, the texts that signal James's homosexuality to the modern reader, clearly occupy this space. These are passages from a journal kept in the early 1620s by a young man named Simonds D'Ewes.[38] As we shall see, the conversations that give rise to the entries are themselves closet transactions; the material form of the document itself is particularly closeted. D'Ewes was the son of Paul D'Ewes, who became one of the Six Clerks in Chancery.[39] After a short and rather unhappy time at St. John's College, Cambridge, from 1618, the younger D'Ewes moved to London to take up legal studies at the Middle Temple in Michaelmas Term of 1620; he was called to the Bar in June 1623. The two entries date from August and October 1622, when he was 20 years old, and record conversations, often secretive conversations, between D'Ewes and his friends, some contemporaries at Cambridge, others from the Inns of Court, both all-male bastions of learning.

As D'Ewes explicitly states, "of things I discoursed with him that weere secrett," and the form of the text inscribes that secrecy. This section of D'Ewes" journal, which runs from January 1622 to April 1624, survives as BL Harley MS 481, a small octavo volume written in a very small, neat hand. Its contents are however partially obscured to the casual reader by the diarist's use of a rudimentary cipher substituting characters of the Roman alphabet with their Greek transliterations and other symbols.[40] This is a very particular sort of cipher – because, as a working cipher, it is redundant. Writing at the same time as D'Ewes, Francis Bacon, who both used and theorized the form, defines a cipher as "a secret and private alphabet, agreed upon by particular persons." Good ciphers should possess three qualities: "that they be easy and not laborious to write; that they be safe, and impossible to be deciphered; and lastly that they be, if possible, such as not to raise suspicion." This last is the most important: the perfect cipher is not the one that takes a long time to crack; it is the one that is never perceived to be a cipher, and so is never subjected to deciphering. "For if letters fall into the hands of those who have power either over the writers or over those to whom they are addressed," Bacon continues, "although the cipher itself may be safe and impossible to decipher, yet the matter comes under examination and question; unless the cipher be such as either to raise no suspicion or to elude inquiry."[41] D'Ewes's cipher is eminently breakable, perfectly readable even after only a few minutes' practice. Ostensibly a tool to ensure secrecy, the cipher in fact publicly signals the secrecy of material, rendering D'Ewes's cipher the textual equivalent of the closet – Miller's open secret. The pertinent entry, one of the lengthiest, is for 29 August 1622, and begins:

> This morning I studied well alsoe and had done soe to in the afternoone, but that my good freind came to mee, with whome I could not thinke it amiss to spend a few howres with him, having not seen him since the commencement, when I was with him and other my good freinds at Cambridge. Of things I discoursed with him that weere secrett as of the sinne of sodomye, how frequente it was in this wicked cittye, and if God did not provide some wonderfull blessing against it, wee could not but expect some horrible punishment for it; especially it being as wee had probable cause to feare, a sinne in the prince as well as the people, which God is for the most part the chastiser of himselfe, because noe man else indeed dare reprove or tell them of ther faults.[42]

"The sinne of sodomy," as discussed by D'Ewes and his friend, leads us not to a physical act, nor even a legal definition, but to a scriptural narrative at once vaguer and yet more precise. While generations of theological commentators have argued over what the sin of Sodom and Gomorrah might be, the scriptural episode is framed by and explained by a concern about judgement and discipline:

> 20   And the LORD said, Because the cry of Sodome and Gomorrah is great, and because their sinne is very grieuous:
>
> 21   I will goe downe now, and see whether they haue done altogether according to the cry of it, which is come vnto me: and if not, I will know.[43]

God reacts to a "cry," which is also "their sinne"; he goes down to investigate the truthfulness of this cry, and then, finding it to be justified, destroys the city. As Michael Warner has argued, judgement was the predominant early modern narrative of Sodom: "Because Sodom was the most prominent example of a judgement passed upon a polis in all the lore of Christendom, this call for discipline soon made Sodom a commonplace." As he goes on to argue, "the topic of sodomy was linked primarily to the topic of national judgement."[44] Thus, when Mervin Touchet, Earl of Castlehaven, was on trial in 1631 accused of a number of crimes including sodomy with his male servants, the prosecution invoked by way of analogy God's investigation into and fatal judgement of Sodom, to explain King Charles's investigation into and, perhaps inevitably, fatal judgement of Castlehaven:

> My Lord Audley, The King hath beene given to vnderstand both by reporte, and by the verdicte of divers gent*lemen* of qualitie in your Countrie [i.e. county], that you stand impeached of sundrie crimes, of a most high and heynous nature. And therfore to trie whether they bee true or noe, (to the end Iustice may receiue her dewe) hee brings yo^w this daie vnto triall, doeing therin like the Almightie Kinge of Kings in the 18th of Genesis ver: 20: 21: who went downe to see whether the synnes of Sodome and Gomorha were soe greivous as the cry of them that came vpp before him: Because the crie of Sodome & Gomorha is great, and their synne greiuous I will goe downe saith the Lord, & see, whether they haue done altogether accordinge to the cry of it, which is come vpp vnto me. And Kings on earth can haue noe better patterne to followe, then that of the Kinge of heauen.[45]

But in D'Ewes' conversation the King cannot fulfill his God-like punishment of the country for its sodomy, since it is "a sinne in the prince as well as the people," and only God can chastise the King "because noe man else indeed dare reprove or tell them of ther faults." If a King must punish the crying sin of sodomy, then a King's own sodomy is impossible to utter, beyond "telling."

D'Ewes goes on to make his case for this allegation:

> I told him a true storye which was a great presumption to this, of an usher of a schoole, a Frenchman, whoe had buggered a knights sonne and was brought into the Guild Hall, when Been was recorder and had surelye receaved his just punishment, but that Mountague then cheife justice, was sent to save him and by the King, as twas thought. Nay, besides Dr Hearne, one of the Kings phisitians offred to have the usher kelled privatelye, soe they would suffer it to passe over in darkenes; and that the childs uncle rann at him with a rapier, after his acquittance, and had slaine him, but that hee was stopped by the people saiing that, though hee had scaped the justice of man, hee could not the judgement of God.[46]

Here justice is foiled by the King. As with so many accusations of sodomy, the central buggery is overlaid with concerns relating to nation, age, and rank: the accused is a foreigner and an usher, the victim a vulnerable young scion of the English gentry. At the same time, the case buys into a drama being waged by competing jurisdictions, as London justice is challenged by the Crown – the case is held in the Guildhall, the most prominent symbol of London's guild system, rather than in the law courts of Westminster Hall; the City's elected Recorder, Been, is overruled by the royally appointed Lord Chief Justice Montagu. As the story progresses, the King, represented this time by his physician, proposes that the usher should be murdered, keeping the whole matter "in darkenes", but then "the people" call for the light of divine justice, recalling the narrative of sodomy as a sin crying up to God for vengeance.

D'Ewes then moves, without pausing, from this case to James' relationships with his two most recent (and most prominent) male favourites, Robert Carr, the Earl of Somerset, and George Villiers, currently Marquis of Buckingham:

> Besides, wee resolved that the King was wearye enough of the Marquess, but for shame would not putt him away. I tolde him of the letter in Sommersetts caskett, found by my Lord Cooke, for which since the King never loved him and finallye that, in other cuntryes, men talked familiarly of it. After which and some other matters passed over (where I tolde him that boyes weere growen to the height of wickednes to paint), wee parted, hee beeing to reach that night to Waltham to my Lord Dennyes and I retired to my study.[47]

Ever since James had first met George Villiers in 1614, rumours had circulated that the favourite's sway was coming to an end; but D'Ewes, like so many others, was mistaken: Buckingham was at James' side when he died in 1625. From Buckingham, it is a natural move for D'Ewes and his friend to turn their attention to his predecessor in the King's affections: Robert Carr, the Earl of Somerset. Following the implication of Somerset and his wife in the murder of Somerset's erstwhile friend, Sir Thomas Overbury, the Earl had been investigated by Sir Edward Coke. We know that Coke had indeed found some letters in Somerset's possession which had angered the King – despatches from his ambassador in Spain, which proved that Somerset, acting as James' secretary, had failed to pass on crucial foreign intelligence to his royal master.[48] But it seems unlikely that these are the letters at stake in this account. Without revealing the contents of the letters, D'Ewes implies that they are secretive, simply by speaking of them as being "in

Sommersetts casket". A casket was a small, lockable box, the repository of valuables, either writings or jewels. Like its larger counterpart, the closet, the casket signalled secrecy through its ability to be locked: the contents took on their particular value partially by being placed in, and locked into, the casket. The space was also easily sexualized: John Lyly wrote in 1580 that *"Euphues* had rather lye shut in a Ladyes casket, then open in a Schollers studie" – the joke being that if Euphues (the book's hero) is sexually gratified by being "shut in a Ladyes casket" then *Euphues* (the book) is "shut," locked up, and unread.[49] So here, whatever the letters may contain, it is what contains them that renders them sexual and secret. Could these letters include James' impassioned plea to Somerset that so appealed to Rowse?

D'Ewes's conversation relating to the King finishes with the observation that "in other cuntryes, men talked familiarly of it". This concern was revived on 2 October when D'Ewes spent an evening with Mr. Masters and William Crashaw:

> Neither could this day add anye great progresse to my studyes, butt at night, going to visite Mr Masters newlye come to towne and finding Mr Crasshaw with him, wee had much good discourse, especiallye of some rare bookes, as Pruritanus, Proscenius, and now Corona Regia or Manes Causaboni. The other two weere sett out 1608 or 1609, of which, because I will speake somewhat of my memorialls, in the Kings time, I will speake the less heere. Pruritanus was infinite profane, but the other the two weere terrible and whollye against the King himselfe, accusing him of athisme, sodomye, etc...[50]

Of these works, the only one that is easily traceable is *Corona Regia*, sometimes called *Manes Causabonii* and it points us to a second discourse circulating about James and sodomy. This mock panegyric to James, published in 1615, bore the title *Is. Casauboni Corona Regia, Id Est Panegyrici Cujusdam Vere Aurei, Quem Jacobo I Magnœ Britanniœ Etc. Regi Fidei Defensori Delinearat, Fragmenta Ab Euphormione Inter Schedus* τοῦ μακαρί-τοῦ *Inventa, Collecta, et in Lucem Edita*, with the imprint of the King's own printer John Bill.[51] Both the authorial ascription and the printing house were fictitious: Isaac Casaubon, the famed scholar who had recently made his home in England, had died the previous year. James reacted to this libel more passionately than to any other, launching an international search for its author, printer, and publisher, assuming that the book originated in the Anglo-Catholic stronghold at Douai.[52] As late as 1639 a

Brussels bookseller, Jean de Perriet, was claiming a reward for his identification of the guilty party.[53]

So what was it about *Corona Regia* that so upset James? At first glance, the text is a eulogy to the King, lacking any outright attack. One answer is suggested by a copy of the book now in the British Library, shelfmark 292.a.42. In this copy, a leaf (sig. D10) has been torn out, and a short passage on the bottom of the preceding page heavily scored. From another copy, we find that this passage gives a remarkably informed account of how James has promoted a series of young, beautiful men – John Ramsey, who allegedly saved his life during the "Gowrie Conspiracy" of 1600; Philip Herbert, who rose to become Earl of Montgomery; Robert Carr, later Earl of Somerset, and the latest favourite, George Villiers – only to drop each one when a younger, more beautiful man came along. In keeping with the text's form of eulogy, however, the passage praises James' policy of "advancing the beautiful," because after all, isn't that only "exalting the good"?[54]

Here again, it is the form that is everything. *Corona Regia* circulated on the international book market with a content that was ostensibly pro-Jacobean; there is nothing concrete here to connect James with the sin of sodomy. For this we have to turn to a closet text like D'Ewes's that explicitly reads *Corona Regia* as engaging with sodomy; D'Ewes clearly uses the term "sodomye" in relation to the prince and the journal's cipher renders it perfectly visible as "zinne of zodomye", and a large "S" in the margin unmasks the one letter that D'Ewes has thought good to change. In the most private of texts, the journal, under a personal cipher, the King's sodomy still jumps off the page.

The past quarter-century has seen momentous advances in gay Renaissance history. Our motivation, our aims, our goals, and our methodologies have all been subjected to a stringent self-conscious analysis. No longer are we allowed simply to respond to the passionate outpourings of what appears to be a jilted lover, to join hands across three hundred years of history. But are our new techniques really so different? D'Ewes's ciphered journal, Somerset's casketed letters, and the ripped page of *Corona Regia* are diverse forms of evidence, but they share a powerful function. In their (ostensibly) occluded, opaque, locked, and mutilated forms, they signal their own open secrecy, their status as closet texts, a queer archive. I suggest that it is this archive, in the transactions it records and the materials it allows to survive, that still indulges the twenty-first-century reader in the Rowsian fantasy of the homosexual in history.

Notes

1. A.L. Rowse, Rowse MSS, as cit. in Richard Ollard, *A Man of Contradictions: a Life of A.L. Rowse* (London: Allen Lane, 1999), p. 272.
2. Michel Foucault, *Histoire de la Sexualité: La Volonté du Savoir* (Paris: 1976); *The History of Sexuality: an Introduction*, trans. Robert Hurley (London: Allen Lane, 1978).
3. Foucault, *History of Sexuality, Volume One, an Introduction*, pp. 42–3.
4. Alan Bray, "Homosexuality and the Signs of Male Friendship in Elizabethan England," *History Workshop* 29 (1990): 1–19, at 2. This is a neat condensation of the ideas he promulgated in *Homosexuality in Renaissance England* (London: Gay Men's Press, 1982; 2nd edn, 1988).
5. Bray, "Homosexuality and the Signs of Male Friendship in Elizabethan England," p. 3.
6. A.L. Rowse, *Homosexuals in History: a Study of Ambivalence in Society, Literature and the Arts* (London: Weidenfeld & Nicolson, 1977).
7. Rowse, *Homosexuals in History*, p. xi.
8. G. Lowes Dickinson, *The Autobiography of G. Lowes Dickinson and Other Unpublished Writings*, ed. Dennis Proctor (London: Duckworth, 1973), p. 11.
9. Rowse, "The Soul of Kings," in *Portraits and Views: Literary and Historical* (London: Macmillan, 1979), pp. 219–23.
10. Rowse, *Homosexuals in History*, p. xii.
11. Ibid.
12. Ibid., p. 46.
13. Rowse, *My View of Shakespeare: the Shakespeare Revolution* (London: Duckworth, 1996), pp. 24–5; see also pp. 12–13; Ollard, *Man of Contradictions*, p. 249.
14. Rowse, Rowse MSS, as cit. Ollard, *Man of Contradictions*, p. 272.
15. Ollard, *Man of Contradictions*, p. 272.
16. Bruce R. Smith, *Homosexual Desire in Shakespeare's England: a Cultural Poetics* (Chicago: University of Chicago Press, 1991), p. 26.
17. Gregory W. Bredbeck, *Sodomy and Interpretation: Marlowe to Milton* (Ithaca, NY: Cornell University Press, 1991), p. x.
18. Rowse, *Homosexuals in History*, p. 48.
19. Ibid., p. 67.
20. Ibid., pp. 57, 60.
21. Ibid., p. 52.
22. Ibid., p. xii.
23. Jonathan Bate, quoted in Arnold Kemp, "'Dark Lady' Scholar Dies At 93" [obituary of A.L. Rowse], *Observer*, 5 October 1997: 9.
24. Rowse, *Homosexuals in History*, pp. 55–6.
25. Michael B. Young, *James VI and I and the History of Homosexuality* (Basingstoke: Palgrave [Macmillan], 2000) 1–2.
26. David H. Willson, *King James VI and I*, p. 337 as cit. Young, *James VI and I*, p. 1.
27. Maurice Lee Jr. *Great Britain's Solomon* (Urbana IL: Illinois University Press, 1990), p. 234–6, 240–2, 247–9, 255, as cit. Young, *James VI and I*, p. 1.
28. Jenny Wormald, "James VI and I: Two Kings or One?," *History* 68 (1983) 187–92 as cit. Young, *James VI and I*, p. 2.
29. Young, *James VI and I*, p. 135.

30   Ibid., *passim*.

31. Rowse, *Homosexuals in History*, p. 61.

32. Patricia Fumerton, "'Secret' Arts: Elizabethan Miniatures and Sonnets," *Representations* 15 (1986): 57–97, at 60.

33. Fumerton, *Cultural Aesthetics: Renaissance Literature and the Practice of Social Ornament* (Chicago: University of Chicago Press, 1991); Alice T. Friedman, *House and Household in Elizabethan England: Wollaton Hall and the Willoughby Family* (Chicago: University of Chicago Press, 1988).

34. Alan Stewart, "The Early Modern Closet Discovered," *Representations* 50 (1995): 76–100. For a critique of this argument, see Lena Cowen Orlin, "Gertrude's Closet," *Shakespeare Jahrbuch* 134 (1998): 44–67.

35. Fumerton, *Cultural Aesthetics*, pp. 76–7, 69, 71–2.

36. D.A. Miller, "Secret Subjects, Open Secrets," in *The Novel and the Police* (Berkeley CA: University of California Press, 1988), pp. 192–220, at 207.

37. Eve Kosofsky Sedgwick, *Epistemology of the Closet* (Berkeley CA: University of California Press, 1990), pp. 3, 71.

38. BL Harley MS 481; published as *The Diary of Sir Simonds D'Ewes (1622–1624): Journal D'un Etudiant Londonien Sous Le Règne De Jacques 1er*, ed. Elisabeth Bourcier (Paris: Didier, 1974).

39. On D'Ewes see Andrew G. Watson, "Introduction" to *The Library of Sir Simonds D'Ewes* (London: British Museum, 1966), pp. 1–92.

40. The volume was first deciphered by Gladys A. Harrison: "The Diary Of Sir Simonds D'Ewes Deciphered, for the Period Jan. 1622–April 1624: With an Index and Introduction, and with Notes for the Year 1622," unpublished PhD dissertation, University of Minnesota, 1915.

41   *Opera Francisco baronis de Vervlamio, Vice-Comitis Sancti Albani, tomvs primvs: Qui continet De Dignitate & Augmentis Scientiarum libros IX* (London: John Haviland, 1623), N3^r–Oo2^r. I am here using (with occasional amendments) the translation in *Works*, ed. James Spedding, Robert Leslie Ellis, and Douglas Denon Heath, 7 vols (London: 1857–59) 4, pp. 444–7, which draws heavily on an earlier translation: *Of the Advancement and Proficience of Learning or the Partitions of Sciences IX Bookes*, trans. Gilbert Wats (Oxford: Leonard Lichfield for Robert Young and Edward Forrest, 1640), Kk4^v–Ll3^v.

42. BL Harley MS 481 f. 16^v. D'Ewes, *Diary*, ed. Bourcier, pp. 92–3 [entry for 29 August 1622].

43. *The Holy Bible, Conteyning the Old Testament, and the New: Newly Translated out of the Originall Tongues: & with the former Translations Diligently Compared* (London: Robert Barker, 1611), Genesis xix.

44. Michael Warner, "New English Sodom," *American Literature* 64 (1992) 19–47; rpt. in Goldberg (ed.) *Queering the Renaissance*, pp. 330–58, at 330–2.

45. Folger Shakespeare Library, Washington DC, MS V.b.328, ff. 4^v–5^r. For recent work on the Castlehaven trial, see Cynthia Herrup: "The Patriarch At Home: the Trial of the Second Earl of Castlehaven for Rape and Sodomy," *History Workshop Journal* 41 (1996): 1–19; "'To Pluck Bright Honour from the Pale-Faced Moon': Gender and Honour in the Castlehaven Story," *Transactions of the Royal Historical Society*, 6th ser., 6 (1996): p. 137–59; "Finding the Bodies", *GLQ* 5 (1999): 255–65; *A House in Gross Disorder: Sex, Law, and the Second Earl of Castlehaven* (New York: OUP, 1999); Stewart, "Queer Renaissance Bodies?: Sex, Violence, and the Constraints of

Periodisation," in Kate Chedgzoy, Emma Francis and Murray Pratt (eds.) *In a Queer Place: Sexualities and Belonging in British and European Contexts* (Aldershot: Ashgate, 2002) pp. 137–53; Nick Radel, chapter 7 of this volume.

46. BL Harley MS 481 f. 16ᵛ. D'Ewes, *Diary*, ed. Bourcier, p. 93 [entry for 22 August 1622].

47. BL Harley MS 481 ff. 16ᵛ–17ʳ. D'Ewes, *Diary*, ed. Bourcier, p. 93 [entry for 22 August 1622].

48. As reported by Sarmiento to Philip III, 20/30 January 1616. Samuel Rawson Gardiner, "On Certain Letters of Diego Sarmiento de Acuña, Count of Gondomar, Giving an Account of the Affair of the Earl of Somerset, With Remarks on the Career of Somerset as a Public Man," *Archaeologia* 41 (1867): 151–86, at 179–80. See Alan Stewart, *The Cradle King: A Life of James VI and I* (London: Chatto & Windus, forthcoming) ch. 16.

49. John Lyly, "Euphues and his World," in *The Complete Works of John Lyly*, 3 vols. (Oxford, 1932), Vol. 2, p. 9.

50. BL Harley MS 481 f. 20ᵛ. D'Ewes, *Diary*, ed. Bourcier, 100 [entry for 2 October 1622].

51. "Isaac Casaubon", *Corona Regia* ('London': 'John Bill', 1615).

52. For correspondence relating to this hunt, see BL Stowe MS 176, f. 170; BL Egerton MS 2592 f.37b; BL Egerton MS 2593 ff. 17, 28; BL Egerton MS 2594 f. 19; BL Egerton MS 2595 f. 197.

53. Mark Pattison, *Isaac Casaubon 1559–1614*, 2ⁿᵈ edn (Oxford: Clarendon Press, 1892) 483.

54. "Et quis reprehendat? promouere pulchros, id verò est bonos exaltare. Ioannem Ramsey Scotum, interfecto Gowero, non minus pulchrum quàm fortem arbitratus, Equitem Auratum, & quasi adhuc affectui non satisfaceres, Vicecomitem creasti. Sed cur in vno hæreres? Philippum Harbert, Fratrem minorem natu Comitis de Pembrook, adolescentem venustate, gratiosum, à cubiculo tibi esse voluisti, quo in gradu beneficio obsequium reddi potuit. Meruit & hic profusiorem beneuolentiam. Comes enim de Mungomeri creatus, variisque muneribus ditatus est. Sed quid placere semper potest? Triennio ferè exacto, pulcher tibi visus est Robertus Carr, puer ex honorariis, præmiisque mox dignus habitus, non lentis gradibus ad summas dignitates ascendit. Laudatem fortunam adolescentis, nisi eam humanitas tua vinceret. Primum quidem Eques Auratus factus est, deinde Vicecomes de Rochester, mox à Consiliis, circa annum ætatis XXVI. postea Comes de Sommerset, denique Magnus Cubicularius tuus. Huic iam maturo, variisque nobilium proscriptorum bonis ditato vxorem addere voluisti, & qualem obsecro? diuortio quæsitam. Hos secutus est incomparabili forma adolescens, Georgius Villiers, à Regina ipsa in cubiculum tuum introductus, vbi eodem dies & Eques, & à Cubiculo factus est, nec multo post à Fisco Regio annuam decem millium Florenorum pensionem accepti." *Corona Regia*, D9ᵛ-D10ᵛ.

3
Male Love and Friendship in the Eighteenth Century

George E. Haggerty

In a 1978 interview Foucault said: "If people see two guys go off together to sleep in the same bed, that's tolerable, but if in the next morning the two get up smiling, if they hold hands, that's unforgivable".[1] Didier Eribon cites this passage in a recent discussion of "Michel Foucault's Histories of Sexuality," and he shows how Foucault's thought developed from an emphasis on transgressive sex acts to a belief that "what makes homosexuality 'troubling' is the homosexual mode of life, much more than the sexual act itself."[2] In Foucault's words: "To imagine a sexual act that doesn't conform to law or nature is not what disturbs people. But that individuals begin to love one another – there's the problem."[3]

Eribon reminds us that Foucault's attitude to the history of sexuality shifted between earlier writings such as *Folie et Déraison: Histoire de La Folie à L'âge Classique* (1961) [*Madness and Civilization*, (abridged, 1973)] and the later *La Volonté de Savoir* (1976), which was translated as *The History of Sexuality, Volume I, an Introduction* (1978).[4] What I find most interesting is Eribon's discussion of Foucault's view of "homosexuality" in the earlier volume. In several paragraphs not included in the English translation of the work, Foucault writes about the last executions for sodomy in the early eighteenth century and asserts: "The new indulgence toward sodomy finds its particular significance both in the moral condemnation and in the sanctions provided by scandal that begin to punish social and literary expressions of homosexuality". He says moreover that:

> Sodomy, formerly condemned under the same rubric as magic and heresy, in the context of religious profanation, is now only condemned for reasons of morality, alongside homosexuality.

70

Homosexuality itself becomes the main focus of the condemnation – added on to sodomitical practices. And at the same time homosexual feelings and desire begin to provoke a new sense of outrage. Two different experiences, previously separate, become confused: the prohibitions on sodomy and the dubious loves of homosexuality. A single form of condemnation will now envelope both of them and will draw an entirely new line of division in the world of feelings. A new moral ensemble is thus formed.[5]

Although he later contradicts this understanding of the emergence of "a new moral ensemble," in his celebrated dictum about the emergence of the "homosexual" as the result of sexological discourse in the later nineteenth century, Foucault here articulates a position that many of us working on the eighteenth century have come to accept: love between men begins to be recognized as an organizing principle of feelings, as a special sort of sensibility (a "propensity" as Hester Lynch Piozzi calls it when talking about Beckford) at this time.[6] Much work on the history of sexuality in England has emphasized sodomitical assault and intergenerational rape as the most available way to analyze and categorize same-sex desire. I would like to focus instead on the "dubious loves" that Foucault mentions here. When love and sodomy are combined in "a new moral ensemble," he seems to say, the possibilities for homophobic identification proliferate.

Love has often been ignored in histories of sexuality, in part because it is the most elusive of the four-letter words and in part because it is has not been understood as central to the question of sexuality itself. Foucault's remarks remind us that emotional relations do have a place, a quite central place, in fact, in understanding the history of male-male relations (and their representation). In *Men In Love*, I tried to place "love" within the history of sexuality.[7] If love has functioned in Western culture precisely because of the ways in which it euphemizes desire (lust), and if heteronormative culture has always been able to use it to short-circuit questions of sexuality and/or same-sex desire, then it is time to reclaim love and understand its place in the study of male-male desire as well. Histories of sodomy rely on trial records and broadside publications for the bulk of their material, where love between men is rarely described. When it does appear, in personal letters or works of fiction, it is often ignored.

As a complement to discussions of the history of sodomy, then, I have proposed male love as an erotic category that can help us talk about the emotional bond between the pairs of friends that appear everywhere in the century. As I argue in *Men In Love*, the love that Gray expresses for Bonstetten, or that Walpole expresses for Conway, is as powerful and as expressive as any love between two people. If relations as erotic-seeming as these can also be considered erotic in fact, then why is it so threatening to acknowledge them as examples of erotic love? When it is used between men, that is, love is meant to imply everything except erotic love. But love is the word that is used (and misused) in Western culture to describe both erotic and emotional bonds between two people. It is a mistake to think that the expression of love is erotic only when the people expressing it are differently gendered. Love has functioned in Western culture (and in other cultures as well) as an ennobling and a transformative power. If this is true for men and women in the courtly tradition, then why is it not available for men as well?

It is available for men, of course, in the rhetoric of friendship.[8] This tradition provides models for male love that are often ignored or explained away. Writers throughout the century invoke this tradition in order to modify the rigidities of masculinity and express their love for one another. Often aware of the complexities of the classical tradition to which they allude, Gray, Walpole, Beckford, and countless others find in the rhetoric of friendship a vocabulary to describe precisely what culture would repress. At the same time, as Foucault's remarks remind us, this love allows a more complete identification that will eventually be used for the purposes of prosecution. (I am thinking of various modes of mockery that are employed in the "molly house" trials but also more specifically in Oscar Wilde's trial for "gross misconduct.") Expressions of love between men in the eighteenth century, then, can be read as expressions of a complex cultural interaction that do more than "queer" the works or writers involved.

In an article that has appeared since my book was published, David Halperin has insisted that expressions of love between men, such as those in heroic drama or in personal letters, are a measure of the limits of eroticism in the eighteenth century. In his essay, "How to Do the History of Male Homosexuality," Halperin argues that erotic pleasure is excluded from friendships and that the love expressed there is to be distinguished from what he calls "sexual love."[9] I hope it goes without saying that I admire David Halperin and that I have learned a great deal from him. Everyone working on topics that involve a historical approach to sexuality owes a debt of gratitude to him for his fundamental work. But admiration and gratitude do not preclude disagreement. Because he is such an important scholar and because this essay

in particular has such far-reaching implications, and attempts categor-
izations that I consider counter-productive for an understanding of
English culture, society, and literature in the eighteenth century, it is
all the more important for me to argue for a different understanding of
how male-male desire was expressed and understood. I hope to complicate our understanding of male-male erotic pleasure by looking at the
ways in which Halperin's uncharacteristically rigid distinctions in this
essay have less force when subjected to a different interpretation of the
historical and literary evidence. Rather than use "love" and "friendship" in their strictest platonic sense, as Halperin does, I would like to
show the ways in which emotional intensity and erotic attachment
worked together in many eighteenth-century relationships between
men. Until we understand that emotional bonds can be as erotic as
much of what qualifies as "sodomy" (or often more erotic), we will fail
to see the full range of male relations in eighteenth-century England.

Antony's friend Dolabella, in Dryden's *All for Love* (1677), for
instance, is one of the Romans sent to Alexandra to convince Antony
to give up his Egyptian diversion and return to the straight path of
virtue. Dolabella is described as one "whom Caesar loves beyond the
love of women," and he uses this lovability to seduce the wavering
hero from the pleasures of Alexandria. Antony becomes wistful when
Dolabella's name is mentioned in this context:

> He loved me too:
> I was his soul, he lived not but in me.
> We were so closed within each other's breasts,
> The rivets were not found that joined us first.
> That does not reach us yet: we were so mixed
> As meeting streams, both to ourselves were lost;
> We were one mass; we could not give or take
> But from the same, for he was I, I he.[10]

Antony's hymn of praise, straining at language as it does and stretching to "reach" the expression of their love, encodes in almost blatant
terms an affection that is more than "platonic." I have elsewhere
talked about how the language of this passage underlines the possibilities of physical affection ("The rivets were not found"; "We were so
mixed/ As meeting streams"; "We were one mass"), and I have suggested that these images stress physicality, fluidity, and bodily
identification in a way that belies any simple "friendship" interpretation.[11] This outburst of male love, moreover, is not a quiet aside that

takes place on the margins of the literary; it is instead one of the definitive speeches of one of the most popular tragedies of the period. This sexualized male relation, in other words, helps to define the heroic. In doing this, Dryden defies the problematic nature of male love by projecting an idealized version of that love into the classical age in order to make it available to his contemporaries.

For Halperin, the language of identification, such as that expressed here, is precisely what distances this relation from what he understands as the erotic in classical terms. After citing my reading of the play, Halperin says:

> The thematic insistence on mutuality and the merging of individual identities, although it may invoke in minds of modern readers the formulas of heterosexual love ... in fact situates avowals of reciprocal love between male friends in an honorable, even glamorous tradition of heroic comradeship: precisely banishing any hint of subordination on the part of one friend to the other, and thus any suggestion of hierarchy, the emphasis on the fusion of two souls into one actually distances such a love from erotic passion.[12]

By insisting on the same classical model of male relations that he articulated throughout *One Hundred Years of Homosexuality*, relations based on hierarchy and status, Halperin reifies male-male relations and makes it impossible for men who see themselves as equal to express their love for one another.[13] He is on particularly shaky ground when he cites this passage from *All for Love*, however. For, as I argue in my discussion of this play, Dolabella is coded as the hyper-sexual love object of both Caesar and Marc Antony, whom Cleopatra can easily enflame and use in her plot to keep Antony from deserting her. Surely Dryden did not choose this character to represent a kind of friendship that was "distanced" from the world of sexual love. It is more likely that he was trying to show how erotic passions function in the context of imperial power. As in Nathaniel Lee's depiction of Alexander and Hephestion in *The Rival Queens*, moreover, the love expressed here is a bond that adds grandeur to the characters it depicts. Unlike Danny Glover and Mel Gibson in *Lethal Weapon*, whom Halperin cites as exemplary non-erotic friends, Antony and Dolabella do not tease each other and the audience with the naughty possibility of same-sex love. Rather, they express it openly, not as a sordid crime to be snickered about, but as a grand and ennobling sentiment that helps to measure their tragic greatness. Halperin wants to deny the possibility of love between friends in any situation in which this love might seem normative or celebratory. But when Restoration and eighteenth-century audiences encountered these classical models of friendship, surely they saw in them something exotic and exhilarating, something unlike what they saw in the world around them. If at the same time they could be inspired to see the possibility of a friendship imbued with eroticism, then that could have, if not a normative, then an idealizing force all its own.

In an essay with a contrasting line of argument, Halperin demonstrates, by using examples from pre- and early-modern culture, situations in which both sexual morphology and sexual subjectivity are richly articulated in literary and quasi-literary texts. He revises our notion of how we can talk about the relation between behaviors and individuals, and he does so by building on Foucault's insights: "We need to find ways of asking how different historical cultures fashioned different sorts of links between sexual acts, on the one hand, and sexual tastes, styles, dispositions, characters, gender presentations, and forms of subjectivity, on the other."[14] In talking about Restoration tragedy, and indeed about later-seventeenth-century culture, it would be wrong to insist that erotically charged male relations were historically inappropriate. Libertine culture regularly celebrated male-male sexual encounters, albeit of a kind different from that which is represented in the plays, and made male-male desire less shocking than twentieth-century readers might suppose. Surely the court of Charles II, which prided itself on the permissiveness of European manners, would have found its way to condone or even encourage the kind of eroticization of male relations that appear everywhere in the work of Dryden, Lee, Thomas Otway, and others.

Moreover, as I argue in *Men In Love*, it is also worth considering the theatrical context. Montague Summers long ago noted the "Uranian" features of the Restoration stage, and he made it clear that male-male intrigues of various kinds were the rule rather than the exception of the Restoration tiring room. In some cases the playwrights themselves were involved in various theatrical scandals, and Nathaniel Lee's impassioned involvement in the theater raised more than a few eyebrows. In addition, the actors who played the parts I have been discussing were often associated with the very sexual practices that Halperin insistently claims they cannot include. When Charles Hart, one of the central actors of the King's Company, introduced the roles of Antony and Alexander in 1677, his young male partner was Thomas Clark.[15] Summers lists Clark among several actors whom he cites as "homosexual." The love scenes then, those between Antony and

Dolabella and those between Alexander and the young Hephestion, would include the dimension of erotic intrigue even if the classical models did not. If Clark, and other actors such as Edward Kynaston and William Mountfort, were involved in sexual intrigues of various kinds, then the kinds of scenes I have been discussing would have a valence far different from that in which male love is seen as a breach of decorum.[16] These plays assert that love in a direct and almost aggressive way. Foucault suggests that friendship makes sex between men somehow socially acceptable. The plays that I am talking about use the bonds between men to make their love visible. Rather than insisting on sex, in other words, the plays insist on the power of emotion. At the same time that they celebrate the love between men, they make that love available for the admiration of everyone.[17]

For Halperin, however, the argument is much more rigidly categorical:

> Sexual love, at least as it is viewed within the cultural horizons of the male world, is all about penetration and therefore all about position, superiority and inferiority, rank and status, gender and difference. Friendship, by contrast, is all about sameness: sameness of rank and status, sameness of sentiment, sameness of identity. It is this very emphasis on identity, similarity, and mutuality that distances the friendship tradition, in its original and discursive context, from the world of sexual love.[18]

I think that by making this distinction between "sexual love" and "friendship" Halperin is imposing difference where none exists. Besides, is it really true that sexual love is "all about penetration"? One kind of male love surely fits this description, but are there not others? Does anything in the eighteenth century suggest that male love can be about something other than penetration? Well, of course it does. The countless examples of passive lachrymose males, of impotent and emasculated heroes, of faltering, stuttering, and assertive masculinity all suggest to me that the eighteenth century is an age when love between men was articulated in a way that could challenge the status quo.

Besides friendship and male love, Halperin proposes four other categories for describing male-male desire through history. These are effeminacy; pederasty or active sodomy; passivity or inversion; and the twentieth-century portmanteau concept of homosexuality. Halperin makes fairly rigid distinctions here, but as in the case of friendship, I think these categories cannot survive careful attention to what is going on in the eighteenth century. As Trumbach and others have shown, effeminacy and sodomy are not always distinct categories in the eighteenth century; nor are pederasty and "active sodomy" in any sense the same.[19] Inversion is not a well-articulated concept in the eighteenth century, nor is passivity. But where they may be said to exist, as in some of the examples I alluded to above, they are not necessarily distinct from any of the other categories.

Beckford, for instance, uses the language of friendship and love when he talks rapturously about his feelings for his young cousin William "Kitty" Courtenay. Now in this case, the role that Halperin calls pederasty, which of course depends on a kind of status hierarchy, is described in terms that are virtually indistinguishable from the language of heroic friendship I have quoted above. In one letter, for instance, he writes to Courtenay's Aunt Charlotte, later to become the wife of Beckford's tormentor, Lord Loughborough, asking her to intercede with the boy, who has not responded to his letters:

> Surely he [Courtenay] will never find any other Being so formed by nature for his companion as myself. Of all the human creatures male or female with which I have been acquainted in various countries and at different periods he is the only one that seems to have been cast in my mold.
>
> When I first began to know him the pleasing delusion would often suggest itself of our having been friends in some other existence. You know he was never so happy as when reclined by my side listening to my wild musick or the strange stories which sprang up in my fancy for his amusement. Those were the most delightful hours of my existence.[20]

This letter goes on to tell of shared musical moments and of a friendship on which he depends for life itself. Beckford uses a vocabulary understood as erotic in the eighteenth century; "wild music" and "strange stories" could hardly be considered innocent, nor would the image of the younger and older boy "reclined" together be anything but provocative. Still, this is the language of friendship: physical and emotional intimacy that defies Halperin's description of pederasty as "male sexual penetration of a subordinate male."[21]

If eighteenth-century pederasty cannot fit easily into the category that Halperin provides, effeminacy is even less determined by a classical model. In "various European cultural traditions," Halperin claims,

> "those men who refused to rise to the challenge [of masculinity], who abandoned the competitive society of men for the amorous society of

women, who pursued a life of pleasure, who made love instead of war – they incarnated the classical stereotype of effeminacy."

Halperin asserts that this stereotype, "which sorts out rather oddly with modern notions of hetero- and homosexuality, goes far back in time. For the ancient Greeks and Romans, a man who indulged his taste for sexual pleasure with women did not necessarily enhance his virility but often undermined it".[22] As Trumbach and others have argued, the connections between effeminacy and sexuality become more explicit in the later eighteenth century, even if the classical model does not insist on this connection.[23] Still eighteenth-century effeminacy defies attempts to associate it with one form of behavior or misbehavior.

Consider, for instance, the friendship between John Lord Hervey and Stephen Fox. Hervey's effeminacy was infamous. He was Pope's Lord Sporus, that "mere-white Curd of Ass's milk ... This painted Child of Dirt that stinks and stings."[24] As I have argued in *Men In Love*, Pope's portrait suggests a confusion of gender ("His Wit was all see-saw between *that* and *this*,/ Now high, now low, now master up now Miss,/ And he himself one vile antithesis") that is, equivalent to a kind of sexual monstrosity.[25] Hervey was attacked publicly as a sexual misfit, charged, for instance, with "a certain, unnatural, reigning Vice (indecent and almost shocking to mention)."[26] The substance of these attacks may be more political and literary than sexual, but it is nonetheless clear that effeminacy and sodomy are to a certain extent interchangeable.

At the same time, Robert Halsband tells in his biography of Hervey of a life of constant political involvement and deep personal friendships. These friendships, especially those with Stephen Fox and Francisco Algarotti, are intensely erotic, and every indication suggests that his only love affairs were with other men. The various parodic versions of Hervey's "gender" ("the world consists of men, women, and Herveys," Lady Mary Wortley Montagu said) should not blind us to the touchingly intense expressions of love that are articulated in the letters to Stephen Fox.[27] In other words, the love between friends, this male love, is, simply, love as it has been defined in heteronormative culture: emotionally extreme and physically expressive. Like Walpole and Gray, Hervey loves his friends and is happy to celebrate that love in letters that are steamy and suggestive.

You have left some such remembrances behind you [he writes to Fox] that I assure you ... you are not in the least Danger of being forgotten. The favours I have received at Your Honour's Hands are of such a nature that tho' the impression might wear out of my Mind, yet they are written in such lasting characters upon every Limb, that "tis impossible for me to look on a Leg or an Arm without having my Memory refresh'd." Or: I have often thought, if any very idle Body had Curiosity enough to intercept & examine my Letters, they would certainly conclude they came from a Mistress than a Friend. ... I love you & love you more than I thought I could love any thing.[28]

Effeminacy and sodomy are labels that disguise these intense personal relations and render them available for public scrutiny and censure. There is no other way to talk about the figure who "Now trips a Lady, now struts a Lord."[29] In public terms, Hervey is an effeminate sodomite, a figure of mockery. But what if the love he expresses defies that label? That is what would be really threatening. It seems to me that we can learn more by looking at these intense loving relations that form the basis of a male-male intimacy and defy the sodomitical label. I would go so far as to claim that out of such circles of male intimacy a new kind of self-awareness gradually emerges. This is the history of sexuality too.

Could the eighteenth century be so transitional that none of Halperin's categories work particularly well in discussing the evidence we have? If eighteenth-century England offers counter-examples in every category and repeatedly suggests the ways in which these categories might blend into one another, then it would seem that in any except in the broadest possible interpretations, such categories have little to tell us. If on the other hand, Foucault's "new moral ensemble" has a resonance that these examples support, then perhaps we need to reassert the claim that love does more to establish a new kind of sexual subjectivity than the histories of sexuality have previously led us to believe. If there is a way to make love a part of the history of sexuality, then it will have far broader cultural implications than have ever been allowed. If the men who loved other men can at last be acknowledged, then the history of male relations can be seen as complex in the ways that all human relations are. This does not seem like a lot to ask; but, as Foucault says, when "individuals begin to love one another – there's the problem."

Notes

1. Michel Foucault, "Sexual Choice/Sexual Acts," in Paul Rabinow (ed.), *Ethics: Subjectivity and Truth*, trans. Robert Hurley Vol. I of *Essential Works of Foucault, 1954–1984*. (New York: New Press, 1997), p. 153.

2. Didier Eribon, "Michel Foucault's Histories of Sexuality," trans. Michael Lucey *GLQ* 7.1 (2001): 72.

3. Michel Foucault, "Friendship as a Way of Life," in Rabinow, *Ethics: Subjectivity and Truth.*, pp. 136–7. Both passages are quoted in Eribon, "Foucault's Histories of Sexuality," p. 72.

4. Eribon, "Foucault's Histories of Sexually," pp. 33–55.

5. Michel Foucault, *Folie et Déraison: Histoire de La Folie à L'âge Classique* (Paris: Plon, 1961; rev. ed. Paris; Gallimard-Tel, 1972), pp. 102–3. This and the following passage are not available in the English translation of this work. The translation here is by Michael Lucey in Eribon, "Foucault's Histories of Sexuality," pp. 39–40.

6. Hester Lynch (Thrale) Piozzi, *Thraliana, The Diary of Hester Lynch Thrale (Later Mrs. Piozzi), 1776–1809.*, ed. Katherine C. Balderston; 2nd ed. (Oxford: Clarendon Press, 1951), Vol. II p. 799.

7. George Haggerty, *Men In Love: Masculinity and Sexuality in the Eighteenth Century* (New York: Columbia University Press, 1999).

8. For a brief summary of the issues involved in considering the rhetoric of friendship, see Peter M. Nardi, "Friendship", in George E. Haggerty (ed.), *Gay Histories and Cultures: an Encyclopedia* (New York: Garland, 2000), pp. 356–58, and Peter M. Nardi (ed.) *Men's Friendships* (Newberry Park, CA: Sage, 1992).

9. David Halperin, "How to Do the History of Male Homosexuality," *GLQ* 6 (2000): 87–123.

10. John Dryden, *All for Love*, ed. David M. Vieth (Lincoln: University of Nebraska Press, 1972), lines 90–6.

11. Haggerty, *Men in Love*, pp. 25–6.

12. Halperin, "How to Do the History," p. 101.

13. David Halperin, *One Hundred Years of Homosexuality and Other Essays on Greek Love* (New York and London: Routledge, 1990). Halperin's ongoing disagreement with the historian John Boswell had precisely to do with the question of mutuality and whether such relations existed between men in pre-modern periods. See John Boswell, *Same-Sex Unions in Premodern Europe* (New York: Random House, 1994), pp. 53–108.

14. David Halperin, "Forgetting Foucault: Acts, Identities, and the History of Sexuality," *Representations* 63 (1998): 109.

15. Clark introduced roles as wide-raging as Horner in *The Country Wife* [1676] and the "mad" partner of Nell Gwynn in James Howard's *All Mistaken, or The Mad Couple* [1667]), as well as every other important part that the King's company presented. See William A. Lennep (ed.) *The London Stage: 1660–1800, Part 1: 1660–1700* (Carbondale: Southern Illinois University Press, 1965), pp. 238, 255, 265.

16. Montague Summers, *The Playhouse of Pepys* (London: Kegan Paul, 1935), pp. 292–6. See also Robert D. Hume and Judith Milhouse, *Producible Interpretation: Eight English Plays, 1675–1707* (Carbondale: Southern Illinois University Press, 1985), p. 134.

17. "As long as friendship was something important, was socially accepted, nobody realized men had sex together. You couldn't say that men didn't have sex together – it just didn't matter. It had no social implication, it was culturally accepted. Whether they fucked together or kissed had no importance.

Absolutely no importance." Michel Foucault, "Sex, Power and the Politics of Identity," Paul Rabinow (ed.), in *Ethics: Subjectivity and Truth.*, p. 171.

18. Halperin, "How to do the History," p. 101.
19. Randolph Trumbach, "The Birth of the Queen: Sodomy and the Emergence of Gender Equality in Modern Culture, 1660–1750," in Martin Bauml Duberman, Martha Vicinus, and George Chauncey, Jr. (eds.), *Hidden From History: Reclaiming the Gay and Lesbian Past.* (New York: New American Library, 1989), pp. 129–40.
20. Guy Chapman, *Beckford* (London: Jonathan Cape, 1940), pp. 81–2. See also Brian Fothergill, *Beckford of Fonthill* (London: Faber, 1979), pp. 98–9.
21. Halperin, "How to do the History," p. 95.
22. Halperin, "How to do the History," p. 93.
23. See, for instance, Trumbach, "The Birth of the Queen," pp. 133–5.
24. See also Martin Battestin (ed.), *Joseph Andrews* [by Henry Fielding. 1742] (Oxford: Clarendon Press, 1967), pp. xxiii, n. 2; 313, nn. 1 and 2; and R.F. Brissenden, *Joseph Andrews* [by Henry Fielding. 1742] (Harmondsworth: Penguin, 1985), p. 342, nn. 219–20.
25. Alexander Pope, "An Epistle to Dr. Arbuthnot," *Poetry and Prose*, ed. Aubrey Williams (New York: Houghton Mifflin, 1969), p. 208.
26. Robert Halsband, *Lord Hervey: Eighteenth-Century Courtier* (Oxford: Clarendon, 1973), p. 117.
27. Quoted in Lady Louisa Stuart, "Biographical Anecdotes," in Lord Whamcliffe (ed.) *Lady Mary Wortley Montagu. Letters and Works* (London, 1837) and Halsband, *Lord Hervey*, p. vii.
28. Halsband, *Lord Hervey*, pp. 90, 102–3, 123.
29. Pope, "An Epistle," p. 208.

In Memoriam – Alan Bray (1948–2001)

Katherine O'Donnell and Michael O'Rourke

Alan Bray was one of those rare scholars who combined being both an historian of queer sexualities and a tireless gay activist. In his work he managed to dismantle the theory/activism binary which hobbles most of what is termed queer historiography. He was careful to avoid the kind of barbed wire prose and obscurantism that renders much pomo-homo criticism untranslatable or inaccessible, and at the same time he was able to skirt the kind of anti-intellectualism which often saturates queer activism. That said, his scholarship was always pitched at the highest intellectual level.

Born in 1948 in Leeds, he was "brought up in significant economic hardship" and his mother died while he was still a child.[1] He attended the Central High School in Leeds where he met a life-long friend, Graham Wilson, before going on to further study at Bangor University. After a brief period in the Anglican seminary Alan moved on to work as a civil servant in the Inland Revenue. He held this post until 1996 having reached the distinguished position of principal and having written *The Clandestine Reformer: a Study of the Rayner Scrutinies* in 1988.

His academic career was as glittering as his time in Lord Rayner's civil service team. In 1982 he published what was to become a land-mark book, one that shone like a beacon for all future scholars of male love, sex, friendship and intimacy. Given Alan's commitment to gay rights it is no surprise that *Homosexuality in Renaissance England* was published by the Gay Men's Press. A hugely influential and brave book it has been widely revered and criticized. Alan Stewart remarks in his essay in this volume how early this piece of scholarship appeared on what Alan would have called the "exploratory maps" created for research into male homosexuality in the early modern period. A measure of its continuing importance is that it remains in print.[2] No less groundbreaking than this short book was Alan's essay "Homosexuality and the Signs of Male Friendship" which was published in the *History Workshop Journal* in 1990 (and reprinted in *Queering the Renaissance* four years later). Alan, a founding member of the Gay History Group, was also editor of *History Workshop Journal* between the years of 1994 and 1997. Up until his death he was an Honorary Research Fellow at Birkbeck College, London. His final project (of which the chapter in this volume provides a snapshot) is an exploration of same-sex unions and ceremonies in pre-modern societies from the eleventh to the nineteenth century. Titled *The Friend* it is forthcoming with Chicago University Press.

One of the major tensions in Alan's life was between his sexuality and his Roman Catholicism and it is one that led to the following study. He was the principal point of contact between Cardinal Basil Hume and Quest, the support group for homosexual Catholics in England when it was an officially recognized Catholic society. When he discovered evidence that the Catholic Church sanctioned and blessed same-sex relationships in memorials dating from the fourteenth to nineteenth centuries Alan embarked on twenty years of scholarship into these tombs and rituals and it was his hope that this evidence would provide a bridge between gay men and lesbians and the Catholic Church. One of the tombs, perhaps the most controversial, which Alan discovered on his tour of country churches in England, was that of Cardinal Newman (founder of the Catholic University of Ireland) and his friend Ambrose St. John on the Lickey Hills near Birmingham. When we invited Alan to speak in Dublin at the conference which engendered this collection of essays, he decided that the best thing for him to present would be his work on friendship. This was all the more pertinent since the conference was held in Newman House on St. Stephen's Green in Dublin. The decision to broach this topic fuelled some controversy in the Irish press in the week preceding the conference, a debate that has continued on the Internet since July of last year.[3] The significant question Alan wanted to ask in this chapter was: what does the significance of the gesture he describes have for the historicization of queer masculinities; for the writing of the history of male love and friendship in the early modern period? Equally importantly he wanted to ask how these questions, which he had been pursuing for a number of years, might alter the early exploratory maps, which he among other historians had constructed twenty years before. Alan was at pains to point out in answering his own questions that when we situate these questions in the terms of the discussion which is going on elsewhere in this volume we have to be cautious. Hence the need to construct a history for this gesture.[4]

Bray's essay provides such a micro-history. The text is recreated from a copy of the paper found in Alan's flat by his executor Graham Wilson but we want to register in this introduction some of the major deviations from it which Alan made in the talk that he presented in Dublin. The emphasis in Alan's talk was very much on friendship and he was gratified that this seemed to dominate many of the other discussions by George Rousseau, George Haggerty and Randolph Trumbach in particular. It is not that friendship hasn't been studied in the context of the history of (queer) masculinity since this would simply not be true (see David Halperin's introduction above) but that the emphasis has tended to be on sex between men. Alan's work and the other essays in this volume which put friendship in the foreground are of course answering a question raised by Foucault when he said, "How is it possible for men to be together; to live together, to share their time, their meals, their room ... their knowledge".[5] Yet Alan's crucial point is that, even though he was indebted to the work of Foucault twenty years ago when he was beginning to construct a history of homosexuality for the Renaissance, it is now time to think about Derrida when we seek to write the history of masculinity and male friendship. He made the bold prediction that it will be Derrida's *Politics of Friendship* and not Foucault's *History of Sexuality, Volume One* which will dominate such discussion in the next twenty years.[6] The reason for this prediction (and this is how Alan's historical work is of importance for recent interventions into queer activism) is ethical. It was Alan's sense that something had been missing in early histories of male homosexuality (including his own) and that while enormous gains had been made by those studies organized around the politics of identity the transition in recent times to the possibility of same-sex marriages has opened up a dilemma for queer historians and activists. In looking at the early modern evidence he sees sworn brotherhood as a response to the ethical uncertainty of friendship. Only by placing friendship in a wider frame of reference as he does in this volume can we begin to understand why it was associated with the Eucharist and the mass. In Alan's terms these were only blessings of friendship in so far as they represented acceptance by these friends of a wider social responsibility.

The question this raises for us is one that Alan feels Derrida was asking in his recent book (a dilemma which was also foreseen by Foucault when he claimed that resistance can be caught up again in the same processes it produces). At the time of Alan's last talk there were no less than nine manuscripts in the press on friendship and the topic of friendship has very much pushed its way back into discussions in a way which it would not have ten years ago. Derrida's book in its closing pages explains a loss of confidence in the Enlightenment idea of the universality of friendship and posits that an abyss has opened up between that confidence and confidence today. According to Alan it isn't hard to see at the end of the last century that the confidence in friendships' universality has given way to nationalism, patriotism, and ethnocentrism or what Derrida calls "the raging quest for identity." For this reason, and this is the faultline in the politics of friendship Alan was talking about, it is more difficult now to see or to recognize that *sexual* identity may have become part of that process and that this is the faultline which the authoritarian Right has grasped can be displaced to other ends. Alan sees no way back, no return to those forms of friendship he describes in the chapter that follows, but it was his hope (one which we historians of sexuality must strive toward realizing) that by trying to begin to recover the ethics one will find space to imagine cultural change. In answer to the big question Alan asked when he began: *How would this change the exploratory maps constructed twenty years ago?* he said this: it would be a shift from studies of sexuality into ethics and from the politics of identity into the politics of friendship.

Alan Bray died on 25 November 2001. We dedicate this book to a wonderful man and his remarkable scholarship.

Notes

1. See the obituary by Alan's lifelong friend Stephen Gee in the *Guardian* on Tuesday 18 December 2001. This can be accessed at http://www.guardian. co.uk/Archive/Article/0,4273,4321882,00.html
2. It was reprinted by Columbia University Press in 1995.
3. See the article by Martina Devlin, "Gay Marriages 'Were Blessed' in Past by Church" in the *Irish Independent*. (http://www.unison.ie/irish_independent /stories.php3?ca=9&si=472503&issue_id=4864). See also "Church Art 'Holds Key' to Gay Tolerance" by Stephen Bates in the *Guardian* on Thursday 9 August 2001. Some of the evidence that follows was presented in the international Catholic Weekly the *Tablet* on 4 August 2001, pp. 1108–9, with a surprisingly warm and positive editorial on page 1103.
4. Some of Alan's problems with John Boswell's approach to same-sex unions can be found in "Boswell and the Latin West and the Debate over the Blessing of Friendship Today" which was posted by Paul Halsall to the bulletin board MEDGAY _L @ Listserv.ksu.edu on 13 May 2002.

5. Michel Foucault, "Friendship as a Way of Life," *Foucault Live (Interviews, 1966–84)* trans. John Johnston, ed. Sylvère Lotringer (New York: Semiotext(e), Columbia University Press, 1989), p. 204.
6. See Jacques Derrida, *The Politics of Friendship* (London: Verso, 1997). The cultural theorist Martin McQuillan, who recently called for a sustained application of Derrida's work to queer discourse, would seem to agree. He said in a review of Derrida's book that *"The Politics of Friendship* is an inadequate title for what is perhaps Derrida's most important work to date." See *Textual Practice* 12.1 (1998), 179. (Foucault, *History of Sexuality, Volume One, an Introduction,* trans. Robert Hurley [London: Allen Lane, 1978]).

4
A Traditional Rite for Blessing Friendship

Alan Bray

This chapter is about a monument on a tomb – and a chance encounter. Shortly after completing my book *Homosexuality in Renaissance England*,[1] now nearly twenty years ago, I gave a talk one evening in Cambridge, and as I was finishing breakfast in college the next morning my host joined me with the invitation: "I want you to see something." Our walk that morning was to the chapel of Christ's College, where we looked at the monument by the communion table that marks the burial there in the same tomb at the end of the seventeenth century of John Finch and Thomas Baines. "What," he asked, "do you make of this?" Later I was to learn how John Finch and Thomas Baines had understood their friendship from the expression that John Finch had used in the Latin inscription he composed for his friend,[2] where he described their friendship as a *"Connubium."* The monument by their tomb makes the same point but more graphically. The two halves of the monument each surmounted by a portrait of one of the two friends are united by the representation of a knotted cloth set between the two tables of the inscription, that corresponds below as it were to the single flaming funerary urn above, in a visual pun on the love knot or the marriage knot; for that is what *"Connubium"* means. It means a marriage.

That chance encounter began the work that was to occupy me over the years that followed, but the scale of the task it required lay in grasping that at this point at the end of the seventeenth century (the monument was completed in 1684) one was standing on the far shore of a land that already by then stretched back for a thousand years. When eventually (at the suggestion of the Oxford historian Diarmaid MacCulloch) I came to the monument of John Bloxham and John Whytton in the chapel of Merton College in Oxford, I realized that I had found there the perspective that I was searching for. This is the great monumental brass that was placed above their tomb when they were buried together at the end of the fourteenth century at the center of the choir and at the foot of the steps to the high altar. The outline of the two figures one sees on their tomb, standing side by side under canopies with their hands joined together in prayer and looking straight on to the viewer, is the familiar iconography employed in the fourteenth century for the common tomb of a husband and a wife.

The Merton College monument has now been moved to a neglected spot in the north transept of the church, but the gaze of John Bloxham and John Whytton still meets the eyes of the viewer across the centuries that divide us from them, and the confidence of that gesture in its original setting is unmistakable. Yet to a modern viewer it is at the same time curiously inexplicable. This is not only because of its marital imagery. The monument is what is known as a "bracket" monument, in which the two figures are presented as if standing on a pedestal (in fact as if they were two saints), and at the base of the monument (at the base of their friendship as it were) the design turns on the three-fold coincidence of the name "Johannes" (John): in the names of the two men shown in the scroll at the base of the bracket and in the lamb with cross and banner depicted above the scroll: the sign of St. John the Baptist. The coincidence is then emphasized by the first names of the two friends being carefully spelt out in full and not abbreviated, as would normally have been the case. In the fourteenth century it was common to take one's first name from a godparent, and what this design seems to be doing is presenting St. John not as their patron, their *patronus*, but as their *patrinus*: as their spiritual godfather and thus each other as spiritual brothers, in an analogy of their friendship here not with marriage but rather with fraternity.

The same confusion to the modern eye recurs in the monument that was placed above the tomb of two English knights, Sir William Neville and Sir John Clanvowe, when they were buried together in 1391 in the same tomb in the church of the Dominican friars in Galata near Constantinople. It has been said that an inhabitant of the England of Richard II could read a heraldic arrangement more easily than a letter. Here the heraldic arms on the two shields are "impaled" like those of the married couple; and the shield on the viewer's left is heraldically incorrect. It is reversed: so that the two shields are inclined towards each other, corresponding to the bodies of the two knights lain together below. A heraldic device is not a realistic depiction; it is a kind of code (like a modern road-sign): and the arrangement of the two heraldic helms above in profile would then correspond, by the same corporal gesture, to the stylized depiction of a kiss. Yet in the British Library there is a manuscript work of heraldry from the 1450s that attributes an impalement of arms of this kind to two knights on the grounds that they were what the author calls "sworn brothryn", i.e. "sworn brothers", although the work does not explain why a device that would normally represent a marital relation should be thought appropriate for what the work describes as a fraternal relation.

The great medievalist Kenneth McFarlane wrote about William Neville and John Clanvowe in his *Lancastrian Kings and Lollard Knights* (and their tomb is discussed in the *Antiquaries Journal* in 1991).[3] Yet neither discussion accounts for that confusion to the modern eye – in which different kinds of kinship terminology seem to overlap and shade into each other and are not clearly distinguished from friendship. That confusion is an evident faultline in the material and one that needs to be weighed in any final judgment on the phenomenon presented by these tombs. A clue to this – but one that was to make my task immensely more painstaking – was the growing recognition that the gesture was not one that ceased with the political and religious changes of the sixteenth century and with the supposedly "feudal" Middle Ages. It survived not only among Catholics but also among traditionally minded Christians in the reformed church also.

A dramatic example of the first is a monument I saw in the church of the Venerable English College in Rome, which at the end of the sixteenth century was a seminary for priests returning on the dangerous mission to win back England for the Catholic faith. Its inscription (in Latin) is:

> To the Reverend Nicholas Morton ... who having lost his dearest friends and all his other goods in his native country for the sake of the Catholic faith died at Rome ... It was his wish to be buried in the same tomb [*sepelirique voluit eodem tumulo*] with the Reverend John Seton with whom he fled from England for the same cause, that of religion, and who came to Rome at the same time...

As one can see from the last lines of the inscription, the monument was placed there by Nicholas Morton's nephew Robert Morton at the point in 1587 when Robert Morton himself entered the seminary, later that year taking priest's orders and returning to England and the mission. The sixteenth century is still a living part of the collective memory of the young Englishmen training for the priesthood in the

English college in Rome today, and as I gathered on my visit they have preserved the recollection that when the news reached the college in 1588 that Robert Morton had been martyred for his priesthood in the Lincoln's Inn Fields it was by this monument, in the church of the college, that the defiant students gathered to sing the *Te Deum Laudamus*. "We praise Thee, O God. We acknowledge Thee to be the Lord ... The noble army of martyrs praise Thee." Robert Morton is the Blessed Robert Morton, beatified by Pope Pius XI in 1929.

There is an example of the survival of such tombs among tradition-ally minded Christians in the reformed church in the chapel of Gonville and Caius in Cambridge, in the monument one can see on the south wall, placed in the chapel by John Gostlin in memory of his friend Thomas Legge in 1619. The depiction of Thomas Legge is con-ventional, but beneath it John Gostlin placed a heart in flames uplifted by two hands with this inscription in Roman capitals: "Love joined them living. So may the earth join them in their burial. O Legge, Gostlin's heart you still have with you. (*IVNXIT AMOR VIVOS SIC IVNGAT TERRA SEPVLTOS GOSTLINI RELIQVVM. COR TIBI LEGGVS HABES.*) It is also at this point in the early part of the seventeenth century that women step into the picture. The earliest example I know of two women being buried side by side in this way is the monument to Ann Chitting and her friend Mary Barber (from 1606) in the church of St. James in Bury in Suffolk, described in the papers of the Suffolk antiquary Henry Chitting (the son of Ann Chitting). From this point the tombs of two women buried together in this way is as common a sight as that of two men. One such from 1710 is the monument to Mary Kendall in its tranquil setting in the chapel of St. John the Baptist in Westminster Abbey that records "that close Union & Friendship, In which She liv'd, with The Lady CATHARINE IONES; And in testimony of which She desir'd, That even their Ashes, after Death, Might not be divided". Another from the end of the century is the lovely monument to Catherine Jennis and her friend Anne Fleming, who are buried together in their vault in Wiveton parish church in Norfolk, at the foot of the steps to the communion table. Was the burial together of two women in this way something new in the seventeenth century? Or does it only then become evident, as the evidence becomes more abun-dant and the light brighter? But whatever judgment one makes on that point, this is evidently not a gesture that was losing its force.

One can on occasion see the political and religious changes of the sixteenth century rather drawing on the gesture than undermining it. One such is the joint tomb that Fulke Greville planned for himself and

Philip Sidney in the retrochoir of old St. Paul's Cathedral in London. Fulke Greville never built that tomb: what he built was rather the monument above his remains in the church of St. Mary in Warwick, in which the inscription to Philip Sidney stands in the place of the family inscription that one would have expected. But the projected design for the monument in St. Paul's is set out in the letter he sent his friend John Coke in the autumn of 1615, where one can see that its design would have corresponded to what remained in the retrochoir of the broken shrine that before the Reformation had once contained the relics of St. Erkenwald, an apt gesture for that hero of the reformed religion which Fulke Greville had presented Philip Sidney as being, in the account he wrote of his life.[4]

The burial together of John Finch and Thomas Baines is not an isolated gesture. It was near this point at the turn of the seventeenth century that the fine monument to Granville Piper and Richard Wise (who died in 1717 and 1726 respectively) was erected in the church of St. Mary Magdalene in Launceston marking their burial together, with an inscription recording their friendship – *"Fidissimum Amicorum Par"* (the most faithful of friends) – with their portraits set between a single flaming funerary urn as in the tomb monument of John Finch and Thomas Baines. It was also near this point that Bishop Herbert Croft and Dean George Benson (who died within a year of each other, the latter in 1691) were buried together within the communion rails of Hereford Cathedral, with a Latin inscription that runs from one ledger-stone to the other, reminiscent of that which John Gostlin left to his friend Thomas Legge, "In life United. In death not divided": *"In Vita conjuncti"* on the one, *"In Morte non divisi"* on the other. The two ledger-stones were laid side by side and are united by a pair of hands stretching from the one to the other exchanging the handfast.

The close detail of these monuments and others like them allows one to identify the written sources that corresponded to that same phenomenon in the world around them: the references in the medieval chronicles to two men being *fratres iurati* or the "sworn" or "wedded brothers" of Middle English; and the traditional stories told about such figures. One also finds glimpses of them, in more mundane circumstances, in the documents with which English men and women have recorded their agreements and their property rights. I have now found such monuments in the parish churches and chapels of England on a scale that stretches from the fourteenth to the nineteenth centuries; and as I have begun to talk publicly about my conclusions more are being pointed out to me, almost by the month. But why is it only now that they are becoming visible? Why have we not recognized and grasped what they represented before?

A clue lies in their setting in the rites of a traditional English Christianity, where these monuments, at the culmination of the friendships they marked so publicly, corresponded to a liturgical practice that could mark their beginning in the same setting. The kiss depicted on the tomb of Sir William Neville and Sir John Clanvowe, in this setting, points to a ritual act that would have been familiar in any Latin church in the fourteenth century, including that of the Dominican friars in Galata: the exchange of the "kiss of peace" – the *osculum pacis* – that preceded Holy Communion or stood in its place and which for the majority of those present represented the climax of the ritual of the mass.

Greek and Slavonic Christianity had a specific office for the creation of ritual brothers, and a Latin *Ordo ad fratres faciendum* was also used among Catholics in the Balkans (and was edited by a learned Dominican there some years ago). I am inclined to think however on the balance of the evidence that this office was not used widely in the Latin West, although it would seem to have been used in Italy in that the fourteenth century manuscript from which the rite is taken describes itself as the Roman Missal. The form used in England and France on the present evidence at least appears rather to have been for the two friends to receive Holy Communion together after – but only after – having exchanged their promises to each other outside the church. In that careful distance one can, I think, detect a reserve about the promises being exchanged, that arguably represents a second fault-line in the evidence.

The social outline of the relation that one sees in documents like those I mention above is both revealing and curiously frustrating. In summary what one sees is this. The vows exchanged are awesome in their scope but they are personal, not contractual or a matter of property: a vow to live together and to stand by each other (and if necessary to die together), vows which are life-long and indissoluble. They did not create expectations of inheritance (in the Latin West at least), nor did they create an impediment to a marriage, and the individual was likely for that reason to have been allowed a degree of freedom of choice that would have been problematic in terms of other forms of ritual kinship. But the very simplicity of the relationship allowed it to be used as part of a family's wider strategy. It avoided those quarrels over property that could divide families, and it crucially allowed kinship relations to be established across social disparities that would have been unthinkable in terms of a betrothal. It also allowed one of the friends to stand in the other's place in the event of death, in the care of children and family. But the extent to which the relation was woven in this way into the world about it also gave rise to ethical reservations about the motives for such friendship that are not evident in the ideal depiction of these tomb monuments. How did friendship differ from a cynical (and mutual) self-advancement? How could it be distinguished in effect from mere collusion? What (perhaps above all) if the fidelity to one's friend drew one or even required one to do something that one knew to be wrong?

The motives that prompted such sworn friendship seem set across a broad spectrum. At one extreme it seems almost a mechanism for resolving a quarrel. At the other it was clearly a heartfelt personal commitment, as it evidently was between those friends who were buried together in the same tomb. For the historian to seize on one of these motives and to present that as the essence of the matter would be to construct a caricature, although that is what some historians who have noticed the phenomenon have done: the late John Boswell attributed the relation to love;[5] the contemporary American historian Brent Shaw has attributed it to a concern for violence;[6] and Kenneth McFarlane a generation ago attributed it to a wish for profit albeit only with reference to the documents he was examining.[7] The striking fact remains that each of them was able to find evidence that substantiated their characterization – and in doing so successfully undermined that of each other. The clue I think to understanding this historical phenomenon in its own terms – from within, as it were – lies paradoxically in that very confusion to the modern eye in the imagery employed on these tomb monuments.

The point is the one J.L. Flandrin makes in his book on the history of the family[8] – the fact that the "family" can be defined in several different ways (in terms of blood relations but also in terms of a common household or in terms of marriage) has tended in modern society to have been a technical point of interest only to sociologists and anthropologists, as in modern society these potentially differing definitions have coincided closely: where the family living together in the same household has conventionally been taken to be the group of parents and their children linked by blood or marriage. In the past these differing definitions have not coincided so nearly, and one of the reasons for this has been the multiplicity of forms of what one might call "voluntary" kinship: kinship created not by blood but by a promise or by ritual. Modern society has recognized substantially only one such form of "voluntary" kinship, in marriage. In the past others have subsisted alongside and overlapped with it. But that overlapping network did not destroy the boundaries of families. Its effect was rather to embed the family within a wider and encompassing ground created by the friendship that kinship was perceived to create, and the "sworn" brotherhood and sisterhood was simply, I think, one of the threads out of which that fabric was made. This is not to say that each of these pairs of friends buried together within the same tomb were made sworn kin by the Eucharist practice one can see in the Latin West (although they may have been and some of them certainly were). But it is to say that the outline of their friendships – a friendship that signified as kinship – explains what the rite effected for those who were.

That is a conclusion which allows one to grasp the coherence of the overlapping imagery in these monuments – that first faultline in the evidence to which I pointed. For the officious historian to attempt to unravel the connections being made is to miss the point that that apparent confusion to the modern eye corresponded with precision to the actual social context in which these relationships figured: a society in which diverse forms of voluntary kinship could at crucial points overlap and by doing so create that interlocking network of obligation which was its frame. It was there that the ethical role of such sworn friendship lay and why Christians recognized it as they did. But it was also there, in that perhaps conflicting and potentially compromising frame that the ethical doubts which accompanied such sworn friendship also lay.

It is not difficult to see the reason for that reserve. To what end might this friendship be put? In the eighteenth-century Enlightenment, Immanuel Kant was to place the moral basis of friendship in an undifferentiated moral benevolence;[9] and the civil society that began to emerge in England towards the end of the seventeenth century was an accurate expression of that view. In the traditional society of this chapter, friendship was rather ultimately inalienable from the particular loyalties in which it was begun, and the ambiguities of that stance were the point on which its ethics turned. Fidelity in such a context easily gave rise to suspicions that were ever to hand of collusion and self-advancement. The point is that the church in the Latin West did not respond to this uncertainty by legislating for the diverse motives that could prompt sworn friendship. The answer it found was a distinctly liturgical solution. Its dilemma might well have been solved, of course, by relegating these vows to the secular world pure and simple. But as the historian John Bossy has argued, the

Eucharist of traditional Christians before and after the reformation divide was recognized as restoring defective human relations in the society about it, and its "social miracle" as he terms it, was the work of kinship and friendship: the peace that was friendship, not peace as the opposite of war or the effect of victory. Its solution lay in an Augustinian view of grace, which necessarily works in a world of defective human relations, and the Eucharist ritual of this chapter provided a liturgical form that allowed the church to respond with integrity to the potential for good in the vows being exchanged, without being compromised by the potential for misuse that inevitably accompanied them. Its theology was that of the grace imparted by the Eucharist which could, with human co-operation, lead those who made the promises towards the ideal to which they pointed.

The monuments I have described in this chapter had an enduring history, as indeed had the Eucharist practice that corresponded to them at the onset of the friendships they mark so publicly. One of the last sights the historian has of that Eucharist practice was on Easter Day 1834, when Anne Lister (the mistress of Shibden Hall in Yorkshire) and her friend Ann Walker solemnized their friendship – described in Anne Lister's diary as a marriage – by receiving Holy Communion together in Holy Trinity Church in Goodramgate, York. One of the last of these monuments – but one of great importance to Catholics – is a simple stone cross (in the form of a Celtic cross) in the burial ground of the fathers of the Oratory of St Philip Neri on the Lickey Hills south of Birmingham. In the upper part is the name, still clearly legible, of the first of the two friends who were laid there together: "Ambrose St John" it reads (in capital letters) "DIED May 24 1875". Below, and in the center of the cross, is the name of his friend whose remains were laid in his grave in 1890: John Henry Cardinal Newman.

Their burial in the same tomb was the emphatic wish of Newman, expressed in a note he wrote on 23 July 1876, the year following the death of Ambrose St. John. "I wish, with all my heart, to be buried in Father Ambrose St. John's grave – and I give this as my last, my imperative will." The note then turns to the inscription for Newman's memorial stone at the Oratory in Birmingham. In 1881 he returned to this note adding to his wish to be buried in Fr St. John's grave these emphatic terms: "This I confirm and insist on, and command." Since this study was first read in Newman House, where Newman founded the Catholic University of Ireland as its first rector in 1854, I ought to say more and may perhaps be forgiven for doing so, especially since Newman had been familiar with the tomb of John Bloxham and John

Whytton in Merton College since his days as an undergraduate. He saw that tomb with the eye of an historian, and through it he knew that his burial with Ambrose St. John expressed a gesture that would have been intelligible to Christians over the centuries.

Newman seems first to have met Ambrose St. John in the spring of 1841. "From his first he loved me with an intensity of love, which was unaccountable," Newman later wrote. "As far as this world was concerned I was his first and last." After that first meeting in 1841, they would be received into the Catholic Church at almost the same time: St. John on 2 October 1845, Newman only a week later on 9 October. There is a painting of them dating from this time, studying in Rome, sitting alone together at a table. The contrast between them is striking, Newman now a mature man of 46: "In 1847 at Rome they used to call him, as being fair and Saxon looking, my Angel Guardian." The gentle humor in that comment disguises much. It is difficult perhaps for us now to grasp how great a social gulf Newman's reception into the Catholic Church created for him and how much it made an outcast of him in Victorian England. He would not meet his friend John Keble again for almost twenty years; and the same was true of many of his friends and companions: he would never see his sister Harriet again. These losses created an enduring bond between Newman and St. John which would never be broken; and Newman returned St. John's love. The most telling trace of this lies in the letters Newman wrote in the days following St. John's death. The calm with which he at first responded to his friend's death gradually gives way to an overwhelming grief, as he repeats over and again in these letters that same phrase: "This is the greatest affliction I have had in my life ...or that I can have," he adds. Towards the end of the month following St. John's death, he writes that "A day does not pass without my having violent bursts of crying, and they weaken me, and I dread them." Fr Tristram of the Oratory recorded the memory of Newman at St. John's requiem mass in his book *Newman and his Friends*.[10]

> The utter misery of the expression on his face at the Mass of the Requiem remains still an unforgettable memory in the minds of those who were present; he insisted on giving the absolutions himself, and as he did so, he broke down continually.

St. John was, Newman wrote, "my earthly light" and "I have ever thought no bereavement was equal to that of a husband's or a wife's, but I feel it difficult to believe that any can be greater, or any one's sorrow greater, than mine."[11]

Here the bond was and remained wholly spiritual. The evidence (if such is needed) is in a letter Newman wrote in the days following St. John's death, recounting a conversation between them before St. John lost his speech in those final days. He went through, he writes, "the history of his whole life, expressed his hope that during his whole priestly life he had not committed one mortal sin". For men of their time and culture that statement is definitive, but they were not afraid to touch and draw close. We find the following in the accounts Newman gave of his last moments with St. John: "Then he put his arm tenderly round my neck, and drew me close to him, and so kept me a considerable time." "I little dreamed," he later wrote, "he meant to say that he was going." "At 7 p.m. when I rose to go ...it was our parting." Their love was not the less intense for being spiritual. Perhaps it was the more so.

Newman's burial with Ambrose St. John cannot be detached from his understanding of the place of friendship in Christian belief or its long history. In a letter sent by Pope John Paul II to the Archbishop of Birmingham, Archbishop John Nichols, in January 2001 to mark the second centenary of Newman's birth, the Pope asked for prayers that the time might come soon when the Church could beatify Newman: "can officially and publicly proclaim the exemplary holiness of Cardinal John Henry Newman." It is likely that his relics will then be brought into the Oratory Church in Birmingham to lie by the altar, and the inheritors of Newman's faith should not separate them now from his final gesture. That gesture was Newman's last, imperative command: his last wish as a man, but also something more. It was his last sermon.

There is no simple passage from this history to the present; but as in our own time the permafrost of modernity is at last beginning to melt, and a more determinedly pluralistic world is emerging, the same suspicions of friendship are beginning to re-emerge with it. Its problematic ethics have, if I may put it this way, an archaeology that can be recovered; and it is my hope in recovering this largely forgotten history that my work may play a part in creating a cultural space for change today, without the destructive confrontations that these doubts may prefigure.

Is that changing world the reason why we can now see these monuments as we have not done before? As the glaciers draw back, as it were, what we are seeing is not a strange new world but a strange old world: kinship; domesticity and affect; locality; embodiment – all of these things, I think. But I would want to add also that we are at times seeing them in something as actual – and as tangible – as the tomb of the two friends buried together in an English parish church. We did not recognize these tombs before because they did not signify, but they are beginning to signify again.

Notes

1. Alan Bray, *Homosexuality in Renaissance England* (London: Gay Men's Press, 1982).
2. It is in the British Library's Sloane Manuscripts: 3329/5^r–6^v.
3. Kenneth B. McFarlane, *Lancastrian Kings and Lollard Knights* (Oxford: Clarendon Press, 1972). Their tomb is also discussed by Siegrid Düll, Anthony Luttrell, and Maurice Keen in "Faithful Unto Death: the Tomb Slab of Sir William Neville and Sir John Clanvowe, Constantinople 1391," *Antiquaries Journal* 71 (1991): 174–90.
4. This is in the British Library's Additional Manuscripts, 64875/166^r–167^v.
5. John Boswell, *Same Sex Unions in Premodern Europe* (New York: Villard Books, 1994).
6. Brent Shaw, "Ritual Brotherhood in Roman and Post-Roman Societies," *Traditio* 52 (1997): 327–55.
7. McFarlane, *Lancastrian Kings and Lollard Knights*.
8. J.L. Flandrin, *Families in Former Times: Kinship, Household, and Sexuality* (Cambridge: CUP, 1979).
9. There is a special issue of *Eighteenth Century Studies* on Kant and the politics of friendship, edited by Peter Fenves. See the introduction, "Politics of Friendship-Once Again," *Eighteenth Century Studies* 32.2 (Winter 1998–99): 133–57.
10. Henry Tristam, *Newman and his Friends* (London: John Lane, 1933).
11. The author had not prepared this paper for publication before his death. Therefore the fault for any absence of references lies with the editors, who were unable to locate the source of this quotation from Newman.

5
The Heterosexual Male in Eighteenth-Century London and his Queer Interactions

Randolph Trumbach

Around 1700 a profound shift began to occur in sexual relations between males in Western societies. In traditional European societies all males had desired both males and females, and most males probably had acted upon both kinds of desire. This had certainly been the case in the pagan Mediterranean world in which adult men had had legitimate sexual relations with both women and adolescent males. The Greeks and Romans had differed only in regard to whether a man's adolescent male partner was to be a free citizen like himself or a slave or a prostitute instead. It was presumed that there would always be a difference in age between the two males. Male honor was maintained if an adolescent with a gender status somewhere between that of a man and a woman allowed himself to be penetrated by a man with a beard that was either fully grown or on its way. But it was profoundly unsettling when a boy failed to change from passive boy to active man once his beard had grown and he had become an adult man. Such individuals formed a small minority of passive adult men who were held in profound contempt. Those passive men came in two kinds: there were those who left their families and became members of a transvestite group of prostitutes or priests like the *galli*; and there were those (the *cinaedi*) who married women and led secret lives of passivity, but who experienced the greatest contempt if their passivity was discovered.[1]

Such a situation does not, of course, exist in any modern Western society. In the twenty-first century the presumption is that nearly all men are heterosexual and more or less exclusively interested in women. There is, however, a homosexual minority. Its size has been much canvassed in the twentieth century, and the estimates have varied from the 10 percent or so that Alfred Kinsey supposedly found to the more recent surveys at the end of the century that have pro-

99

jected a minority of between 1 and 5 percent of all men. An occasional modern historian has tried to show the existence in the ancient world of such a homosexual minority, but most recent historians would agree that the men of the ancient Mediterranean desired both women and adolescent males and that they usually acted on both of these desires. A transition to something like the modern Western system must therefore have occurred at some point.[2]

If historians (prior to the last 25 years) had allowed themselves to discuss such a question, it is likely that many would have looked to the conversion of the ancient world to Christianity to find the moment for this transition in sexual behavior. But in the last generation it has become clear that the transition to the system in force at the end of the twentieth century is a distinctive feature of modernity. Some historians have made it very recent indeed – a matter of the last hundred years – and cited the late nineteenth century sexological discussions. But other historians like myself presume that the modern world in most of its aspects – whether economic, religious, political, affective, or artistic – first appeared in the generation or two after 1700, and that the division of sexual life into a heterosexual majority and a homosexual minority (as a distinctive aspect of modernity) must therefore also first have occurred in those same two generations. The rise of Christianity may have brought with it a new sexual asceticism, though it has been argued that this asceticism was already present in late pagan antiquity. But Christianity did not change the nature of desire, and it is likely that its impact on actual behavior was extremely limited. A mere quick perusal of an ancient Christian ascetic text such as *The Sayings of the Desert Fathers* (the *Apophthegmata Patrum*) shows this. The monks in the Egyptian desert were warned against both boys and women because it was presumed that they desired both and in their weakness might act upon either kind of desire.[3]

As late as 1400 this was still the prevailing system in Western Christian societies, as Michael Rocke has now demonstrated with statistical certainty for fifteenth-century Florence. In the second and third generations of that century at least 15,000 Florentine males were accused of sodomy and over 2,400 were convicted by the principal magistracy responsible for overseeing sodomy. From this Rocke has estimated that at least two-thirds of all Florentine males were implicated by the time they reached the age of 40, and these figures do not cover all the magistracies. This strongly suggests that almost all males had sexual relations with other males at some point in their lives and did so repeatedly. The importance of this finding cannot be stressed too much. The most perspicacious readings of the ancient Greek and Roman sources have also demonstrated a similar world, but these readings and observations have been challenged or ignored by those who have been convinced that homosexual behavior has always been limited to a small deviant minority.[4]

Sodomy was nonetheless illegal in Florence. Preachers such as Bernardino of Sienna regularly denounced it. But Bernardino also accepted that it was widespread. He even said that mothers were proud that their attractive adolescent sons caught men's eyes and deliberately sent them into the streets dressed in the most alluring clothes. The Florentines apparently lived out their sexual lives under two different moralities, one that was Christian and disapproved of sodomy, and another that was masculinist and patriarchal and promoted it. Such a contradiction could also be found in other parts of the sexual life of Christian Europe: Christians were charged before the Inquisition with holding that simple fornication between unmarried men and women was no sin, and married couples divorced each other even though the Church held that marriage was indissoluble. Christians also resorted to magic instead of using the channels of grace provided by the Church. These contradictory moralities existed together in the minds of individuals; and at some moments and in some roles, one morality prevailed over another in the life of an individual. But the presence in all males of sexual desire for other males no longer has to be teased from literary sources. It can now be demonstrated statistically for Florence.[5]

This must mean that the distinction between a homosexual minority and a heterosexual majority cannot have existed in Florence. If this distinction can be shown not to have existed in a single European society, it is extremely unlikely to have existed in any of them. Certainly in the present world all Western societies are organized sexually by the same distinction between homosexuals and heterosexuals. It is true that this distinction became dominant in different Western societies at different moments in the last three hundred years. But it is apparent when one compares Florence with either the ancient pagan or the later Islamic Mediterranean, that the sodomy of Florence was nothing new. It was simply more open and therefore better documented. The question needs to be raised whether it had grown more open in the course of the fifteenth century. There had certainly been relatively few cases in the fourteenth century when the penalties had been far more severe. But as the penalties were moderated into a series of graduated fines (which were often not paid), the number of denunciations increased. Many Florentines therefore thought that sodomy was wrong, but they did not think it was so wrong as to merit severe punishment. This was the compromise between the two moralities by which many Florentines lived. But in their adolescence and young manhood, most Florentine males lived entirely according to the masculinist morality and not the Christian one.

The sodomy which most Florentine males practiced was strictly organized by differences in age. From the time boys entered puberty at 15 (for physiological reasons, puberty began later than it does today) until their beards began to grow at 19 or 20, they were anally penetrated by older men. These men were usually unmarried and in their later twenties. Between 19 and 23 there seems to have been a transitional phase when a young man could be both active and passive, but he was always active with someone younger and passive with someone older. Adolescent boys occasionally took turns at being active and passive with each other. But young adult men never allowed themselves to be passive with their adolescents. Older men sometimes fellated their adolescent partners instead of penetrating them. Most men seem to have stopped pursuing boys once they married in their thirties. A few adult men (12 percent) never married, and some of these had boys throughout their lives. Some men in their twenties had sex both with female prostitutes and with boys. A very few adult men (3 percent) allowed themselves to be penetrated; they had presumably failed to make the transition from passive boy to active man. No adult transvestite men appear in the fifteenth-century records, but there is evidence for such men in the sixteenth century, and they certainly appear in the sixteenth- and seventeenth-century records for Spain and Portugal. All of the four positions typical of age-structured systems in the Mediterranean world can therefore be found in Renaissance Florence: the active man, the passive boy, the passive man who tries otherwise to live a conventional life, the transvestite passive man. But as in all such systems, most activity was between men and adolescents. And it must be stressed that this was not simply a preference for younger partners of the kind that can be found among the male homosexual minority after 1700. It was instead a desire for the smooth, small, lightly muscled bodies of boys, and it was a desire that was always destroyed (whether in Greece, Rome, Islamic countries, or Christian Europe) by the growth of hair on the thighs and the face.

Patterns similar to Florence's turn up throughout southern Europe. Elsewhere in Italy there were fewer prosecutions than in Florence since the penalties were usually more severe. At Venice there were known places where men picked boys up. There was group sex and gang rape.

There were long-lasting love affairs. There was the occasional adult man who was sexually passive and there were a few transvestite men. The entire age-structured Mediterranean system was present. In Spain and Portugal the Inquisition records document similar patterns. In most cases sodomy occurred between men in their twenties and boys between 15 and 19 with the men active and the boys passive. These boys were often dressed and painted like women. Florentine boys do not seem to have done this. The Iberian material also presents more clearly cases of adult transvestite men who dressed constantly as women, used women's names, and in some cases even constructed artificial vaginas to conceal their penises. But such men as a typical part of the Mediterranean pederastical system were a decided minority in a world in which most sexual acts were between men and adolescents.[6]

Information about northern Europe is much sparser because there were fewer trials. In Basel, for instance, there were only eight trials in the first 50 years of the fifteenth century. The penalties were severe: four men were exiled and three were burnt at the stake. But in 1475 when a chaplain at the cathedral confessed to having several times sodomized a choirboy who lived in his house, the boy claimed that the priest had persuaded him by saying that "if everybody who committed this act was burnt at the stake, not even fifty men would survive in Basel." These fragments, when read in the light of the southern European materials, reveal a now-familiar world of widespread sexual acts between men and adolescents, with a great deal of implicit tolerance and very few cases brought to trial because the penalties were felt to be too severe.[7]

The Reformation in northern Europe would seem to have made no difference. Even in Geneva a man in 1610 confessed, under torture for high treason and murder, that he had had sexual relations with 20 other males and thereby revealed the existence of a world that usually went undisturbed.[8] But it is England that has been most extensively studied. The fragmentary evidence comes in three kinds: there are a few trials for sodomy; there are the biographical anecdotes about gentlemen and kings; and there are the plays and poems. Literary scholars who have studied the third category have sometimes claimed to find evidence for egalitarian sexual relations between two adult men in some of the plays from early in the century, but these are certainly misreadings, and those who have studied the Restoration plays are agreed that the sodomy in them is structured by differences in age. Every case of sodomy brought to court was for relations between men and adolescents. And even the most hostile anecdotes about King James I and his lovers took for granted that the king was dominant with younger men. Robert Carr became the king's favourite when he was 20 and "smooth-faced" and fell from favor when he grew his beard, lost his looks, and then married. In England (possibly because of a different physiological regime than in the south) a young man's passivity could last till the age of 25. Different court factions regularly vied with each other to present the king with a favorite of their choosing, and they seemed to have taken for granted that it lay within the power of any handsome young man to satisfy the king's desire, presuming, evidently, a universal capacity in this regard. The comments on James' behavior could be either condemnatory or non-committal, establishing in Protestant England the continued presence of two opposing moralities of sodomy. During those years of his marriage that James evidently slept with his wife (because of the cycle of her pregnancies), there is no evidence that he had male favorites. The favorites came only after he had ended sexual relations with his wife. No one thought the king was an effeminate passive sodomite interested only in men or boys.[9] Such mollies would be found in England only in a hundred years' time. The real difficulty with the English material is that the two kinds of passive adult man which from the Mediterranean evidence we would expect to be present have so far not shown up except for the case of John Rykener. He called himself Eleanor and was found in women's clothes having sex with another man in a London street on a night in 1394. He had worked regularly as a prostitute but had also had sex with women.[10]

This age-structured system in Europe began to disappear over the course of the eighteenth century, first for men and then for women. It was replaced by a system that structured same-sex relations by gender differences and divided the world into a homosexual minority and a heterosexual majority. In the eighteenth century the change seems to have been limited to northwestern Europe (England, France, and the Netherlands). It had reached central Europe by the middle of the nineteenth century; but it did not appear in southern and eastern Europe until the early twentieth century. When it first appeared around 1700, it probably came as part of the major societal shift that produced the dominant modern culture of the last three centuries. The likelihood of this is confirmed by the experience of Japanese society which between 1910 and 1950 moved similarly from an age-structured to a gendered system which divided the world into a homosexual minority and a heterosexual majority.[11] The beginning and slow growth of equality between men and women probably accounts for the change. Certainly in traditional societies like that of native North America where same-sex relations were structured by the presence of a third-gender minority, women had relatively higher standing than they did in the age-structured societies of the Mediterranean or East Asia. But in neither kind of traditional society was the sexual world divided into a homosexual minority and a heterosexual majority. The modern sexual system was therefore in some respects radically different from all preceding systems.

In the thirty years after 1700 it becomes possible to identify a new kind of sodomite in English society who (in the slang of the streets) was called a molly. A molly was an effeminate adult man who desired to have sex only with men or boys. His speech and gait were similar to a woman's; his clothes tended to be elegant and he occasionally dressed as a woman for a ball. Among his fellow mollies he was often known by a woman's name. Some men like the Princess Seraphina always dressed as women, they were referred to by everyone as she and her, and they lived by prostitution. All mollies differed from the effeminate men of both traditional systems. They were closest in role to someone like the North American *berdache*. But whereas it was legitimate for the Native American *berdache* to be penetrated by the men and boys from the majority, in the modern system the molly was supposed to be strictly avoided by the men and boys from the majority. The molly did desire such men, sometimes as their only object, but the men who yielded were concerned to hide this very carefully since any contact with a molly could be used to put them into that despised category. Mollies also had sex (and perhaps mainly) with each other, whereas the *berdaches* strictly avoided each other. Mollies also differed from the two types of passive men in age-structured systems because it was no longer the case that most sexual acts between males were between men and boys. It is true that adult mollies sometimes pursued boys and that for a while in the early eighteenth century there continued to be men who desired both women and boys. It was also the case that throughout the next three centuries some men in totally male institutions such as prisons or ships at sea satisfied themselves with boys who were present. But it was no longer acceptable for a boy to be passive. Boys among themselves talked with constant horrified fascination about mollies, but a boy approached by such a man tended to panic. Masturbation was severely discouraged with threats of mental and physical debility because it led males to a fascination with their penises instead of with women's bodies.[12]

The appearance of the molly's role was accompanied by the development in the majority of men of a new sexual role which allowed them to desire only women. Men now determinedly pursued the populations of streetwalking female prostitutes who filled the principal thoroughfares of most Western cities for the next 250 years. They seduced unmarried women with such callous vigor that within a hundred years illegitimacy climbed to unprecedented levels. In the end every sexual act was threatened by the venereal diseases clients contracted from prostitutes and passed on to their wives and children. Whore-mongering no longer injured a man's reputation. Instead it was crucial to be known not to be a molly. Blackmailers could terrify a timid man by swearing to charge him with sodomy, since the charge once made was difficult to disprove. But there was no term to distinguish this male majority. They were simply men and not mollies.[13]

Throughout the next three centuries, some of the males from this heterosexual majority, either as adolescents or as adult men, continued to have sex with men from the sodomitical or homosexual minority.[14] These sexual interactions became increasingly controversial over the course of the twentieth century. The appearance early in the twentieth century of adolescence as a distinct stage of social and sexual development began to curtail severely the sexual interactions between adolescent females and males and heterosexual and homosexual adult males. These interactions had been relatively commonplace and unremarkable in the eighteenth and the nineteenth centuries when most female prostitutes for instance had been adolescents between the ages of 15 and 22, at a time when puberty both for males and females began around 15. It is therefore the purpose of the rest of this chapter to describe some of the sexual interactions in eighteenth-century London between sodomites and heterosexual males of all ages.

There were at least three kinds of contact between adult men: sodomites met men who were not sodomites either while drinking in a public house or as they urinated together at a "pissing post" or sat next to each other in a "bog house" or public toilet. These contacts must often have been by mutual consent, but the sources tend to describe only those which went awry. The two different kinds of male prostitute were the other principal means for making sexual contact. Transvestite homosexual prostitutes had sex both with other sodomites and with men who were not sodomites. It is not easy to say whether a sodomite's heterosexual partner knew that he was having sex with another man. These transvestite males sometimes blackmailed their customers. When the cases came to court the victim occasionally claimed not to be a sodomite himself and this may or may not have been true. Soldiers were the other kind of male prostitute who engaged in blackmail. The adolescent male prostitutes (like the telegraph boys) who turn up easily enough in nineteenth-century sources, are not so conspicuous in the eighteenth century, but a number of the blackmailing soldiers were certainly late adolescents. The cases do not usually stress their prostitution, but it is very likely that this was the means by which contact between the blackmailer and his victim was made initially.

Sodomites who preferred boys engaged in a few cases with prepubescent boys aged 10 to 15, but in most cases the boys were over 15. Contemporaries noted that some men preferred boys to adult men, but the preference was not singled out and was condemned only in so far as all forms of sodomy were. The desire of some sodomites for boys rather than men seems to have arisen out of their uneasiness with the effeminacy of adult sodomites, and these men presumably would have been repelled by an adult transvestite male. Subordination by age rather than by effeminacy was of course the tradition in sodomitical relations before 1700, when all men had felt desire for both women and boys. It is therefore not surprising that when in the eighteenth century sex occurred between two males neither of whom was a sodomite, it tended to continue to be organized by differences in age. This can be seen in sexual relations in all-male institutions such as schools and colleges, or ships at sea, where there were likely to be few if any women. Sexual relations between heterosexual males were not of much significance in eighteenth-century prisons since these were not yet segregated by gender, but by 1810 when they were, the pattern of domination by differences in age is found. But the sexual life of all same-sex institutions after 1700 has been complicated by the fact that there have always been present in them a certain number of homosexual men exclusively attracted to other males. Eighteenth-century sailors in their ships at sea therefore faced the choice of having sex either with a (probably) heterosexual adolescent boy or with an effeminate adult sodomite, and in some ships, like the *Africaine*, they chose to do both.

In most of the complaints made to the eighteenth-century magistrates that a man had tried to seduce another male, it is not possible to tell which were made by late adolescents and which by adult males. These complaints make up the bulk of the manuscript materials on sodomy in the quarter-sessions' rolls. The printed trials and the newspapers deal more often either with the seduction of adolescents or with raids on the molly-houses in which adult sodomites had consensual sodomy with each other. The attempted seductions recorded in the manuscripts usually took the form of quite open lunges made at another man's privates while drinking together in a public house; but they were sometimes also made in a public latrine or in the street. Sometimes more than a lunge was made; actions that became complicated and took long enough seem to imply some degree of initial interested consent which eventually changed to anger or alarm. But sometimes after the charge was made, it was withdrawn, after the two drinking companions decided to forget the matter. William Green in 1788 charged that Thomas Impey had attempted an unnatural crime when they were drinking together. But the next day, Green refused to maintain his charge, and said that he had been drunk and could not recall the matter. The magistrate had no choice but to discharge Impey, so he fined Green five shillings for being drunk by his own confession. Similarly, Peter Campbell charged that Francis Philpott had touched him several times in Catherine Street and unbuttoned his breeches in Fleet Market; but since they had then agreed to go together to have a drink in a public house in Fleet Street, the magistrate dismissed the matter.[15]

The aggressive sexual acts of sodomites against other men took two forms across the century. Either the sodomite pushed his hand into the other man's breeches and took hold of his privates, or he took out his own penis and put it into the other man's hand. Either action might occur in the street or in a public house, and they might be accompanied by kisses or enticing words. In 1704 Humphrey Bower said that William Gage had met him in the street, touched him, and affectionately invited him to have a drink in a shop near Charing Cross. Gage, "being willing to see what his meaning was," went along. When they were seated in an inner room, Gage put his hand into Bower's codpiece and "used all the enticing actions he could." After they left the house and were again in the street, "Gage drew his yard privately and put it into Mr. Bower's ... hands." In the same year, John Hodges and Henry Turner met Thomas Turner in the street at one o'clock in the morning. Thomas Turner claimed that Henry Turner assaulted him, but the other two said that Thomas Turner put his privates into the hands of John Hodges and tried to persuade Hodges to bugger him.[16] In 1726, Thomas Coleman put his privates into the hand of Richard Hudson; another man did the same thing to Bartholomew Cornell in 1727; and nearly fifty years later, Godfrey Walley made the same complaint of John Batten.[17]

Three men complained together that Samuel Dassell put his hand into their breeches in 1707. In 1727 William Saise unbuttoned the breeches of Thomas Batterton, took hold of his privates, and asked him several times to lie with him; and in the same year Thomas Beach did exactly the same things to William Gibson.[18] In another part of town, also in 1727, John Harvey forced his hand into the breeches of Isaac Hughes, took hold of his privates, kissed him, and asked him to lie with him. Thomas Chamberlaine also kissed Edward Radvell, putting his tongue into his mouth; but in this case, Chamberlaine made the other take hold of his privates. William Davenport was more explicit in his acting out, since when he took hold of John Marshall's privates, he also put his bare backside into Marshall's lap. Fifty years later, men were still thrusting their hands into other men's breeches, as John Weston did to Robert Armstrong.[19]

The most elaborate attempted seduction that I have found occurred in 1761 when John Lowther and John Bushnell followed each other from one pissing post to another through several neighborhoods. Lowther remained ever hopeful that Bushnell would comply with his desires. Bushnell was intrigued enough to see how the matter would end and had decided to lure the other man on with the intention of eventually charging him with sodomy. Bushnell began by saying that "John Lowther came up to me and brushed on my elbow ... stared me full in the face, and then crossed the way into Pope's-Head-Alley, and turned to the wall to make water ... I then went past him, and looking back, observed the defendant looking after me." Lowther now followed Bushnell to a courtyard "and turned himself against the wall as if going to make water." Lowther stayed in that position for a little time and then turned toward Bushnell. He had unbuttoned the flap of his breeches, and "shook his private parts at me, making a great panting noise much like a person out of breath with running." Lowther then buttoned up and walked on to a second courtyard, where he again stood against the wall to pee, took out his penis, shook it at Bushnell, and panted loudly. When Lowther performed this ritual a third time in a third courtyard he came closer to Bushnell, put his head on the other man's shoulder, and stared him in the face, as though he meant to kiss him. The two men continued their way through the courtyards. All told, Lowther stopped to pee, shook his penis, and panted at Bushnell eight times as they walked through a series of eight courtyards. After he "made water the eighth time," Lowther came closer, took his penis in his hand and rubbed it against Bushnell's waistcoat. He then tried to take Bushnell's hand; but Bushnell drew back his hand. So Lowther caught Bushnell by the thigh and squeezed his penis through his breeches for a minute. Lowther then pushed his hand into Bushnell's breeches. He could only get four fingers in; so with his free hand he tried to unbutton Bushnell's breeches, but he could get only one button partly undone. All this while, Lowther's own breeches were undone and his penis hanging out. Bushnell now thought Lowther had gone quite far enough. He seized him by the collar and called for help to his friend who followed them by prearrangement. Lowther struggled free and ran. But the two men pursued him, crying out "Stop, Sodomite." He was soon caught. When he came to trial his neighbors said they had all known Lowther's reputation as a sodomite. He was fined £20, imprisoned for three months, and sentenced to stand in the pillory near his own house.[20]

None of the men in these accounts were dressed as women, and mollies who cross-dressed were probably always a minority, as opposed to the larger number who were effeminate in gesture, movement, and speech. A few individuals seem to have dressed as women most of the time. It is likely that they were either prostitutes themselves or bawds for male prostitution. James Dalton's friend, Sukey Haws, was such a man. So was John Cooper who was usually known as the Princess Seraphina. In 1757 a third man wrote a letter to Lord Tankerville offering to meet him for an assignation. When he was arrested he was found to be carrying a number of such letters which might "either pass for a begging letter of a man in distress or to offer his person for the basest purposes." When his neighbors were questioned, it was found that "he lay in bed every day till after twelve; that he constantly breakfasted in bed, wore a bedgown, and a woman's cap and knot: his paint and patch boxes [for makeup] were found in his toilet."

In 1764 John Gill was arrested at eleven o'clock on a Tuesday night as he was having sex with a man in a coach (one of the standard locales for female prostitution). He was known in his neighborhood as Miss Beasly and had been dressed in earrings and a bracelet, women's satin shoes and white silk stockings, and an outside petticoat trimmed with silver lace. Later in the same year the constables on a Monday night cleared the streets around Covent Garden of 22 female prostitutes, as they thought. But it turned out that two of the prostitutes were men dressed in women's clothes. It would be intriguing to know (but there is, alas, no evidence) whether the sexual partners of these male prostitutes, or the women with whom they walked the streets, knew the anatomical identity of these men beneath their women's clothes.[21]

Some of these transvestite prostitutes engaged in blackmail as three examples show. Susannah or Sukey Haws was

> a man who was what they call a bug to the mollies, and sometimes acting in that capacity with those who were not established in

clubs, picking 'em up as if to commit that damnable crime of sodomy; and when they had got an handle, or any foundation to proceed upon, they would extort money from them before they parted, or dog them to their own houses, and there, by daily threatening, they would make a considerable advantage of them.[22]

John Stevens was another of these "bugs." In 1729 Stevens, who was a waterman from Blackfriars who was notorious for going about dressed "in woman's apparel in a very impudent and insolent manner, insulting the neighborhood,"[23] tried to blackmail Thomas Foster.

Charles Vaughan in 1790 was a well-known character who attended all the masquerades in women's clothes, and went similarly dressed to other places of entertainment. He was known as Fat Phillis. Vaughan in the past had apparently made his advances to several noblemen and gentlemen using various names and characters. He was well-known in the magistrate's office. In April 1790 Vaughan tried to extort money from the Hon. and Rev. Mr. Cuff. Vaughan's accomplice was George Smith, a gentleman's servant who had met Vaughan six months before at the races at Newmarket when he was out of work. Vaughan and Smith charged Cuff with taking liberties with one of their friends at the playhouse on a Wednesday night. The theaters were common enough places of sexual encounter for both female prostitutes and male sodomites. Vaughan seems to have had some knowledge of the world in which fashionable and aristocratic sodomites moved, and he probably had successfully blackmailed some of them in the past. But in this case he judged wrongly. Instead of paying up, Cuff took Vaughan to the magistrates and was congratulated by the bench for his public spirit in bringing an old offender to justice.[24]

Soldiers appeared more frequently as blackmailers than any other group of men, especially during times of war when there would have been many of them passing through London. Their role as blackmailers may have been the result of being young underpaid men stationed in London with not enough to do. But it is also likely that soldiers in their uniforms were frequently solicited for sex by sodomites. Soldiers were therefore better informed about the sodomite's world in London than were most poor men. It may have been easy to turn from prostitution to blackmail; blackmail was probably more financially rewarding than prostitution; and it was certainly less threatening to a young man's masculine self-image. Soldiers blackmailed as lone operators, in pairs, and in gangs. A soldier on his own accused the Rev. Mr. Smith, the chaplain to the Duke of Northumberland, of sodomy. The magistrates carefully examined the evidence (one wonders whether Mr. Smith looked sexually ambiguous), found the soldier guilty, and sentenced him to six months in jail.[25] Some blackmailing soldiers became professional robbers. Shortly after Peter Green was discharged from prison in 1787 for extorting money from a gentleman by threatening to swear sodomy against him, Green and a fellow soldier, John Francis, assaulted an apothecary in St. James's Park on a Saturday night and took from him a gold watch, a great coat, and three guineas. They struck their victim several times, and, under a bright shining moon, would have taken his other coat from him, but stopped when others came walking in the Park. There is the possibility, of course, that Green's second victim was also a sodomite who had been using the Park to pick someone up, but there is no evidence to show this.[26]

Groups of soldiers seem to have acted together as blackmail gangs. In August 1790 four privates from the Coldstream Guards who were stationed in the Tower of London began to extort money from Henry Sharp. Sharp lived in James Street, Covent Garden, and was a porter to a carpet warehouse in the Piazza. Three of the soldiers, William Smith, George Platt, and Phillip Roberts, charged that Sharp had made advances to a fourth soldier, James Tempelman. Sharp paid them on several occasions a total of £8 12s. With the help of a friend, Sharp brought three of the four soldiers to the magistrate in early November. Roberts, however, could not be found at the time and was reported to have been absent for two days from his regiment. But when Sharp returned home from the magistrate, he found Roberts waiting for him. He did not give him a chance to ask for money but took him instead to the magistrate. All four soldiers were convicted of highway robbery, which brought the death penalty with it.[27] A year later two other soldiers from the Coldstream Guards made an indecent assault on a gentleman and then tried to extort money from him by threatening to swear sodomy against him. But the victim managed to seize his tormentors. He complained to their commanding officer; a court martial was immediately held; and the two men were sentenced to 300 lashes each, which they received in the Tilt-yard at Whitehall.[28]

The presence of blackmailing gangs in St. James's Park was of long standing. In July 1721 as Joseph Stone walked through the park at eleven o'clock on a Monday evening, he was set upon by four men in the "walk between the Mall and the Road about the first bench near Whitehall." They knocked him down and took his hat, his wig, and his money. Stone recognized one of the men as William Casey by his face and his voice. He had seen him drinking several times in Thieving

Lane. Casey almost strangled Stone with his neck cloth and said that if he cried out they would swear sodomy against him. But as they left, Stone did cry out murder. So Casey came back and stamped on him and said, "Damn you, are you not dead yet?" Stone could not identify Martin Mackowen so well when he was tried along with Casey – the remaining two men were apparently not arrested. Mackowen was acquitted but Casey was found guilty and sentenced to death.[29] In the middle of the century, in a single year in 1759, there was a rash of these attacks on men in the park. London was then probably full of soldiers because of the war in progress. There was a barracks close to the park and some soldiers were familiar with sodomites as sexual customers. In that year John Fielding therefore had to commit to Newgate several individuals who had charged supposedly innocent men in the park with sodomy as a means of robbing them. A month before these arrests were made an elderly gentleman was attacked at eight o'clock in the evening as he walked near the Bird Cage Walk in the park (a traditional pick-up place for sodomites). Two men took from him his hat, his shirt, a pair of gold sleeve buttons, a blue coat, a waistcoat, and a pair of silver buckles: they stripped him down, in other words, to his shoes, stockings, breeches, and wig.[30]

John Parker, a gentleman's servant, was also attacked in Bird Cage Walk in 1759, by James Brown, a soldier. Parker was going through the park on an errand for his master. Another servant in the park, on an errand for his master Lord Harcourt, observed what occurred. An accomplice of Brown's, who was genteelly dressed, clasped Parker around the waist, forcibly took him aside, and began to fondle him. Brown then "surprised" them in their act. He threatened Parker that he would charge him with sodomy and have him hanged if he did not pay him. Parker gave him five shillings, but refused to part with his shoe buckles. Brown and his accomplice therefore took Parker to the guard to charge him with sodomy. Lord Harcourt's servant appeared, however, and gave evidence against the soldiers. Brown was tried, found guilty of robbery, and sentenced to hang. His accomplice got off more lightly since his part in the robbery was judged not to be proven. The newspaper report praised Lord Harcourt's servant for having had the "curiosity as well as humanity to watch" and for thereby being "the happy means of preserving the young man's character." But there is, of course, the possibility that both these servants were sodomites who had made a detour on their masters' business so that they could pass along the Bird Cage Walk on the chance of a sexual encounter and that Lord Harcourt's servant was a sodomite with presence enough and heart enough to come to the rescue of a brother sodomite. It is clear that public opinion and the law would have been much less sympathetic to the young servant's plight if Brown had been able to show that the man was in fact a sodomite.[31]

The eighteenth century did not make a sharp distinction between those sodomites who liked men and those who liked boys, even though they recognized the existence of the two categories. John Dunton in the 1710 edition of his poem "The He-Strumpets: a Satyr on the Sodomite Club" (which he had first published in 1707 as a commentary on one of the earliest series of arrests of adult effeminate men) declared that in "this club of Sodomites/These doat on men, and some on boys." But Dunton expressed no shock at the preference of some for boys. His concern was that all sodomites "quite abandon female joys" and become "men worse than goats/Who dress themselves in petticoats," and in this regard, were more brutish than the beasts (who themselves "he-lechery detest") and were in fact the "perfect Devil." In the early-eighteenth-century English evidence, however, when the modern system was still coming into existence and had not yet entirely replaced the old, it is not always easy to separate the traditional man who liked boys and women from those modern sodomites who liked boys, and it is very likely that in those years men coexisted who had grown up in different generations and therefore in different cultural systems. It is not likely that Richard Kirby, who took a barber's young servant down into a cellar in London in 1699 and told him to "turn his face to the wall", was a modern sodomite; nor were military men such as Lord Stanhope and Lord Huntingdon who could meet "over a glass of champagne in Paris with two or three pretty smiling unthinking fellows that know nothing and do everything." Stanhope was born in 1673 and died in 1721. But Lord Hervey who was born 23 years later in 1696 was a modern sodomite though he married and had a mistress as well. His passion for males, however, was directed not at adolescents but at young men in their early twenties just at the moment that they would have entered manhood: he usually cast himself with them in a passive female role. When he was 30 he fell in love with Stephen Fox who was 22. Ten years later in 1736 when Hervey's last child was born and Fox married, Hervey at 40 began a new relationship with a 24-year-old Italian. Francesco Algarotti, in whose Italian world men still liked boys and women, seems to have been able in England to have sexual encounters both with women and with effeminate adult men like Hervey. Hervey seems to have been like the majority of modern sodomites whose preference was for young men in their twenties and thirties. But in his generation he lived with men like Stanhope who liked both boys and women.[32]

Modern sodomites whose preference was for adolescent males turn up in the eighteenth-century London cases for sodomitical assault in which males of a variety of ages complained of the sexual advances of another male. The historian of the early twenty-first century tends to divide these complaining males into three groups: the prepubescent under 15; the adolescents between 15 and 20–23; and the adult men. But there really is no sign that the eighteenth-century judges and juries made these distinctions. Still, it is probably useful to take up first and separately what must have been the cases of physically prepubescent boys. There were not many of them. In fact, between 1730 and 1830 only five of 70 cases before the Old Bailey involved boys younger than 14 which was the age of legal consent for boys.[33]

Captain Robert Jones was a man who seduced a prepubescent boy, the 12-year-old nephew of his jeweller. Once Francis Henry Jay became accustomed to having Jones look at him in the street and tip him with halfpennies, Jones told the boy he had a buckle to mend and asked him up into his lodgings. There he put the boy into an elbow chair, and after he had kissed him a little, he told the boy to lie with his face on the chair, came up behind him, and "put his c[oc]k into my b[unghol]e" for about five minutes. The boy said he did not cry out from the pain because he was ashamed to. After "some wet stuff that was white" came from Jones, and the boy had wiped it off himself, Jones "spouted some on the ground." Jones now kissed the boy, gave him some money, and told him not to tell anyone. All this had taken half an hour. He asked the boy to return the next morning, and during the ten minutes they were together "he made me rub his c[oc]k up and down until some white stuff came again," but this time there was no penetration, probably because the first encounter had left the boy too sore. The next day the boy returned for the third time and masturbated Jones again. But the boy became frightened. "I was taken very ill after this," he said; "I was ill a week; I had a pain in my thighs and legs that I could not stand." Jones eventually came to the jewelry shop and ordered a buckle. But when Francis's uncle ordered him to deliver the buckle, he declined to do so.

The boy's family was religious, and went to church on Sundays, and the boy recited the catechism afterwards at home. So he answered "yes" in court when he was asked if he thought he "had been doing a wrong thing." And when he was therefore pressed "how came you to go the second and third times," he could only answer that he "thought my uncle might get business by it." The pain from the first encounter had left him so sore that he "straddled as I walked." But the lure of the money had drawn him a second and a third time even though "I was quite ashamed of it when I was with him." Jones brought witnesses to court to try to prove that he was "addicted to women." But the jury believed the boy and Jones was condemned to hang. Jones, however, was well connected. On the day of his hanging he was respited, and a month later pardoned on the condition that he went abroad, where, it was claimed, he lived at Lyon "with a *lovely Ganymede* (his footboy)." In his encounter with the jeweller's nephew, Jones had seductively prepared the boy for their first encounter, and it may be that if he had not penetrated him on the first occasion and caused some physical hurt that eventually frightened the boy away, that the boy, despite his guilt and shame, would have returned steadily, drawn by the money and perhaps the excitement of the encounter with this affable gentleman. There was considerable public outrage when the king pardoned Jones. But the outrage was simply that this encouraged sodomy. None of it made anything of the boy's age.[34]

For a man like William Beckford at the end of the eighteenth century, it is likely that a prepubescent boy's prettiness was a definite alternative to the effeminacy of an adult sodomitical partner. Beckford was severely ostracized for most of his life because of a scandal over a boy. In 1779 when Beckford was 19 he met and fell in love with William Courtenay, the eldest son of Viscount Courtenay, who was 11 years old. The boy was very pretty and was nicknamed "Kitty." Three years later when Courtenay was 14 and a student at Westminster School, Beckford found opportunities to see the boy alone and it is possible that their friendship became sexual. Shortly thereafter Beckford went abroad with his head full of Courtenay and wrote the boy indiscreet letters which were probably discovered. The boy's new uncle by marriage, Lord Loughborough, in all likelihood decided to lay a trap to catch the lovers. Beckford had in the meanwhile married at his mother's insistence, but he continued to dream of Courtenay. In 1784 Beckford visited the Courtenay family seat accompanied by his wife. After the couple's visit had ended, Courtenay's new tutor was supposed to have said that through the keyhole of a locked door he had seen Beckford sodomizing Courtenay. The scandal made its way into the newspapers and Beckford was thereafter ostracized from respectable society. His ostracism (no formal legal charges were made) was probably facilitated by his ambiguous social status as a young man of fabulous wealth whose family had only recently been trying to gain admission to aristocratic society.

At the moment the scandal broke Beckford had become profoundly disillusioned with Courtenay. Courtenay was now between 16 and 17, and it was beginning to be apparent that he would grow into an adult effeminate sodomite. In his early forties Viscount Courtenay (as he had become) was threatened with a legal prosecution for sodomy as Beckford himself had not been. Courtenay's only solution was to go abroad into exile where he died 24 years later. Beckford had found the emerging young homosexual "quite lost in flowers and foolery ... still more girlish and trifling than you are aware of." Courtenay had become obsessed with clothes – balloon hats and silvered sashes, Beckford said. Six years after the scandal, Beckford complained of Courtenay that things had only gotten worse: "*c'est un berdache, s'il en fait jamais; il se pare comme un poupée et se fard comme un p——*": which was to say, he is a passive sodomite if there ever was; he decks himself out like a milliner's dummy and paints himself like a whore. Beckford liked pretty boys exactly because they were not effeminate sodomites. When he visited Portugal he pursued them tirelessly (at a moment when southern Europe still lived under the older male regime of desiring both boys and women), and he met there a 16-year-old Italian choirboy whom he eventually brought back to England and made his steward after the boy had grown up and married. In Beckford's case his relations with his social inferior endured and the love affair with his young lord failed because he could not manage the boy's relations. But it is apparent that Beckford wished to have nothing to do with Courtenay after the boy had grown up into an effeminate sodomite. For Beckford, and probably for many Englishmen with such tastes, boys were an alternative to adult effeminacy. But a masculine sodomy was an illusion in a world in which all sodomites were supposed to be effeminate. And Beckford himself had been held in contempt for singing in what was thought to be a eunuch's voice. Nonetheless, when as a contemporary of Beckford's, Jeremy Bentham, set out in 1785 in an unpublished essay to justify (and is it possible that Bentham was inspired to write by the newspaper reports on Beckford?) sodomy as morally indifferent and therefore not deserving of punishment, he characterized sodomy as an act between a man and an adolescent and ignored its more recent associations with adult male effeminacy. It may be that his knowledge of the literature of the ancient Greeks and Romans and their moral acceptance of age-structured relations blotted out for him the actualities of his own day as it did for some of his French and German contemporaries, but it must also have been that in 1800 sexual relations between an adult and an adolescent were still less disturbing than sexual desire between two adults of the same gender.[35]

A man such as George Duffus liked older adolescents. He met Nicholas Leader and Mr. Powell at sermons on a Sunday evening and had religious discussions with them afterwards, and on several other occasions. Then, in both cases, the discussion having continued very late into the evening, Duffus asked to share a bed for the night. Once they were in bed, he made his advances. In Leader's case, Duffus first hugged and kissed him, called him his dear, and when asked what he meant, answered, "No harm, nothing but love." He tried several times to get on top of Leader and eventually seized him by the throat, turned him over, and entered him briefly. But the continued struggle caused Duffus to ejaculate in his own hand, which he then wiped on the tail of Leader's nightshirt, telling him, "now you have it." Leader said he allowed Duffus to stay the rest of the night so as not to disturb his sleeping grandmother, and that the following morning Duffus told him, "that I need not be concerned at what he had done to me, for he had done the same to several others, and named in particular, a cabin-boy."

Duffus' approach in bed with Powell was similar. He told him that his wife was out of town and asked to stay. In bed he began to kiss Powell. He took hold of his privates and said, "How lean you be. Do but feel how fat I am'; but Powell would not touch him. When Powell turned away, Duffus got on him, held him down, put his penis between his thighs, and ejaculated. He then offered the same sort of moral reassurances that he had made to Leader: that Powell "need not be troubled or wonder at what he had done, for it was very common, and he had often practiced it with others." But Powell, after refusing an offer of reciprocation, said that he "was a stranger to all such practices," and that if he "had known what sort of man he had been, I would never have lain in the same bed with him."[36]

Duffus was a pious, self-confident, aggressive, married man, who was, evidently, accustomed to getting his way with the pious young men with whom he had established his moral authority, and whose scruples he was certain he could calm. He might have to use a little initial force, but eventually he expected to succeed. He had, presumably, succeeded in the past, but in these two instances he had, unfortunately for him, misjudged the moral pliability of his companions. Sodomy was for Duffus a thing to which any man might be brought; but it was no sin, but an act of love. Yet it seems unlikely that Duffus was tied to traditional libertine culture. Duffus' kissing and his offer of reciprocal sex made him a modern sodomite, even though he met his friends in a meeting-house and not in a molly-house. But, for Powell, it is clear that a man who would do such a thing at all was a different kind of man than himself. If, however, Duffus was in fact a new sodomite rather than an old libertine writ large, he did not live up to expectations in two regards. He was not effeminate, since Powell had not been able to tell in advance what kind of man he was. And he was not sexually exclusive: his wife was out of town. One thing was certain about Duffus. He was very religious. It is a characteristic that has some-times been noted in the twentieth-century sexual deviant: the devout Catholic father who cruises the highway toilet; the religious husband who thinks that sex with his daughter is preferable to adultery. It has been suggested that this "breastplate of righteousness" protects an indi-vidual from his own negative judgment of himself, as well as from the judgment of others, and that an individual committed to a rigid moral system says to himself that once one rule is broken, none of the rules apply.[37] So, for instance, if Duffus found himself adulterous, why not be sodomitical as well. But there is also the possibility, that Duffus, as a man accustomed to religious discussion, had formed an independent conscience for himself, and that he found sodomy, as he said, "no harm, nothing but love."

Most of the sex that occurred on British naval vessels over the course of the eighteenth and the early nineteenth centuries seems to have been structured by differences in age. Between 1706 and 1809 in 14 of 17 cases discussed by Arthur Gilbert, an adult man had sex with a boy of 16 or younger, and most of the boys seemed to have been 12 or 13. In only three of the cases was the encounter between two adults. Some boys clearly did not know what semen was and said that the man had "pissed in his arse" or that "it was the same as if he was making water." The sex involved was usually anal, but one man made the boy fellate him also. All these men but one were the penetrators, and the one exception handled "their private parts, and taking them into his mouth, thrusting his fingers up their fundaments, blowing into them, and ... making them ease themselves into his hands, and asking them to do it in his mouth."[38]

The situation on board the ship *Africaine* in 1816 was more compli-cated. Some adult men were passive with other men, some men were both active and passive, and some men had relations with boys and with men. The *Africaine* was in fact known as a "man-fucking ship." A boatswain's mate declared that "God must put it into men's heads to commit the unnatural crime of buggery" and therefore "if God was to put it into his head to fuck a man he would as soon do it as fuck a woman," in fact, "he would do it to the skipper, any of the officers or ship's company, even to Jesus Christ if he was in his coffin." James Cooper was both active and passive with Raphael Seraco. Emmanuel Cross did it both with William Dane and with a 14-year-old boy, and Raphaelo Treake did it with two boys and with several men. One of the English midshipmen accused the two principal witnesses of being sodomites, and by this he probably meant that they were effeminate sodomites of the modern kind. But one of these men was a black Spaniard from Santo Domingo and the other a Portuguese sailor from Madeira, and it is likely that for them sodomy with a boy did not exclude a sexual interest in women. Indeed it is possible that the heightened sexual life of the ship was produced by the interaction between (heterosexual) men, adult sodomites, and boys from England, with Mediterranean sailors who in the traditional way liked both boys and women.

The English officer W.L. Crutchly, however, not only had a boy who either masturbated him or allowed himself to be penetrated; he was also charged with and convicted of embracing and kissing another man, and kissing had in England in the course of the eighteenth-century come to be taken as a sure sign of effeminate sodomy.[39]

The public schools or boarding schools for boys from the English elite were a second all-male institution in which sexual relations occurred between males who in adult life seem to have turned out to be exclusively heterosexual in their desires and sexual practices. As late as 1990–91 in a survey of the general population, men who had gone to a boarding school were three times as likely to have had some sort of sexual contact with another male (15 percent as opposed to 5 percent) as were the general male population. But even these public school boys were a decided minority in their own class, and it is apparent from anecdotal evidence that the extent of sexual activity (as opposed to mere romantic longing) varied widely from one school to another. In adult life, however, public school boys were no more likely to be homosexual than men from the general population (2 percent as opposed to 1.75 percent). It is sometimes said that from the early nineteenth century onward the schools were reorganized to cut down on the homosexual activity between older and younger boys by excluding younger boys, giving each boy a separate bed, and organizing a school's domestic life through several constituent houses each under a master and a dame rather than through large unsupervised communal dormitories where boys slept together naked in featherbeds. But this system was in fact introduced in the generation after 1750 in the schools to which aristocrats sent their sons, which dovetails neatly with the assertion that the modern homosexual role and its complementary heterosexual mate were firmly established for men by 1750. But sexual relations between older boys and younger ones, and sometimes between boys and schoolmasters, continued to occur.[40]

Eighteenth-century prisons often mixed men and women together promiscuously and were therefore not really totally sex-segregated institutions. But by the second decade of the nineteenth century, men and women were separated from each other. In some male prisons, disorderly apprentices, adult male criminals, and men and boys committed for homosexual acts were kept from each other in separate galleries and were not allowed to associate when they were let out of their cells for exercise or to warm themselves before the fire. In Cold Baths Field Prison in 1818 there was a top gallery for males confined for attempting sodomy, but they were able to talk to other kinds of prisoners from cell to cell during the night. On a gallery beneath were the apprentices who were never allowed to mingle with the sodomites. And on the lowest gallery were imprisoned soldiers. But in the gallery for boys, the cells slept two or more; there was "very much reason to fear that the most abominable actions have been committed with each other"; and one "boy," Robert Jones, became venereally infected because he had "almost constantly slept with a young man named Joseph Bowyer." Heterosexual males, in other words, although separated from the sodomites, slept together and had sex in which the young men penetrated the boys. There seem to have been opportunities in some prisons for sodomites to mingle with each other and even with other men at recreation; sometimes a younger sodomite in his teens might be confined with groups of older sodomites varying from nine to 21 men; but there is no direct evidence that these men managed to have sex with each other in prison. The prison sex that can be documented was between heterosexual males and structured by differences in age.[41]

From the preceding discussion it follows that in prisons, ships at sea, and boarding schools, there were three different sexual categories of males, namely, heterosexual men, boys, and adult effeminate sodomites. The boys were the most complicated category: some were prepubescent and some had entered puberty; most boys would eventually become heterosexual and a few homosexual, but these realizations would not necessarily have been achieved during their time in prison,

at sea, or in school. In prisons, especially in the nineteenth and twentieth century, heterosexual men had sexual relations with both homosexual and heterosexual men, structuring their actions with the former
by effeminacy and with the latter by age. But boys eventually would be
sent to separate prisons where they would have relations with each
other which were most often structured by age. Boys after 1945 were
no longer to be found in ships at sea, and from the middle of the nineteenth century onward there was probably an increasing tendency to
separate them from the men. But from the *Africaine* case, it is apparent
that ships witnessed the most complicated set of relations, with heterosexual men having sexual relations structured by age with both heterosexual adults and with boys, and relations with homosexual men
structured by the effeminacy of the latter. In schools adult schoolmasters would have been either heterosexual or homosexual, and some of
the latter had relations with boys that were age-structured. Among the
boys themselves, differences in age were crucial to attraction; still,
younger boys were often valued because they were pretty and could
serve as substitutes for women; but their age was probably more deter-
minative of their passivity. It is therefore likely that while after 1700 it
was only a minority of homosexual men who structured their sexual
relationships with males by differences in age, in all-male institutions
heterosexual men were very likely to use these differences to establish
sexual dominance.

Notes

1. K.J. Dover, *Greek Homosexuality* (Cambridge, MA: Harvard University Press, 1978); Craig A. Williams, *Roman Homosexuality* (New York: OUP, 1999).
2. Anne M. Johnson, et al., *Sexual Attitudes and Lifestyles* (Oxford: Blackwell Scientific Publications, 1994); Edward O. Laumann, et al., *The Social Organization of Sexuality* (Chicago: University of Chicago Press, 1994); Amy Richlin, "Not Before Homosexuality: the Materiality of the *Cinaedus* and the Roman Law Against Love Between Men," *Journal of the History of Sexuality* 3 (1993): 523–73; Rabun Taylor, "Pathic Subcultures in Ancient Rome," *Journal of the History of Sexuality* 7 (1997): 319–71.
3. Paul Veyne, "Homosexuality in Ancient Rome," in P. Aries and A. Bejin (eds.), *Western Sexuality* (Oxford: Blackwell, 1985); Benedicta Ward, *The Sayings of the Desert Fathers* (Kalamazoo, MI: Cistercian Publications, 1975).
4. Michael Rocke, *Forbidden Friendships* (New York: OUP, 1996).
5. Richard Trexler, "Florentine Prostitution in the Fifteenth Century: Patrons and Clients," in *Dependence in Context in Renaissance Florence* (Binghamton, NY: MRTS, 1994): 373–414; J.P. Dedieu, "La Défense De Mariage Chrétien," in Bartolomé Bennassar (ed.), *L'Inquisition Espagnole (Xve-XIXe siécle)* (Paris: 1979), pp. 313–38; Randolph Trumbach, *Sex and the Gender Revolution*, Vol.

I, *Heterosexuality and the Third Gender in Enlightenment London* (Chicago: University of Chicago Press, 1998), Chap. 11; Franco Mormando, *The Preacher's Demons: Bernardino of Siena and the Social Underworld of Early Renaissance Italy* (Chicago: University of Chicago Press, 1999).

6. Guido Ruggiero, *The Boundaries of Eros: Sex Crime and Sexuality in Renaissance Venice* (New York: OUP, 1985), Chap. 6; Luiz Mott, "Pogode Português: a Subcultura Gay em Portugal Nos Tempos Inquisitorias," *Ciência E Cultura* 40 (1988): 130–9; David Higgs, "Lisbon," in David Higgs (ed.),*Queer Sites: Gay Urban Histories Since 1600*, (New York: Routledge, 1999), pp. 112–37; Rafael Carasco, *Inquisición y Represión Sexual en Valencia: Historia de los Sodomitas (1565–1785)* (Barcelona: Laertes, 1985).

7. Helmut Puff, "Localizing Sodomy: the 'Priest and Sodomite' in Pre-Reformation Germany and Switzerland," *Journal of the History of Sexuality* 8 (1997): 165–95.

8. William Monter, "Sodomy and Heresy In Early Modern Switzerland," in S.J. Liccata and R.B. Petersen (eds.), *Historical Perspectives on Homosexuality*, (New York: Haworth Press, 1981).

9. Alan Bray, *Homosexuality in Renaissance England* (London: Gay Men's Press, 1982); Michael B. Young, *King James and the History of Homosexuality* (New York: New York University Press, 2000); David M. Bergeron, *King James & Letters of Homoerotic Desire* (Iowa City: University of Iowa Press, 1999); Cynthia B. Herrup, *A House in Gross Disorder: Sex, Law and the 2nd Earl of Castlehaven* (New York: OUP, 1999). The most useful of the literary studies, because it is the clearest on the pederastical nature of the sources, is Steve Brown, "The Boyhood of Shakespeare's Heroines: Notes on Gender Ambiguity in the Sixteenth Century," *SEL: Studies in English Literature* 30 (1990): 243–63. See also, Bruce R. Smith, *Homosexual Desire in Shakespeare's England: a Cultural Poetics* (Chicago: University of Chicago Press, 1991); Terrence Johnson, "Representation of Male Homosexuality on the English Restoration Stage," unpublished PhD thesis, University of California, Los Angeles, 1992; Mario DiGangi, *The Homoerotics of Early Modern Drama* (Cambridge: CUP, 1997). In three essays Joseph Cady has tried to argue that the phrase "masculine love" in the Renaissance indicates desire between two adult men, but an attentive reading of his texts shows that they are usually referring to relations between men and boys. Cady, "'Masculine Love', Renaissance Writing, and the 'New Invention' of Homosexuality," in Claude J. Summers (ed.), *Homosexuality in Renaissance and Enlightenment England: Literary Representations in Historical Context* (New York: Haworth Press, 1992), pp. 9–40; "Renaissance Awareness and Language for Heterosexuality: 'Love' and 'Feminine Love'," in C.J. Summers and T.-L. Pebworth (eds.), *Renaissance Discourses of Desire* (Columbia, MI: University of Missouri Press, 1993), pp. 143–58; "'The 'Masculine Love' of the 'Princes of Sodom': 'Practicing the Art of Ganymede' at Henry III's Court: the Homosexuality of Henry III and his *Mignons* in Pierre L'Estoile's *Memoires-Journaux*," in J. Murray and K. Eisenbichler (eds.), *Desire and Discipline: Sex and Sexuality in the Premodern West*, (Toronto: University of Toronto Press, 1996), pp. 123–54.

10. Ruth M. Karras and David L. Boyd, "'*Ut Cum Muliere*': a Male Transvestite Prostitute In Fourteenth-Century London," in L. Fradenburg and C. Freccero (eds.), *Premodern Sexualities* (New York: Routledge, 1996).

11. Gregory M. Pflugfelder, *Cartographies of Desire* (Berkeley, CA: University of California Press, 1999).

12. For England, Randolph Trumbach: "London's Sodomites: Homosexual Behavior and Western Culture in the Eighteenth Century," *Journal of Social History* 11 (1977): 1–33; "The Birth of the Queen: Sodomy and the Emergence of Gender Equality in Modern Culture, 1660–1750," in M. Duberman, M. Vicinus and G. Chauncey, Jr. (eds.), *Hidden From History: Reclaiming the Gay and Lesbian Past* (New York: New American Library, 1989), pp. 129–40; "Sodomy Transformed: Aristocratic Libertinage, Public Reputation and the Gender Revolution of the 18th Century," in Michael S. Kimmel (ed.), *Love Letters Between A Certain Late Nobleman And The Famous Mr. Wilson* (New York: Harrington Park Press, 1990), pp. 105–24; "Are Modern Lesbian Women and Gay Men a Third Gender?," in Martin Duberman (ed.), *A Queer World: the Center for Lesbian and Gay Studies Reader* (New York: New York University Press, 1997), pp. 87–99; "London," in Higgs (ed.), *Queer Sites*, pp. 89–111. "Sodomitical Assaults, Gender Role, and Sexual Development in 18th Century London," in Kent Gerard and Gert Hekma *The Pursuit of Sodomy: Male Homosexuality in Renaissance and Enlightenment Europe* (New York: Haworth Press, 1988), pp. 407–29; and *Sex and the Gender Revolution*, pp. 59–65, has dealt with sexual relations between men and adolescents and between adolescent males: this material will be reconsidered in this essay. Netta Murray-Goldsmith, *The Worst of Crimes: Homosexuality and the Law in Eighteenth-Century London* (Brookfield, VT: Ashgate, 1998) deals with the blackmail of sodomites, as does Trumbach, *Sex and the Gender Revolution*, pp. 55–8. Trumbach uses the material to investigate the heterosexual identity of the male majority. G.S. Rousseau's presentation of a sodomitical circle around the late adolescent John Wilkes and his older tutor – see G.S. Rousseau, "'In the House of Madame Van der Tasse': Homosocial Desire and a University Club during the Enlightenment," in Gerard and Hekma (eds.), *The Pursuit of Sodomy*, pp. 311–48, rep. with an introduction in G.S. Rousseau, *Perilous Enlightenment* (Manchester: University of Manchester Press, 1991), pp. 109–37 – has been seriously questioned by Arthur Cash, "Wilkes, Baxter, and D'Holbach at Leiden and Utrecht: an Answer to G.S. Rousseau," in Paul J. Korshin (ed.), *The Age of Johnson*, Vol. 7 (2000): pp. 397–426. Rictor Norton, because he does not realize the nature of the pederast system before 1700, doubts that there is a modern homosexual identity: *Mother Clap's Molly House: the Gay Subculture in England 1700–1830* (London: GMP Publishers, 1992); *The Myth of the Modern Homosexual: Queer History and the Search for Cultural Unity* (London: Cassell, 1997). Cameron McFarlane, *The Sodomite in Fiction and Satire, 1660–1750* (New York: Columbia University Press, 1997), doubts all change, but he does not understand the sources and reduces everything to fiction. A.D. Harvey, *Sex in Georgian England: Attitudes and Prejudices from the 1720s to the 1820s* (London: Duckworth, 1994), accepts that adult male effeminacy grows more important but cannot see the difference with the period before 1700 because he also does not realize the pederast nature of the earlier system. Philip Carter accepts the reality of the change in systems, but believes that older ideas of effeminacy as brought on by moral corruption persisted: "Men about Town: Representations of Foppery in Early

Eighteenth-Century Urban Society," in H. Barker and E. Chalus (eds.), *Gender in Eighteenth-Century England: Roles, Representations and Responsibilities* (New York: Longman, 1997) 31–57; "An 'Effeminate' or 'Efficient' Nation? Masculinity and Eighteenth-Century Documentary," *Textual Practice* 11 (1997): 429–43; "James Boswell's Manliness," in T. Hitchcock and M. Cohen (eds.), *English Masculinities 1660–1800* (New York: Longman, 1999) 111–30. Raymond Bentman usefully distinguishes the conventions of heterosexual and homosexual friendship in "Thomas Gray and the Poetry of 'Hopeless Love'," *Journal of the History of Sexuality* 3 (1992): 203–22 and "Horace Walpole's Forbidden Passion," in Martin Duberman (ed.), *Queer Representations: Reading Lives, Reading Cultures* (New York: New York University Press, 1997), pp. 276–89. Tim Hitchcock, *English Sexualities, 1700–1800* (New York: St. Martin's Press [now Palgrave Macmillan], 1997) is the most satisfactory but his analysis does not present all sexualities as part of a single system. For sexual roles in the theater see Laurence Senelick, "Mollies or Men of Mode? Sodomy and the Eighteenth-Century London Stage," *Journal of the History of Sexuality* 1 (1990): 33–67 and Kristina Straub, *Sexual Suspects: Eighteenth-Century Players and Sexual Ideology* (Princeton, NJ: Princeton University Press, 1992). For France, see: Michel Rey, "Parisian Homosexuals Create a Lifestyle, 1700–1750: the Police Archives," in *'Tis Nature's Fault: Unauthorized Sexuality during the Enlightenment*, ed. R.P. MacCubbin (Cambridge: CUP, 1987) 179–91, and "Police and Sodomy in Eighteenth-Century Paris," in Gerard and Hekma (eds.), *Pursuit of Sodomy*, pp. 129–46; Jeffrey Merrick, "The Marquis de Villette and Mademoiselle Raucourt: Representations of Male and Female Deviance in Late Eighteenth-Century France," in J. Merrick and B.T. Ragan Jr. (eds.), *Homosexuality in Modern France* (New York: OUP, 1996), pp. 30–53; Jeffrey Merrick: "Sodomitical Inclinations in Early Eighteenth-Century Paris," *Eighteenth Century Studies* 30 (1997): 289–95, "Commissioner Foucault, Inspector Noël and the 'Pederasts' of Paris, 1780–3," *Journal of Social History* 32 (1998): 287–307, and "Sodomitical Scandals and Subcultures in the 1720s," *Men and Masculinities* 1 (1999): 365–84. For the Netherlands, see Theo van der Meer: *De Wesentlijke Sonde van Sodomie en Andere Vuyligheeden: Sodomienten ver volgingen in Amsterdam, 1730–1811* (Amsterdam: Tabula, 1984), *Sodoms Zaad in Nederland: Het Ontstaan van Homoseksualiteit in de Vroegmoderne Tijd* (Nijmegen: Sun, 1995), "The Persecution of Sodomites in Eighteenth-Century Amsterdam: Changing Perceptions of Sodomy," in Gerard and Hekma (eds.), *Pursuit of Sodomy*, pp. 263–307, "Sodomy and the Pursuit of a Third Sex in the Early Modern Period," in Gilbert Herdt (ed.), *Third Sex, Third Gender: Beyond Sexual Dimorphism in Culture and History* (New York: Zone Books, 1994), pp. 137–212; D.J. Noordam: *Riskante Relaties: Vijf Eeuwen Homoseksualiteit in Nederland, 1223–1733* (Hilversum: Verlorn, 1995) and "Sodomy in the Dutch Republic, 1600–1725," in Gerard and Hekma (eds.), *Pursuit of Sodomy*, pp. 207–28; L.J. Boon, *Dien Godlosen Hoop van Menschen: Vervolging van Homoseksuelen in de Republiek in de Jaren dertig van de Achttiende Eeuw* (Amsterdam: De Bataafsche Leeuw, 1997).

13. Trumbach, *Sex and the Gender Revolution*, pp. 55–7, 70–322.
14. George Chauncey, *Gay New York: Gender, Urban Culture and the Making of the Gay Male World, 1890–1940* (New York: Basic Books, 1994), Chaps. 1–4, pro-

vides the best account of sexual relations between homosexual and heterosexual men; see also Trumbach, "Are Modern Lesbian Women and Gay
Men a Third Gender?"

15. Corporation of London Record Office (CLRO): Guildhall Justice Room Book,
Notebook 37 (9 Aug. 1788), Notebook 29 (12 Jan. 1785).

16. London Metropolitan Archive (LMA): MJ/SR/2032, Recog., 72; CLRO: S.R.
(September 1704), Recog. 30, 31.

17. CLRO: S.R. (August 1726), Poultry Compter List; S.R. (July 1727), Poultry
Compter Kalendar; LMA: MJ/SR/3266, Recog. 256.

18. CLRO: S.R. (October 1707), Newgate Calendar; S.R. (May 1727), Recog. 12,
and Poultry Compter List; S.R. (July 1727), Wood Street Compter Kalendar.

19. LMA: MJ/SR/2481, New Prison List; MJ/SR/2483, Recog. 137, Bond, 7;
CLRO: S.R. (May 1727), Recog. 21; LMA: MJ/SR/3363, Recog. 118.

20. *The Trial of John Lowther for an Assault on John Bushnell* (London, 1761).

21. James Dalton, *A Genuine Narrative of All the Street Robberies* (London, 1728),
pp. 31–43; *Proceedings at the Old Bailey* (SP hereafter), no. 6 (1732): 166–170;
the *London Chronicle* (*LC* hereafter), 4–6 January 1757, 17–19 July 1764,
11–13 September 1764; *London Evening Post*, 17–19 July 1764, for John Gill.

22. Dalton, *A Genuine Narrative*, p. 32.

23. CLRO: S.R. (October 1729), Recog. 78.

24. *LC*, 29 April–May 1, 6–8 May 1790.

25. *LC*, 5–7 July 1787.

26. *LC*, 22–25 December 1787.

27. *LC*, 4–6 November, 11–13 November, 7–9 December, 9–11 December 1790,
13–15 January 1791.

28. *LC*, 4–6 August 1791.

29. *SP*, 30–31 August, 1 September 1721.

30. *LC*, 1–4 December 1759.

31. *LC*, 6–8 December 1759.

32. John Dunton, *Athenianism* (London, 1710), 2 vols., II, pp. 93–9; Trumbach,
"Sodomy Transformed," in Kimmel (ed.), pp. 108–13; Robert Halsband, *Lord
Hervey: Eighteenth-Century Courtier* (Oxford: Clarendon Press, 1973), index
s.v. Stephen Fox and Francesco Algarotti.

33. Antony Simpson, "Masculinity and Control in Eighteenth-Century
London," unpublished PhD thesis, New York University, 1984, p. 429, n. 8,
and pp. 828–9; Trumbach, "Sodomitical Assaults," in Gerard and Hekma
(eds.), p. 427, n. 13.

34. *SP*, no. 6, part 1 (1772): 315–23; Norton, *Mother Clap's*, pp. 170–1. The discussion in the newspapers of Jones's pardon may be followed in one of
them, the *London Evening Post* (1772), 1–4 August: 4; 4–6 August: 1, 4; 6–8
August: 1; 8–11 August: 1, 4; 11–13 August: 4; 13–15 August: 1; 15–18
August: 4; 18–20 August: 4; 25–27 August: 3; 1–3 September: 4.

35. Beckford's 11 principal biographers over the past century and a half have
varied widely in their interpretation of his sexual life. For the most part I
follow Brian Fothergill, *Beckford of Fonthill* (London: Faber and Faber, 1979).
The French quotation comes from Guy Chapman, *Beckford* (London:
Jonathan Cape, 1937), p. 232. For Beckford in Portugal, see Boyd Alexander
(ed.), *The Journal of William Beckford in Portugal and Spain, 1787–1788*
(London: Rupert Hart-Davis, 1954); and for homosexual behavior in

Portugal, see David Higgs, "Lisbon," in *Queer Sites*; Jeremy Bentham, "Offenses Against One's Self: Pederasty," ed. Louis Crompton, *Journal of Homosexuality*, 3 (1978): 383–405; 4 (1978): 91–107: on which see also, Crompton, *Byron and Greek Love: Homophobia in Nineteenth-Century England* (Berkeley, CA: University of California Press, 1985).

36. *Select Trials at … the Old Bailey* (London, 1742), 4 vols., ed. R. Trumbach, Garland Reprint (New York, 1985), I, 105–8.

37. Laud Humphreys, *Tearoom Trade* (Chicago: Aldine, 1970).

38. Arthur N. Gilbert, "Buggery and the British Navy, 1700–1861," *Journal of Social History* 10 (1976–77): 72–98.

39. Arthur N. Gilbert, "The *Africaine* Courts-Martial: a Study of Buggery and the Royal Navy," *Journal of Homosexuality*, 1 (1974): 111–22. Jan Oosterhoff, "Sodomy At Sea and at the Cape of Good Hope During the Eighteenth Century," in Gerard and Hekma (eds.), *Pursuit of Sodomy*, pp. 229–35, at 234.

40. Anne M. Johnson, *Sexual Attitudes and Lifestyles*, pp. 204–6; for collections of twentieth-century anecdotal evidence, see Alisdare Hickson, *The Poisoned Bowl: Sex, Repression, and the Public School System* (London: Constable, 1995), and Royston Lambert with Spencer Milham, *The Hothouse Society: an Exploration of Boarding-School Life through the Boys' and Girls' Own Writing* (London: Weidenfeld and Nicolson, 1968); for the eighteenth-century public schools, see Randolph Trumbach, *The Rise of the Egalitarian Family: Aristocratic Kinship and Domestic Relations in Eighteenth-Century England* (New York: Academic Press, 1978) pp. 252–85.

41. Parliamentary Papers, *Third Report from the Committee on the State of the Police of the Metropolis* (London, 1818), pp. 12–13, 37, 50, 76–7, 85–8, 164–8.

6

How Queer Was the Renaissance?

Mario DiGangi

In a recent article entitled "Tobacco and Boys: How Queer Was Marlowe?" Stephen Orgel refutes the longstanding myth of Christopher Marlowe as "a universally dangerous, seductively persuasive radical."[1] The scandalous statements attributed to Marlowe by his contemporaries Thomas Kyd and Richard Baines – that "all they that love not Tobacco & Boies were fooles" and that Christ "used" John the Evangelist "as the sinners of Sodoma" – have been generally taken as evidence of the queer eroticism at the core of his transgressive persona.[2] According to Orgel, however, this dominant account of Marlowe's sexuality is based on misreadings of the Baines document and of the playwright's own work, which upon more careful scrutiny indicates that Marlowe's "lust" ran not for boys but rather for "upward mobility," a "place in the service of some powerful courtier".[3] Ultimately, Marlowe does not seem very queer at all, and this may well be because "homosexuality is our problem, not Marlowe's."[4]

Borrowing the title of my chapter here from Orgel's essay, I mean to signal my similar intention to question the widespread account of male same-sex desire in early modern England as fundamentally transgressive or queer. Like Orgel, I also hope to explain why we do not find attributions of same-sex transgression where we might most expect to find them: in overtly defamatory statements. Orgel points out that in the depositions or "libels" of Baines and Kyd, "homosexuality in the charges against Marlowe is primarily an aspect of his blasphemy and atheism": Marlowe is reported to have said not that he himself was a sodomite but that Christ and St. John were. And despite the notorious "tobacco and boys" remark, there is no implication in the libels that "Marlowe systematically debauched the youth of London" or committed sodomy.[5] We find a comparable absence of overt slander for male same-sex activity in contemporary texts such as court records and satiric stage plays. By analyzing the discursive construction (and omission) of same-sex activity in legal and theatrical representations of social disorder, I aim to raise questions about the kind of evidence we possess regarding the presence of male same-sex relations in early modern England, and about the methodologies used to interpret that evidence. Through consideration of their social function and provenance, I will also situate representations of same-sex transgression within certain local and national contexts. Such a placement helps us to understand the circumstances under which male homoerotic relations in this culture were licensed or repressed, and the particular ways in which gender ideologies impacted on the social perception and evaluation of those relations.

Transcriptions of slander depositions from sixteenth- and seventeenth-century English courts give the immediate impression of a society with few inhibitions about the public discussion of illicit sexuality. In church court records, one finds sexually graphic statements such as appear in the following allegations made by women against other women:

> "she is a droncken whore...if I may not call her so then I will call her droncken queane";
> "you laie with a sailor 2 monthes before you wer married";
> "Thou art a privat queane and a base queane and ... thou keepest privat knaves in thy hous or els thy bed would not goe jigge and jogge so often as it doth";
> "It is no honest womans parte to put her hande into a mans codpiece and pull out his members and kisse it and say she liked it better then her husbandes";
> "my husband doth not looke lyke thy husband for my husbandes pricke was never burnt with the pocks nor halfe of it cut of in Newgate Market as thy husbandes was" ;
> "away you whore you lay with a fleminge for 2 shillings and with an English man for halfe a crowne I would have used an English man better than a fleminge you whore."[6]

Like the vast majority of defamatory statements made against women in the period, these slanders essentially boil down to the charge of "whoredom" – not prostitution, but sexual promiscuity. Yet their inventiveness, frankness, and attention to detail reveal the various rhetorical strategies available for expressing perceptions of sexual impropriety. In slander litigation cases, the same words – usually "whore," "quean," or "jade" – come up again and again, arranged and qualified in myriad patterns, embedded within compelling narratives meant to arrest the attention of listeners and to persuade them of the plausibility of the alleged misconduct.[7]

In her important study *Domestic Dangers*, Laura Gowing, from whom I have taken the above examples, identifies a significant pattern behind these fragmented, localized, forms of speech. "Insults of women," she writes, "were overwhelmingly personal and sexual," whereas insults of men "were less likely to attack their own sexuality ... . On the whole, sexual insults of men revolved around their control of women's sexuality: cuckoldry represented a husband's failure to control his wife, bawdry an investment in another woman's promiscuity." Summarizing her findings, Gowing observes that:

> the language of slander divided sexual honour starkly by gender. There was no way of calling a man a whore, or condemning his sexual promiscuity; nor of calling a woman a cuckold, or calling her to account for her spouse's misconduct. Women remained the focus of sexual guilt and responsibility.[8]

If early modern English provided no words for calling a man a whore or a woman a cuckold, it is because such positions were not intelligible within dominant ideology – they did not make sense in a culture that, theoretically, equated manhood with the control over sexuality (one's own and others'), and womanhood with sexuality to be controlled. This is why those few early modern words that can designate a "male whore" – for instance, "Ganymede" and "ingle" – refer not to adult men but to adolescents or boys. Early modern sexual ideology defined "whore" as *de facto* a "feminine," or subservient and objectified, position. Thus, in Shakespeare's *Troilus and Cressida*, Thersites' attempt to "call a man a whore" renders his meaning unintelligible. A vicious satirist, Thersites repeats to Patroclus the common rumor about his shameful sexual behavior: "Prithee be silent, boy ... Thou art thought to be Achilles' male varlet."[9] When Patroclus demands clarification of the insult – "'Male varlet,' you rogue? What's that?" – Thersites responds, "Why, his masculine whore."[10] "Masculine" here refers not to Patroclus' manliness: to the contrary, to be at once male and a whore is antithetical to masculinity or manhood. To be a male whore, whatever one's biological age, is to be a "boy" socially. Lest "boy" strike us as a rather mild insult, we might recall the tragic conclusion of Shakespeare's *Coriolanus*, in which Aufidius enrages his former military rival and intimate friend by deriding him as a "boy." Thersites' insulting designation of Patroclus as Achilles' male whore further debases Patroclus through an implied analogy with Helen of Troy, whose unfaithfulness to her husband occasions the Trojan War, a glorified conflict between "a whore and a cuckold."[11] The insult, in sum, works not primarily by ridiculing same-sex desire, but by reducing the warrior Patroclus to something less than a man: a boy, wife, or servant to Achilles – his "varlet," his "whore."

In *Romeo and Juliet*, a comparable instance of sexual defamation provokes the display of masculine violence that jolts the play into tragic mode. Searching for Romeo, Tybalt scornfully addresses his usual companion: "Mercutio, thou consort'st with Romeo."[12] Just as Patroclus questions the meaning of Thersites' "male varlet," so Mercutio angrily dwells upon the offensive term "consort": "'Consort'? What, dost thou make us minstrels? And thou make minstrels of us, look to hear nothing but discords.... Zounds – 'Consort'!"[13] Nicholas Radel has argued that by mobilizing the sexual connotation of "consort," Tybalt "turns the normally erotic discourse of friendship into a discourse of sodomy," hence slandering Mercutio. Reacting to this slander, Mercutio "deflects the word toward a third definition, one with a musical valence."[14] I would further remark that Tybalt's use of "consort" subordinates Mercutio to Romeo – it positions Mercutio as one who merely accompanies or follows Romeo, like a servant or a boy. As with Patroclus, then, the sexual slander works via the social slander, through the imputation of low status and insufficient masculinity. This reading is corroborated by a subsequent episode in which a Capulet manservant debases a consort of musicians as "minstrels."[15] Mercutio's anger at being taken for a "minstrel," a common entertainer, indicates that he has understood Tybalt's remark as a slight against his social status.

These scenes from *Troilus and Cressida* and *Romeo and Juliet* present rare instances of men slandering other men for being – well, what exactly? Effeminately passive? Excessively lustful? Erotically servile? Or are these men imagined as some monstrous aggregation of gender, sexual status, and economic deviance? It is precisely the point that neither Patroclus nor Mercutio is overtly defamed as a "sodomite," and that it is only with Thersites, Shakespeare's most foul-mouthed and scurrilous character, that we approach anything like defamation for same-sex activity. If Thersites' epithet "masculine whore" can stand as an example of Shakespeare's linguistic inventiveness, his creation of new significations from the deft juxtaposition of familiar signifiers, then his avoidance of the word "sodomite" can stand as an instance of his social conservatism, his accordance, at least in this case, with the norms of his society. For, as Laura Gowing explains, despite the fact that the slander depositions of nearly 6,000 English men and women survive for the period between 1572 and 1640, and despite the sharp increase in defamation suits heard in London between 1600 and 1610, none of the depositions "feature any allegations of homosexual behavior."[16]

This fascinating piece of social history deserves extended consideration. Gowing herself provides two "equally important" explanations for the absence of defamation cases involving same-sex conduct. First, because the 1534 buggery statute made male-male sodomy a secular crime, it was not a "technically actionable allegation" at the church courts.[17] Consequently, surviving sixteenth- and seventeenth-century legal records involving sodomy derive not from the church courts, but from the secular Assizes, which handled serious felonies, and the Quarter Sessions, which handled lesser felonies and misdemeanors.[18] Gowing's second explanation for the absence of same-sex slander litigation adopts Alan Bray's theory regarding the paucity of sodomy indictments in Renaissance England: "Renaissance thought pictured sodomy through distant metaphors, not the realm of daily life; and it was daily life with which these defamers were most concerned. Their insults focused around the street, the market, and the household."[19] In *Homosexuality in Renaissance England*, Bray observes that despite the harsh condemnation of sodomy in the written law the courts rarely prosecuted it in actual practice.[20] Bruce Smith's detailed analysis of the sodomy laws in *Homosexual Desire in Shakespeare's England* supports Bray's findings: describing sodomy indictments as statistically insignificant, Smith points to a single conviction for sodomy during the sixteenth century, in a case involving the rape of a five-year-old boy.[21] Both Bray and Smith provide plausible explanations for the infrequency of sodomy trials in early modern England. Bray posits a general inability to recognize in everyday homosexual behavior the exaggerated theological account of sodomy as a monstrous sin of cosmic proportions; Smith, approaching the issue from the opposite direction, concludes that the increasing precision of the legal definition of sodomy – as, essentially, anal penetration – left all other kinds of male-male sexual activity (and all kinds of female-female sexual activity) outside the scope of juridical detection.

As Gowing, Bray, and Smith recognize, the legal and theological discourses of sodomy seem far removed from the realm of "daily life" that

Gowing identifies as the focus of concern in sexual defamation cases. In other words, what people encountered in everyday life seemed far from the "sodomy" commonly associated with monstrous crimes against nature, the church, or the state. Because of sodomy's associations with the weightiest of crimes, the discourses of sodomy operated primarily at the highest levels of society. For instance, in the diary he kept between 1622 and 1624 Sir Simonds D'Ewes expressed his fear that "some horrible punishment" would fall on London, where the "sinne of sodomye" was "frequente" and practiced by "the prince as well as the people." Recording with impunity his "secrett" knowledge of King James's sodomy, D'Ewes observed that it is up to God to chastize sinful princes "because noe man else indeed dare reprove or tell them of ther faults."[22] When sodomy entered into public visibility, it did so as a scandalous eruption – as those who accused others of sodomy for political advantage ensured that it did. The massive social dislocation implied by the charge of sodomy became a plausible threat when political order and national security were at stake: for instance, in the cases of elite men such as King James and his favorites, Francis and Anthony Bacon, and the Earl of Castlehaven.[23] It therefore seems reasonable to conclude, as Gowing does, that in early modern England sodomy was indeed not visible in "the street, the market, or the household."

Yet Gowing's claim actually reaches well beyond that conclusion, for it implies that English subjects did not recognize (and hence did not target through slander) even lesser, everyday, forms of same-sex disorder. This assumption deserves more scrutiny. In *The Homoerotics of Early Modern Drama*, I argued that same-sex relations in this period were evaluated in terms of their perceived accordance with and promotion of social order or disorder. Any same-sex relationship could signify as orderly or disorderly, depending on a variety of circumstances.[24] Moreover, the perception of a same-sex relationship as disorderly was not equivalent to a perception of sodomy. Same-sex relationships existed on a spectrum ranging from the normative and valorized – male friendship, hierarchical patronage and service relations – to the transgressive and feared – relations that challenged or inverted social hierarchy – to the extreme of "sodomy." If, then, we use this more flexible taxonomy to determine what kinds of same-sex relations might have been encountered in "the street, the market, and the household," we come up with considerably more than nothing. In theory, it is conceivable that "lesser" (or less easily classifiable) forms of male-male sexual incontinence than "sodomy" could have been targeted by the kind of slander that brought other litigants to ecclesiastical courts.[25]

What is curious is that there does not appear to have been much concern to discipline disorderly homoerotic relations as such.

This is even more surprising when we consider how much the London theater contributed to the visibility and identification of homoerotic relations. Beginning in the 1590s, plays regularly introduced and circulated sexual terminology of various kinds. Specialized words such as "Ganymede," "ingle," "catamite," "cinedo," and "pathic" described sexually subordinated young men, especially in urban settings; less narrowly circumscribed words such as "minion" and "favorite" identified objects of same-sex dotage, especially in courtly settings; and familiar adjectives such as "monstrous," "preposterous," "unnatural," and "strange" generally denoted unauthorized erotic desires and practices.[26] If this vocabulary never made the transition from the stage to the street, it may well be because the majority of homoerotic relations – whether the validated intimacy between male friends or the licensed desire of an adult man for an attractive youth – operated unremarkably (albeit complexly) within socially normative parameters. Thus in the case of orderly same-sex relations, a distinct vocabulary of identification was conspicuously lacking. With its direct association to theological and legal discourses, the highly loaded condemnatory term "sodomite" would not, of course, apply to the orderly adult male who enjoyed a male friend or an attractive page. In fact, there was no term available by which to identify such a man: none was needed because there was no social need to distinguish one virtuous gentleman from another virtuous gentleman who happened to have a close male friend or servant.

Furthermore, when male-male relations were represented as disorderly, as in satiric plays and poems, unruly homoerotic desire was depicted as just one element in the overall social, economic, and moral misconduct of stereotypically debauched gentlemen, courtiers, or wealthy citizens. In such cases, no specialized term was needed by which to identify the adult male who exploited the friend, minion, or Ganymede since his sexual license was just one component in a much larger cluster of transgressions through which he was identifiable as a satiric type.[27] Ultimately, then, one could argue that London playgoers understood theatrical representations of disorderly same-sex relations simply as literary fictions – exaggerated, fanciful situations that necessarily failed to correspond with the prosaic transactions between men outside the theater. Nonetheless, it is hard to believe that theatrical depictions of disorderly same-sex relations could have meaningfully signified anything to playgoers who experienced no recognition, however obliquely registered or mediated through generic conventions, with the transgressions presented on the stage.[28] And it is precisely under the cover of the patently fantastic or the merely conventional – in other words, through aesthetic forms that in their distance from everyday experience disarm skepticism and scrutiny – that ideology can weave its subtle webs.

Assuming, then, that in early modern England "everyday" same-sex relations were occasionally recognized as having crossed into impropriety, why was there apparently no resort to sexual slander as a mechanism of social control? The answer, I believe, lies in what might be called the "supplemental" or "proximate" place of the erotic in the perception of social disorder. As with sodomy, disorderly homoerotic relations became intelligible as such only in the presence of more fundamental kinds of social and economic disorder. This explanation for the juridical invisibility of same-sex disorder gains support from Martin Ingram's observation that the church courts "made virtually no effort to punish autoerotic activities and sexual irregularities which took place between husband and wife" or in "extramarital sexual activities which fell short of full intercourse."[29] The church courts were most vigilant in prosecuting cases involving bastardy because it posed the most serious social and economic threats to the local community.[30] Regarding the church courts' limited surveillance over many forms of male-female sexual activity, Ingram concludes that "local communities did not normally intrude themselves into people's lives to seek out cases of immorality: they usually waited until the circumstances became blatant or a matter of common knowledge and insistent gossip."[31] It makes sense that a similar reticence would characterize juridical and community interference into male same-sex activities as well.

If same-sex relations did, for whatever reason, break into socially disruptive behavior, the disruption could have been identified and corrected by the usual methods. For instance, the smaller secular courts attempted to control disorderly alehouses, which were blamed for keeping servants and apprentices from work and for functioning as brothels. Yet when the brewer William Firthe was reported to a court of hundred in 1582 because "he keeps apprentices, boys, and servants in his house at night," the perception of his inappropriately intimate congregation with young men arises as a contributing factor to the charge of misconduct.[32] Likewise, in 1597–98 a Norfolk innkeeper was reported for allowing four men "to keep bad governance at night time in his said house to the great disturbance of his neighbors."[33] Another target of local discipline, nightwalking, was sometimes linked to sexual misconduct, as in the 1576 presentment of John Baker and William Newton for "leading a lascivious [liciviosa] life and being "common night watchers."[34] Describing an unusually explicit case of 1609 in which a London merchant was called before the Quarter Sessions for abusing his servant and "correcting him unreasonably with whipcords, being quite naked," Alan Bray remarks that "the courts were apparently unconcerned with sexual relations between masters and servants unless a scandal was involved or an illegitimate child was produced."[35] To put this reductively in the terms of my own argument, an unruly servant, master, or neighbor was, as far as the operations of social discipline were concerned, simply an unruly servant, master, or neighbor.

London plays, however fantastic and removed from everyday life, provide insight into the logic of this principle. In Ben Jonson's *Volpone*, for instance, the ambitious servant Mosca is intelligible not as a sexual transgressor who happens to be a servant, but as a transgressive servant who happens to be erotically involved with his master. The homoerotic affection between Mosca and Volpone signifies as disorderly because it becomes a vehicle through which Mosca can transcend his low place in the social hierarchy. Struggling for dominance, Mosca and Volpone ultimately betray each other, are tried, and incarcerated – not for sodomy, but for various moral, economic, and social crimes.[36] At his sentencing, Mosca is branded in overtly status-marked terms as a "parasite," the "plotter" of "lewd impostures," and a "fellow of no birth or blood" who has "abused the court" with his "impudence" in dressing as a gentleman.[37] Similarly in Middleton's *Michaelmas Term*, the London draper Quomodo instructs his servant Shortyard to disguise himself as a gentleman for the purposes of fleecing Easy, a landed gentleman from Essex: "Drink drunk with him, creep into bed to him, / Kiss him and undo him, my sweet spirit."[38]

Presenting himself as Master Blastfield, Shortyard establishes a publicly recognized relationship as the "sweet bedfellow" of Easy and subsequently manipulates their intimacy to acquire his lands. Eventually betrayed by his own schemes, Shortyard is apprehended and punished as a "rogue," "coz'ner," "villain," and "slave": during his sentencing, his explicitly homoerotic methods of cozenage go unmentioned, even by Easy himself .[39] A similar de-emphasis on sexuality in the punishment of status transgression applies as well to heteroerotic relationships, as in Shakespeare's *Twelfth Night*. Malvolio attempts to use his sexual access to Olivia as a means of social advancement; however, his punishment emphasizes his fundamental transgression as one of status boundaries. Malvolio's humiliating incarceration as a madman symbolizes the loss of social identity and domestic authority that comes from the violation of his proper place in the household.

A final defamation case from the period will help to illustrate the "proximate" relation of same-sex behavior to social disorder and discipline that I have been positing. In 1613, William Sandes reported to the London court that his minister, Mr Searle, slandered his parishioners in the following manner during a sermon:

> We have some sodamites in the parishe which do abound in pride, fullnes of bread idlenes not strentheninge the hand of the needye And they thinke to rule the minister and the whole parishe, or they go aboute to rule the minister and the whole parishe. But I hope that my heart shall be as the heart of righteous Lott and have no conversacon with them for their sinnes are greater than the sinnes of Sodome and Gomorrhe they contemne or refuse the sacraments and service of God but do they thincke to escape the vengeance of God no I doubt not but fire and brimstone will come from heaven and consume them wee have them here today but wee shall not have them here againe foure or fyve sondaies followeing.[40]

Does the deposition suggest that the minister used "sodomy" in a coded sense, underhandedly to accuse his enemies of sexual license? Or does the apparently non-sexual use of "sodomy" instead reveal the contradictory, multivalent quality of early modern sodomy discourse, split as it was between broadly theological and narrowly juridical levels of meaning? Had he indeed spoken these words, Searle would certainly not have been the first minister to blast sodomites from the pulpit: the "Sermon against Whoredom and Uncleanness," one of several state-sponsored homilies designed to be read during weekly church services, warns that God destroyed Sodom and Gomorrah for "the filthy sin of uncleanness":

> Whose heart trembles not at the hearing of this history? Who is so drowned in whoredom and uncleanness that will not now forever after leave this abominable living, seeing that GOD so grievously punisheth uncleanness, to rain fire and brimstone from heaven...? Mark this history (good people) and fear the vengeance of GOD.[41]

If the "Sermon against Whoredom and Uncleanness" was delivered and received as orthodox doctrine, then why did Searle's sermon against sodomy strike William Sandes as defamatory? For one, Searle is reported to have referred to presumably recognizable members of the congregation: the "sodomites" who "thinke to rule the minister and the whole parishe." Unlike the universal and national "Sermon against Whoredom," Searle's sermon is particular and local. I would argue, however, that Sandes represents as Searle's greatest offense the accusation against local "sodomites" not of "the filthy sin of uncleanness," but rather of the considerably more palpable and consequential dereliction of their social duties as respectable Christians: notably, idleness, excessive consumption, lack of charity, and a proud conviction of their superiority to the minister and the parish.[42]

There is nothing intrinsic to early modern European conceptions of homoeroticism *per se* that would explain why the English paid so little attention to the correction of same-sex disorder. As Michael Rocke relates in his book *Forbidden Friendships*, in 1432 Florence established the Office of the Night, a "special magistracy" for discovering and prosecuting sodomy.[43] The Office of the Night encouraged community participation in its policing efforts by offering rewards to local informants and by guaranteeing their anonymity. In addition, "whole neighborhoods acted at times in collective, informal ways to rid themselves of a sodomite or to convince a neighbor to reform."[44] For instance, in 1468 an informer testified against a mercer whom neighbors caught twice in his shop at night with a boy; the neighbors jeered at him and enjoined him to put an end to his disgraceful behavior. In England, communal surveillance and shaming customs such as the skimmington and cucking stool were customary methods of local discipline; like the ecclesiastical courts, however, they punished infractions of gender order, sexual chastity, and household discipline, not same-sex activity. Clearly, the vast differences obtaining between fifteenth-century Florence and late-sixteenth-century England – among the most relevant of which might be the particularly vigorous excoriation of the "unnatural" vice of sodomy by the Roman Catholic Church – mean that no simple conclusion can be drawn from this discrepancy in attitudes towards same-sex activity.[45] Nonetheless, the discrepancy does support a conclusion Randolph Trumbach came to in an early essay on "sodomitical subcultures" in early modern Europe, namely, that male same-sex activity in early seventeenth-century England was acknowledged yet not deemed threatening or objectionable enough to warrant public attack.[46]

If in early modern England male homoeroticism was not subjected to constant scrutiny, masculinity was, and it is important to consider those occasions on which failures of masculinity were associated with same-sex transgression. In *Shakespeare and Masculinity*, Bruce Smith describes the ideals of male behavior deemed appropriate for men at different social levels: masculinity did not manifest itself in the same forms for a merchant as for a knight.[47] Yet the ideology of masculinity established certain fundamental principles across the social field. Overall, early modern manhood conferred the responsibility to police the sharply drawn ideological boundary between men and women. A married man had the duty of keeping in check his own sexuality as well his wife's: the common slander of cuckoldry gets its power from the normative correlation between sexual mastery and manhood.[48] Moreover, a man was supposed to secure the social order by acting "like a man" – rational, controlled, strong, authoritative – hence avoiding the "womanish" traits of irrationality, immoderation, weakness, and submissiveness. For common men, the achievement of masculinity largely consisted in effective "oeconomy" or proper governance of the household, the basic unit of English society.[49] For gentlemen and noblemen, the social expectations of conspicuous consumption and civilized manners, especially in London and at the court, introduced further considerations regarding the gendering of personal comportment.

It is on urban and courtly settings that early modern writers focus when they examine male effeminacy and its relation to homoerotic desire. Alan Bray has argued that early modern men faced an inherent danger in the ambiguity of sexual signification, because the signs of male friendship – kissing, embracing, sharing a bed, intimate conversation – were also the signs of sodomy.[50] But men were also evaluated according to the different signifying system of gender. Stephen Orgel, Laura Levine, and Mark Breitenberg have all demonstrated the constant preoccupation with assessing and policing the boundaries of male identity in early modern England.[51] Particularly confusing are the potential associations and dissociations that could obtain between effeminacy and homoeroticism in this culture. Because "effeminate" could describe any man who acted "womanish," and because any object of desire, whether male or female, could incite womanish passion in a man, male effeminacy existed in a complicated, unpredictable relationship to same-sex desire.

We can see this ideological matrix at work in Ben Jonson's representation of the courtier Amorphous in his satirical comedy *Cynthia's Revels*.[52] Amorphous ("the deformed") embodies social transgression through the outward signs of dress, mannerisms, and speech, in all of which he is excessive and affected – in short, womanish. Bragging about his refined "behaviours," "garments," "countenance," and "gestures," Amorphous "speaks all cream, skimmed, and more affected than a dozen of waiting women."[53] Having no masculine integrity, Amorphous is slandered for being "so made out of the mixture and shreds of forms that himself is truly deformed."[54] He ultimately reflects the effeminacy of the other vain courtiers attacked in the play: the "proud and spangled sir, / That looks three handfuls higher than his foretop," the "mincing marmoset / Made all of clothes and face," the "subtle Proteus" who "can change and vary with all forms he sees," and the "neophyte glazing of his face, / Pruning his clothes, perfuming of his hair."[55]

At stake in this parade of "male deformities" is the definition of proper comportment for the English gentleman. In an essay on "The Semiotics of Masculinity in Renaissance England," David Kuchta explains that courtesy book writers did not consider the mere display of the male body to be effeminate. Instead, the evaluation of a courtier as either "masculine" or "effeminate" depended on the perceived correspondence between his clothing and social status:

> Conspicuous consumption was considered a rightful and manly honor bestowed upon [the courtier] by his noble status and position at court. Rich clothes proclaimed high status. Conspicuous consumption made the social order conspicuous. Effeminacy, on the other hand, was the misuse of these arbitrary status symbols, and thus a threat to the social order by the base materiality of the nouveau riche.[56]

Whereas the masculine courtier displayed an unaffected sprezzatura, a nonchalance or ease about his appearance and his status, the effeminate courtier vainly showcased his clothing or dressed above his degree.

In *Cynthia's Revels*, Amorphous epitomizes the effeminate courtier described by Kuchta, for through his strategic deployment of superficial forms he gains access to a court at which he has no rightful place. His effeminacy also distorts the ideal of masculine friendship or "acquaintance" between gentlemen, which Jeffrey Masten has analyzed so productively.[57] Early in the play, Amorphous attaches himself to Asotus, a citizen's son who has groomed himself as a "pretty formal young gallant."[58] Amorphous initially perverts the conventions of friendship by flattering a man of lower social status: "I think I shall affect you, sir... . your sweet disposition to travel, I assure you, hath made you another myself in mine eye, and struck me enamored of your beauties."[59] Asotus, who finds Amorphous "ravishing", likewise gushes, "I would I were the fairest lady of France for your sake, sir."[60]

These affected homoerotic exchanges, culminating in Asotus' wish that he could be a French lady for Amorphous' sake, should not be taken as evidence that Jonson regards male same-sex relations as necessarily gender-transitive or effeminate. As Jonathan Goldberg has insisted, the structures of Renaissance homoeroticism did not simply mime heteroerotic configurations; and cultural representations of male homoerotic desire did not necessarily require the mediation of a cross-dressed figure.[61] Asotus' fantasy of being "the fairest lady of France" instead reveals his desire to occupy an elevated social status through which he might validate Amorphous' courtly masculinity, much as the Petrarchan mistress provided her suitor with an opportunity to display his social and rhetorical accomplishments. Asotus and Amorphous are legible as effeminate precisely because their conspicuous consumption and display of courtly signs has not been authorized by the "fairest lady" of the court, the monarch Cynthia. In the end, Jonson does not present homoerotic desire as a cause of effeminacy or a symptom of effeminacy; rather, he shows effeminacy to be a perversion of the orderly, normatively masculine, homoerotics of friendship.

I stress this point because Kuchta's theorization of Renaissance effeminacy remains blind to the possibility that "masculine" men might engage in same-sex relations. One of his sources, Giovanni della Casa's influential courtesy book *Galateo*, indeed seems to associate effeminacy with homoeroticism in advising against "extremely fancy" garments that look like "Ganymede's hose." Kuchta concludes from this advice that courtesy manuals defined masculinity "in opposition to a series of 'wanton and sensual imperfections,'" including "prostitution, homosexuality, and effeminacy."[62] Aligning the anachronistic term "homosexuality" with "effeminacy," Kuchta thus implies that same-sex desire was uniformly linked to gender inversion in the Renaissance court. On the contrary, the court was structured by relations of friendship and patronage in which the signs of valorized male intimacy might be indistinguishable from the signs of homoerotic desire.[63] When della Casa refers to gaudy clothing as "Ganymede's hose," he is certainly stigmatizing effeminacy. Ganymede's effeminacy, however, derives not from his engagement in same-sex acts but from his youth, beauty, and submissiveness to an adult male.

Observers of the English court who resented the excessive power King James bestowed upon his favorites likewise defamed his objects of desire as effeminate Ganymedes unworthy of political responsibility. The intimacy that Somerset and Buckingham enjoyed with the King was sometimes explicitly attributed to their feminine charms as "smooth-faced," "delicate," "curious," and "lovely" young men.[64] Yet when in the *Basilicon Doron* James exercised his kingly right to define appropriate standards of masculinity for the court, he dispensed the utterly conventional, conservative advice to "specially eschew to be effeminate in your cloathes, in perfuming, preening, or such like."[65] A similar cognitive dissonance has often been remarked regarding the explicit condemnation of sodomy in the *Basilicon Doron*. What explains the apparent discrepancy between James's theory and practice is that in the Renaissance, effeminacy, like sodomy, was an offense ascribed to someone else, not a position that one adopted for oneself.[66] The defamation of Somerset and Buckingham as effeminate arose not from loathing of homoerotic desire, but from resentment that they could attain such powerful positions without the masculine credentials – maturity, wisdom, judgment – that would justify the honor bestowed on them.[67] Whether or not James's tastes ran towards feminine men is besides the point as far as his sovereignty was concerned: by not seeing "effeminacy" either in his favorites or in his own will to patronize whomever he pleased, the king, like his enemies, located it somewhere else.

In a discussion of the power of contemporary homophobia to besmirch a multitude of "queer" identities and behaviors, Michael Warner observes that "stigma is messy and often incoherent."[68] As my analysis has suggested, the stigma attached to disorderly same-sex relations in early modern England appears so messy and incoherent because there was no discrete discourse or site of "queerness" in that culture.[69] Queering the Renaissance, then, should not involve the attempt to locate queerness in discrete sexual identities, roles, or acts; rather, it requires us to discover how queerness could subtly, unpredictably, fluctuate into and out of visibility from the very practices and pressures of everyday life – as it was lived in the street, marketplace, household, or court.

Notes

1. Stephen Orgel, "Tobacco and Boys: How Queer Was Marlowe?" *GLQ: a Journal of Lesbian and Gay Studies* 6 (2000): 564.
2. Richard Baines quoted in Jonathan Goldberg, "Sodomy and Society: the Case of Christopher Marlowe," in David Scott Kastan and Peter Stallybrass, (eds.) *Staging the Renaissance: Reinterpretations of Elizabethan and Jacobean Drama* (New York: Routledge, 1991), pp. 75, 78.
3. Orgel "Tobacco and Boys": 568, 573.
4. Ibid.: 566.
5. Ibid.: 567.

6. Quoted in Laura Gowing, *Domestic Dangers: Women, Words, and Sex in Early Modern London.* (Oxford: Clarendon Press, 1996), pp. 66, 70, 71, 79, 81, 90.
7. Lisa Jardine cautions against taking depositions as reliable accounts of actual events: "as texts they are explicitly *purposive* – they shape the story told to a desired outcome ... . the depositions show how some ostensibly verbal incidents between individuals, as they spill over into the community space (the village green, the pump, outside the house) become recognized as events, which generate particular expectations on the part of the audience". *Reading Shakespeare Historically* (London: Routledge, 1996), p. 28.
8. Gowing, *Domestic Dangers*, p. 63.
9. William Shakespeare, *Troilus and Cressida*, in *The Norton Shakespeare*, ed. Stephen Greenblatt (New York: Norton, 1997), 5.1, 13–14.
10. *The Norton Shakespeare*, 15–16.
11. Ibid., 2.3.65.
12. Ibid., 3.1.40.
13. Ibid., 3.1.41–4.
14. Nicholas F. Radel, "Queer Romeo and Juliet: Teaching Early Modern 'Sexuality' in Shakespeare's 'Heterosexual' Tragedy" in Maurice Hunt (ed.) *Approaches to Teaching Shakespeare's Romeo and Juliet* (New York: MLA, 2000.), p. 93.
15. *The Norton Shakespeare*, 4.4.138.
16. Gowing, *Dosmetic Dangers*, pp. 33, 65.
17. Ibid., p. 65.
18. Alan Bray, *Homosexuality in Renaissance England* (London: Gay Men's Press, 1982), pp. 38–50.
19. Gowing, *Domestic Dangers*, p. 65.
20. Assize and Quarter Session records from approximately 1560 to 1680 reveal only three cases involving same-sex behavior; records of the Home County Assizes, which are largely complete for the period between 1559 and 1625, show only four indictments for sodomy (Bray, *Homosexuality*, p. 71).
21. Bruce R. Smith, *Homosexual Desire in Shakespeare's England: a Cultural Poetics* (Chicago and London: University of Chicago Press, 1991), p. 48.
22. Quoted in Smith, *Homosexual Desire*, p. 176.
23. On Castlehaven see Cynthia B. Herrup, *A House in Gross Disorder: Sex, Law, and the 2nd Earl of Castlehaven* (New York: OUP, 1999).
24. Mario DiGangi, *The Homoerotics of Early Modern Drama* (Cambridge: CUP, 1997).
25. According to Martin Ingram, after 1500 the "common law rapidly encroached on the church courts' slander jurisdiction," making damage instead of the insult itself the actionable offense. After 1583, defamations could be tried in church courts only if characterized by three "incidents": 1) the slanders had to concern "spiritual matters"; 2) they had to concern *only* spiritual matters; 3) they could not involve compensation for damages. Under these guidelines, the slander of two men for sexual immorality or misconduct would theoretically be as actionable as the slander of a woman as a "whore" or of a man as a "cuckold." Martin Ingram, *Church Courts, Sex and Marriage, 1570–1640* (Cambridge: CUP, 1987), p. 296.
26. In his taxonomy of the "prehomosexual" discourses of homosexuality, David Halperin distinguishes the subordinate boy in a pederastic relationship – in early modern parlance, the "Ganymede" or "ingle" – from the

"passive" or gender-inverted man who actively desires to be penetrated by another man. Halperin identifies the latter figure, who is essentially characterized by gender deviance, as the *"cinaedus," "*catamite," "pathic," "minion," or "molly"; see "How to Do the History of Male Homosexuality", *GLQ: a Journal of Lesbian and Gay Studies* 6 (2000): 102, 107. Nonetheless, in early modern English usage, terms like "cinedo," "catamite," and "pathic" could also refer to the "Ganymede," the young man who engages in sodomy not for personal pleasure but for money, gifts, or patronage. For instance, in 1598 John Florio defined "Cinedo" as "a buggring boy, a wanton boy, an ingle"; Simonds D'Ewes wrote that Francis Bacon kept a servant for "his catamite and bedfellow"; and in Jonson's *Sejanus*, Sejanus is accused of having "prostituted" his body as the "noted pathic of the time" (DiGangi, *Homoerotics*, pp. 70, 73, 121). This discursive overdetermination helps to corroborate Halperin's theory of the synchronous existence of different pre-homosexual models in pre-modern Europe.

27. Renaissance satirists often depicted sodomy as an "aristocratic vice" associated with the vices of pride, gluttony, and sloth (Smith, *Homosexual Desire*, p. 166). Halperin remarks that in the sodomitical/pederastic model "there was not necessarily anything sexually or psychologically abnormal in itself about the male sexual penetration of a subordinate male" (p. 95).

28. Mary Bly has recently advanced an important argument about the deliberate production of male homoerotic discourse on the London stage. According to Bly, the managing syndicate of the Whitefriars Theater realized the profit to be made from marketing satirical, bawdy plays to male playgoers with a taste for the homoerotic. In Whitefriars plays, gender-blurring and sexually ambiguous women, played by flirtatious boy actors, speak "queer puns" – words like "bit," "case," and "meat" that referred to male and female genitalia alike (*Queer Virgins and Virgin Queans on the Early Modern Stage* (Oxford: OUP, 2000), pp. 12–14).These "queer virgins," Bly maintains, produced in male playgoers feelings of erotic pleasure and control, even affording them the opportunity to fashion a kind of nonce homoerotic community. Bly's argument has significant implications for my own, in so far as she posits, in a specific local context (the Whitefriars theater in 1607–8), an on-going public recognition and consumption of representations of disorderly, but not necessarily sodomitical, homoerotic relations.

29. Ingram; *Church Courts*, pp. 239–40.

30. Ibid., p. 261.

31. Ibid., p. 245.

32. Quoted in Marjorie Keniston McIntosh, *Controlling Misbehavior in Early Modern England, 1370–1600* (Cambridge: CUP, 1998), p. 76. McIntosh analyzes reports of social misconduct from 267 public courts held in 255 villages, market centers, and hundreds. She classifies conduct that was "regarded as socially harmful or disruptive by jurors" but not expressly against the law into ten offenses, which she then groups into clusters: the Disharmony cluster – scolding/quarreling, eavesdropping, nightwalking; the Disorder cluster – sexual misconduct, unruly alehouses, being of "bad government" or "evil reputation"; the Poverty cluster – (hedgebreaking, vagabondage/living idly, and receiving subtenants (pp. 9–10). McIntosh

notes that despite the official jurisdiction of the church courts over sexual offenses, cases of sexual misconduct did appear in the local public courts when they were perceived to threaten "good order within their communities" (p. 70).

33. Ibid., p. 79 n.79.
34. Ibid., p. 67.
35. Bray, *Homosexuality* p. 50.
36. DiGangi, *Homoerotics*, p. 74–8.
37. Ben Jonson, *Volpone; or, The Fox.*, ed. R.B. Parker. (Manchester: Manchester University Press, 1983), 5.12.107–12.
38. Thomas Middleton, *Michaelmas Term*, ed. Richard Levin (Lincoln: University of Nebraska Press, 1966), 2.3.136.
39. *Michaelmas Term*, 5.1.20, 36, 37. Will Fisher has argued persuasively that in early modern discourse "illegal monetary practices were always already sexualized": counterfeiting and usury were figured as unnatural sexual practices, and vice versa ("Queer Money" *English Literacy History* (*ELH*), 66 (1999): 11). Although illicit monetary and sexual practices might have been discursively equated, the above examples from *Volpone* and *Michaelmas Term* suggest that categories of economic and social transgression were more readily available and deployable as signifiers of disorder than were categories of sexual transgression; while terms like "parasite," "slave," and "cozener" might take on homoerotic connotations in particular contexts, they primarily identified base socio-economic conditions or activities.
40. Gowing, *Domestic Dangers*, pp. 55–6.
41. "A Sermon against Whoredom and Uncleanness," in Lloyd Davis (ed.), *Sexuality and Gender in the English Renaissance: an Annotated Edition of Contemporary Documents*. (New York: Garland, 1998), p. 13.
42. Mark Jordan argues that "there is no text of the Christian Bible that determines the reading of Sodom as a story about same-sex copulation. On the contrary, there is explicit scriptural evidence that the sin of the Sodomites was some combination of arrogance and ingratitude"; (see *The Invention of Sodomy in Christian Theology* (Chicago: University of Chicago Press, 1997), p. 32). In the interpretations of medieval Christian exegetes, Sodom does become associated with sexual irregularities generally and with same-sex copulation specifically, but such sexual sins are also identified as the product of the Sodomites' "brazen arrogance bred of opulence" and the "madness of their fleshly appetites" (pp. 33, 35).
43. Michael Rocke, *Forbidden Friendships: Homosexuality and Male Culture in Renaissance Florence* (New York: OUP, 1996), p. 45.
44. Ibid., p. 83.
45. Ibid., pp. 19–20, 36–7.
46. Randolph Trumbach, "Sodomitical Subcultures, Sodomitical Roles, and the Gender Revolution of the Eighteenth Century: the Recent Historiography," in Robert Purks MacCubbin (ed.), *'Tis Nature's Fault: Unauthorized Sexuality during the Enlightenment* (Cambridge: CUP, 1987), p. 118.
47. Bruce R. Smith, *Shakespeare and Masculinity* (Oxford: OUP, 2000), p. 57.
48. Elizabeth A. Foyster, *Manhood in Early Modern England: Honour, Sex and Marriage* (London: Longman, 1999), pp. 67–87.

49. Lorna Hutson, *The Usurer's Daughter: Male Friendship and Fictions of Women in Sixteenth-Century England* (London: Routledge, 1994), pp. 32–41; and Foyster, *Manhood*, pp. 87–93.

50. Alan Bray, "Homosexuality and the Signs of Male Friendship in Elizabethan England," in Jonathan Goldberg (ed.), *Queering the Renaissance* (Durham: Duke University Press, 1994), pp. 40–61.

51. Stephen Orgel, *Impersonations: the Performance of Gender in Shakespeare's England* (Cambridge: CUP, 1996); Laura Levine, *Men in Women's Clothing: Anti-Theatricality and Effeminization, 1579–1642* (Cambridge: CUP, 1994); Mark Breitenberg, *Anxious Masculinity in Early Modern England* (Cambridge, CUP, 1996).

52. The brief discussion of *Cynthia's Revels* that follows borrows some material from my extensive treatment of the play in "'Male Deformities': Narcissus and the Reformation of Courtly Manners in *Cynthia's Revels*," in Goran Stanivukovic (ed.), *Ovid and the Renaissance Body*, (Toronto: University of Toronto Press, 2001), pp. 94–110.

53. Ben Jonson, *Cynthia's Revels: Or the Fountain of Self-Love*, in G.A. Wilkes, (ed.), *The Complete Plays of Ben Jonson*, Vol. 2 (Oxford: Clarendon Press, 1981), 1.3.24–25, 2.3.81–82.

54. *Cynthia's Revels*, 2.3.77–78.

55. Ibid., 3.4.12, 22–23, 42–43, 55–56.

56. David Kuchta, "The Semiotics of Masculinity in Renaissance England," in James Grantham Turner (ed.), *Sexuality and Gender in Early Modern Europe: Institutions, Texts, Image* (Cambridge: CUP, 1993), p. 241.

57. *Cynthia's Revels*, 1.4.66. Jeffrey Masten, *Textual Intercourse: Collaboration, Authorship, and Sexualities in Renaissance Drama* (Cambridge: CUP, 1997), pp. 28–37.

58. *Cynthia's Revels*, 1.4.30.

59. Ibid., 1.4.111, 119–21.

60. Ibid., 1.4. 57, 122.

61. Jonathan Goldberg, *Sodometries: Renaissance Texts, Modern Sexualities* (Stanford: Stanford University Press, 1992) pp. 112–16.

62. Kuchta, "The Semiotics of Masculinity," p. 239.

63. Masten, *Textual Intercourse*, pp. 28–37; DiGangi, *Homoerotics* pp. 134–41.

64. Quoted by Michael B. Young, *King James and the History of Homosexuality* (New York: New York University Press, 2000), pp. 74–5.

65. Quoted in Ibid., p. 73.

66. The discrepancy is further explained by the difference between the gender-deviant discourses of "effeminacy" and "inversion" and the discourse of pederasty or "active" sodomy, which need not be associated with gender deviance (Halperin, pp. 92–9). Whereas his critics derided James's favorites as effeminate Ganymedes or gender-inverted minions, James apparently viewed his relations with his favorites in terms of the "masculine" model of pederasty based on difference of status between partners.

67. Robert Shephard has argued that "while stories and gossip about James's homosexual proclivities did occasionally appear, they are far less numerous than the tales alleging sexual transgressions on [Queen] Elizabeth's part." Shephard finds that whereas ordinary people circulated luridly detailed rumors about Queen Elizabeth's supposed sexual misconduct, slanders

against James usually concerned his religious policies. "Sexual Rumours in English Politics: the Cases of Elizabeth I and James I" in J. Murray and K. Eisenbichler (eds.), *Desire and Discipline: Sex and Sexuality in the Premodern West.* (Toronto: University of Toronto Press, 1996), p. 111.

68. Michael Warner, *The Trouble with Normal: Sex, Politics, and the Ethics of Queer Life* (New York: Free Press, 1999), p. 37.

69. Jonathan Goldberg, *Queering the Renaissance* (Durham, NC: Duke University Press, 1994), pp. 6–7.

7

Can the Sodomite Speak? Sodomy, Satire, Desire, and the Castlehaven Case

Nicholas F. Radel

Can the Sodomite Speak?

I will begin with a few questions, not the least of which is the one contained in my title: "Can the sodomite speak?" Clearly, I ask this particular question with tongue in cheek, troping as I do Gayatri Spivak's famous query about the subaltern in postcolonial culture.[1] We cannot even be sure there is a sodomite in the early modern period, let alone wonder if he (or possibly she) can speak. But however facetiously I ask the question, I do so to raise the problem of power relations in and around early modern sodomy, for recent discussion of that subject has tended to elide issues of individual power and agency. Before proceeding, though, I want to complicate my opening question by asking some others. Does speaking imply agency or subjectivity? If so, what kind? And if sodomy can be spoken, if the sodomite can speak, does he feel desire? Why or why not? What exactly is the relationship between speaking, desire, and sodomy? Twenty years after the late Alan Bray initiated the discussion of sex and sodomy in early modern England, the answers to these questions are not yet obvious.

In Bray's formulation of the issues surrounding same-sex behavior and sodomy in sixteenth- and seventeenth-century England, sodomy certainly did not define a subject position. Sodomy was a religious and symbolic discourse designating what was outside the created order of existence. Charges of sodomy could appear in the presence of other social or political disruptions, but they symbolized disorder in other, specifically non-sexual institutions.[2] Bray's lead was followed by Jonathan Goldberg, who searches for sodomy throughout Renaissance texts, but not for evidence of subjectivity or desire *per se*. For Goldberg, sodomy is a sign of social and political dislocations that helps reveal the institutions in which normative same-sex desire took place. He explores sodomy deconstructively, as a relation to other discursive spaces of male-male desire such as pedagogy or friendship that were decidedly not sexual in the modern sense of the term – though Goldberg is careful not to disavow the place of sex in these institutions.[3] For both of these critics, it would be superfluous to ask if the sodomite could speak or if there was a relation between sodomy and desire, for there was, strictly speaking, no sodomite, and no sodomy was imagined in the space of desire. If sodomy was imagined in an individual, it was an accusation thrust upon a figure who was revealed in order to be repressed, someone who, as Goldberg puts it in his discussion of the New England patriarch William Bradford's *Of Plymouth Plantation*, became the sign of a disavowing of homoeroticism within normative homosocial relations.[4]

Other critics have responded differently. While Bruce Smith doesn't talk about sodomy itself in his discussion of Shakespeare's sonnets, he suggests that their speaker invents "a new mode of discourse about homosexual desire where none existed before." In fact, that speaker records "an experience of sexual desire that seems distinctively modern."[5] Smith theorizes a voice of same-sex desire in the sonnets who speaks himself in a different relationship to sex and to men than had been articulated before, certainly in a relationship different from those that Bray or Goldberg imagined. Gregory Bredbeck goes a step further, proposing that early modern textualities might "ascribe a subjective potentiality to the rhetoric of homoeroticism,"[6] and suggesting that while we cannot find an "*actual* sodomite" in literature, we can find "a delineation of the *conditions* for his existence."[7]

It is not my goal to adjudicate these possibilities, which dance tantalizingly around each other even as they suggest that no single theory of Renaissance sodomy will account for the multivalent nature of this discourse. Instead, I want to focus on another possibility – one that retains the symbolic and relational aspects of sodomy as these were explored by Bray and Goldberg while seeming to bring the sodomite into view as a speaking agent or subject. I want to suggest that sodomitical desire was thinkable in the early modern period – at least when it was someone else's. This is not so much a thesis as a point of meditation, one I will explore by looking at the intersection of two (only apparently) unrelated discourses of sodomy: the texts of the trial of Mervyn Touchet, 2nd Earl of Castlehaven, and sixteenth- and seventeenth-century satire. Seen side by side, these different types of text suggest that under certain circumstances it was possible to imagine the sodomite localized as a voluntary agent of desire and that such imaginings authorized specific power relations within homoerotic institutions such as mastery.

The trial of Mervyn Touchet

In 1631, Mervyn Touchet, the 2nd Earl of Castlehaven, was brought to trial before the House of Lords for the rape of his wife and for sodomy. Castlehaven's trial began when his son, James, hereafter referred to as Lord Audley, accused his father of attempting to disinherit him in favor of a serving man, Henry Skipwith.[8] Audley charged that his father was extremely generous to Skipwith and that Castlehaven had encouraged Skipwith to cuckold him, Lord Audley, and to have sex with the Countess of Castlehaven as well. The ensuing investigation revealed that Castlehaven's household at Founthill was in extreme disorder. Skipwith, it seems, was not Castlehaven's only favorite. The Earl had shown preference for an earlier one, John Amptil, by marrying him to his own daughter. Among Castlehaven's present servants, there were two more favorites, the Irish Catholic, Lawrence or Florence Fitzpatrick,[9] and an Englishman, Gyles Broadway. Unlike Skipwith, who confessed primarily to having an affair with Elizabeth Brydges, Lord Audley's wife, Gyles Broadway testified, among other things, to lying with the Countess of Castlehaven, while, it was alleged, her husband held her down. And Fitzpatrick confessed to sleeping with the Earl's whore, Blandina, and that Castlehaven "made him lie with him at Founthill and at Salisbury, and once in the bed, and emitted between his thighs, but did not penetrate his body...."[10]

Additional accusations were made, and as Cynthia Herrup makes clear in her recent book about the trial, a host of prior social and political complications helped shape the case that was emerging against Castlehaven. Although he was a peer of the realm, Castlehaven failed to take an active role in Parliament, and was not well known in London. His family had a problematic relationship with the Crown, not least because of its many Irish connections: the Touchet family had long held properties in Ireland; Castlehaven's father lived in and seemed to maintain his loyalties to Ireland; and his brother was charged as a recusant. Castlehaven himself had a tendency to prevaricate in religion, though he confessed at his trial to having settled this issue firmly in favor of Protestantism. Castlehaven's youngest sister, the Protestant prophet, Lady Eleanor Davies, had offended King Charles, who drove her from the court.

If anything seems clear about this trial, it is that the sexual crimes, including the allegations of sodomy, gave shape to a series of political problems associated with Castlehaven and his family. To use Alan Bray's formulation, sodomy in this instance "symbolized" far greater social and political issues. Herrup makes clear that:

> "[if] we look closely at the trial, at the explanations offered, and at their unarticulated implications, it is the violation of the precepts of a properly run household, neither sodomy nor rape nor religion nor favoritism *per se*, that was the most critical of the Earl's abominations. Focusing on the household shows us not the importance of any one crime, but what all of the allegations had in common, the de-legitimation of conventional authority."[11]

Yet I still want to resist the tendency of recent readings to see sodomy as completely inscribed into the political or social disruptions it symbolizes and to see it as completely separate from contemporary discourses that both articulate and delimit acceptable homoerotic behavior. If the trial is not about same-sex activity *per se*, it is about the discursive production of certain kinds of same-sex desire and the proscriptions that surround them. The Castlehaven documents do not simply articulate sodomy as a product of social disorder; they actually help articulate the conditions under which homoeroticisms would be tolerated or not in the period. By failing to see this, we have failed to see exactly how some discourses of erotic behavior intersect with ideologies of social control.

That we have done so, I want to argue, proceeds from two things: first, our habit of looking only at the Earl, whose authoritarian role as the head of the household allowed his sexual behavior to constitute a civil and social threat; and, second, our tendency to constitute early modern history in this case simply as a product of important legal discourses and ideologies of hierarchy and status. If, however, we look at that other figure who was executed for sodomy along with Castlehaven, the servant Lawrence Fitzpatrick, we can begin to see that the trial enacts its tensions more fully around issues of (homo)erotic behavior than at first seems to be the case. Recent readings of the trial simply do not account fully for the animus that falls upon this servant, a person whose "place" does not put him at the center of power and authority in the culture. This argument only becomes clear, however, if we see the trial in relation to Tudor-Stuart satire – and it is there I will begin.

Tudor-Stuart satire: the literary record

Within the tradition of early modern satire, a clearly articulated erotic dynamic between better-born men and lower-born others assumed the silence of servants or favorites of lower social status. But the fact of their "silence" was also cynically manipulated – articulated as silence or not – to serve the interests of moralizing writers and the erotic status quo. Satiric works of the sixteenth and seventeenth centuries demarcated the boundaries of social control of homoerotic activity by simultaneously ascribing and prohibiting erotic "agency" to scapegoated figures who were seen as needing to be controlled in situations that needed to be corrected. In doing so, they reveal the ways the demarcation of same-sex activity as sodomy and the normative silences about homoerotic activity were, in certain cases, discursively intertwined.

Perhaps more than any others in the period, the discourses of satire bring into close proximity illegible or unmarked homoeroticism and stigmatized sodomy, for these works perform a complex negotiation around the sexual "agency" of their ubiquitous Ganymedes, ingles, catamites, and pages. In using the term "agency" I assume no more than the works' problematized representations of these figures as usurping the prerogative to control either their own erotic availability or the men who desire them. If, as critics such as Jonathan Goldberg have argued, one of the effects of an open secret about the (homo)erotics of master/servant relations in the period would have been to allow homoerotic activity to flourish without falling within the more legible purview of sodomy, the satires reveal how class or status issues directed this homoerotic illegibility, and they suggest that the failure to read homoeroticism within the normative constructions of desire in the period could depend – at least in some cases – upon a construction of sodomy as a scapegoated and marginalized behavior in a particular individual: a minion or person of lower status on whom blame could be deflected and who could be seen as willfully attempting to undermine the established order. Such a response to sodomy ensured, at least in part, that sexual transgression could always be articulated elsewhere than within the centers of power. Its articulation there, of course, would tend to secure the status quo of that center.

In Tudor-Stuart satire, various Ganymedes, ingles, and minions seem, at times, to serve in their silence as symbols of the open secret of master/minion erotic relations revealed. So, for example, John Marston uses a Ganymede figure in the third of his *Certaine Satyres* (1598) to color his portrait of the sodomite at the center of his railing: "But ho, what

Ganimede is that doth grace/The gallants heeles. One, *who for two daies space/Is closely hyred.*"[12] Or, in *The Scourge of Villanie* (1598), he introduces Luscus, who, tiring of his wife, finds a "*Ganimede,*" a "peece of lustfull flesh" to help him "redresse" his "*Priape.*"[13] Other examples would include the ingles and catamites accompanying the victims of satiric abuse in Michael Drayton's *The Moone-Calfe*, Everard Guilpin's *Skialetheia*, and Ben Jonson's "On Sir Voluptuous Beast." These figures may seem to escape a fully delineated inscription as sodomites because their presence on the streets of London is simply taken for granted. Like a mistress, the Ganimede or ingle is legibly inscribed as silent within an erotic dynamic fully comprehensible to the satirist and his audience. Although Bruce Smith has correctly argued that the tradition as a whole represents these figures as falling within the boundaries demarcated by the category of sodomy,[14] the discursive contest to control their meaning can be more complexly imagined.

The usual portrait of a powerless partner who is the silent adjunct to his social betters, a portrait that insured a non-threatening (if not wholly normative) construction of homoerotic desire, is not the only or standard revelation of these satires. Part of the point of satirists like Marston and Jonson seems surely to be the exposure of the ingles', the servants', and the minions' availability within a hierarchical dialectic that gives shape to sodomitical transgression. So, in some cases, Elizabethan and Stuart satirists imagine some place of active control for the subservient figures who are usually represented as adjuncts to more powerfully inscripted men.

We might look at a work attributed to Thomas Middleton: in dramatizing the horrors of the London streets and the sodomitical disintegration of the London gentry who frequent them, Middleton creates "Ingling Pyander" in his *Micro-Cynicon* (1599). Pyander, the hermaphroditic or cross-dressing descendent of Sodom, actively seduces the speaker of the poem, inciting his lust by impersonating a woman and engendering his homophobic disgust at the discovery of Pyander's secret. The poem exposes the speaker's depravity through his association with Pyander, but its humor is fully developed around the exposure of Pyander as the source of sodomitical transgression. The speaker, looking for our sympathy, rails against Pyander:

> O, so I was besotted with her words,
> His words, that no part of a she affords!
> For had he been a she, injurious boy,
> I had not been so subject to annoy.
> A plague upon such filthy gullery![15]

Pyander's willful depravity serves to locate and identify the equally willful, sodomitical lust of the better-born speaker. Not the unthreatening object of the speaker's homoerotic lust, Pyander, in his subversive "agency," becomes the literal "subject" of the poem, something like a subjectivized sodomite, at least for the speaker. Pyander's "action" presumes his control over his sexual transgression, and he is most threatening because his actions dramatically reveal what typically remained silent, his own availability and perhaps his own desire. Middleton may be having a joke at the expense of his speaker, but he seems in absolute earnest as he reveals the source of social disorder in London not simply in the better-born speaker but in the usually not-spoken-for sodomite on the street.

Other examples throughout the period replay in different ways a similar concern with the ingle's agency. So, in Epigram 26 of Guilpin's *Skialetheia* (1598), "To Pollio," lexical ambiguity renders the gentlemanly Pollio indistinguishable from his ingle:

> Th'art a fine fellow trust me *Pollio*,
> And euery one reputes thee so to be,
> Both for thy ingles face, and goodly show,
> Of thyne apparraile and thy naperie...

The intriguing word play here (Does Pollio have an ingle with a fine face, or is his face a fine ingle's face?) hints at the collapse of an important social distinction between master and servant, gentleman and favorite, sodomite and Ganymede – and thus suggests that the ingle can perform in the actively desiring capacity of the gentleman.

In the following Epigram 27, "Of the Same," Guilpin makes this hint explicit:

> *Pollio* at length's fallne in my good conceit,
> Not for his wanton face and curled haire,
> Nor his fatte buttocke, nor that I delight
> In his french Galliard, which is nothing rare,
>   Nor for that others thinke him to be so,
>   (For others credits cannot better me,)
>   But for he thinks himself a fine fellow,
>   For his owne state who better knowes then hee?[16]

Again through lexical ambiguity, the speaker suggests that Pollio may have assumed the position of an ingle, and in so doing, may actively work to incite the speaker's desire. It is hard to determine precisely whether Pollio has fallen in the speaker's good opinion of him, or if he has fallen into the speaker's good opinion. Although he is literally the aristocratic figure, Pollio's identification with (and as) the ingle places him in a rhetorical position similar to Pyander's, a willfully desiring Ganymede who subverts natural hierarchies. So this poem, too, reveals tension around the threatening possibility that the ingle can become a "subject" and not simply remain an object of desire. Although it is, finally, the gentleman Pollio here who is the source of sodomy, his sodomy is imagined as deriving from his own aping of his inferior, the ingle.

Later in the century (c. 1675), John Wilmot's infamous lyric, "The Disabled Debauchee," encodes a series of sexual transgressions remembered by its now impotent speaker, among which is a memorable contest between himself, Chloris, and a good-looking favorite:

> Nor shall our love-fits, Chloris, be forgot,
>   When each the well-looked linkboy strove t'enjoy,
> And the best kiss was the deciding lot
>   Whether the boy fucked you, or I the boy.[17]

While I can hardly do justice in the space provided to the nuance of this poem belonging to so different a period from the others, it is nevertheless worth pausing briefly over its portrayal of the sexual underling as well. For Rochester's speaker, too, plays – at least phantasmatically, and again through lexical ambiguity – with the possibility that the linkboy may be an actively soliciting subject of desire. It seems impossible to determine here who kisses whom in the contest for the boy, who has to produce the "best kiss," and who gets to choose the sexual partner: the boy himself, Chloris, or the debauchee? But the poem certainly, and scandalously, seems to hold out the possibility that the boy himself may get to decide whether to fuck or be fucked. So, if the more relaxed tone of Rochester's poem signals a very different context, it, in its own way, reflects the tendency of the earlier satires to locate the sources of sodomy in the lower-born. Once again, we find that the possibility of a favorite's willingness to participate in sodomy helps define not only the social but the sexual dysfunctions of his superior as well.

Tudor-Stuart satire, then, presents not one but at least two distinct possibilities in its representation of homoerotic legibility and sodomy.

So long as it imagines its Ganymede figures as silenced adjuncts to their more powerful partners, those figures simply remain symbols of the misplaced affections of their betters. Sodomy is figured as the vice of the better-born, and though the "sodomite" may be disorderly in his lack of discretion and proportion, he does not seemingly threaten an order that otherwise allows him sexual access to a wide variety of pleasures outside marriage. The ingle or catamite may be drawn within the general boundaries of sodomy, but he does not threaten to undermine the social order of which he is a part. He may thus remain an available figure of desire in spite of being revealed as such.

But in others of these texts, sodomy is imagined as a transgression of hierarchy or status in which the Ganymede or ingle can be seen as the threatening (or at the least scandalous), active agent of desire. In this, the satires rehearse a tendency to see the Ganymede as a "sodomite," a willful agent of disorder, someone whose actions help explain the causes of social disintegration in the form of his own desire. Which brings me back to the case against Castlehaven.

Service and the sodomite

When Castlehaven was brought to trial before the House of Lords for the rape of his wife and for sodomy, his conviction was secured in large part on the testimony of Lawrence Fitzpatrick and Gyles Broadway. It is not entirely clear after 350 years exactly how the state compelled the two servants to testify against Castlehaven, but, as Caroline Bingham points out in her analysis of the case, it is almost certainly true that Fitzpatrick and Broadway had been assured by Lord Dorset, the prosecutor, that they would be granted immunity from prosecution if they did so.[18] It is also unclear whether or not Fitzpatrick might have escaped implication in the Earl's crimes had he remained silent, for unlike Broadway, whose case was complicated by his lying with the Countess and her testimony against him, there was no evidence of Fitzpatrick's "sodomy" but his own testimony.

It is on his case, then, that I want to focus. As critics such as Mario DiGangi have made clear, sexual relations between masters and minions were not specifically proscribed in the period and were generally illegible as sodomy[19] – an argument that may be extended to any number of hierarchical male-male social arrangements. In other words, they may or may not have been known, they may or may not have signified, but they remained insignificant so long as they did not violate other, established ways of conducting business. So, it seems possible – indeed probable– that Fitzpatrick's silence could have prevented him from ever having been labeled a "sodomite." We have no evidence of the extent to which Fitzpatrick himself may have conspired with Castlehaven to commit sodomy or may simply have been taken advantage of by his master, nor can we be entirely sure that these were the only options available to explain his actions. Finally, we cannot be certain to what extent the servant's unrepentant Catholicism, which he expressed fully at his trial and execution, implicated him in the general religious and political issues surrounding the case.[20] I want to suggest, however, that Fitzpatrick's fate is at least partially explained by a convoluted logic controlling master/servant relationships in which the sodomy of the lord is fully realized only in the discursive production of active agency in the sodomitical servant.

I will begin by asking what it means that Fitzpatrick came to be singled out as a "sodomite" in an historical moment that might otherwise prefer to keep such actions illegible. This is the first of many seeming illogicalities in the handling of Fitzpatrick, especially if we compare his situation to that of Henry Skipwith, another lower-born figure in the case who seemingly escapes prosecution. On his own testimony, Skipwith was forced to have sex with Castlehaven's daughter-in-law. The Earl apparently wanted Elizabeth Brydges, Lady Audley, to bear Skipwith's child. This crime, which was so much an affront to patrilineal order, seems to have been part of what was most repellent to the prosecution in the case, for in the Lord Steward's "exhortation" at the sentencing, he tells Castlehaven to think that "...you have abused your own daughter! And having both honour and fortune to leave behind you, you would have had the impious and spurious offspring of a harlot to inherit!"[21] We need to keep in mind that it is probably not the affront to Lady Audley's person that is most grievous to the Lord Steward, but "the offense against the social order."[22]

Other actions of Skipwith's would seem to bring him within the realm of homoerotic attachment to Castlehaven. The Earl's steward, Walter Bigg testifies that Skipwith was entertained as Castlehaven's page for eight years and that "[he] spent of my lord's purse per annum 500L. and he gave him at one time 1,000L. and hath made divers deed of land unto him."[23] The Earl himself confesses that "Skipwith lay with him when he was straitened in rooms"; the Countess of Castlehaven testifies that her husband "would make Skipwith come naked into his chamber, and delighted in calling up his servants to show their privities; and would make her look on, and commended those that had the largest"; and Fitzpatrick says that "Henry Skipwith was the special favourite of my lord Audley, and that he usually lay with him."[24]

Yet there seems to be no record of a trial against him.[25] Despite what may seem to us a strong suggestion of the homoerotic in his behavior and his clear identification with the Ganymede, minion, or favorite in early discourses, Skipwith's culpability seems to remain illegible beneath complex layers of discourse that effectively shield knowledge of it. In this case, these may be discourses of service and obligation, and even, perhaps, one of romantic love, depending on how we interpret Skipwith's testimony "that in the end he usually lay with the young lady, and that there was love between them both before and after."[26] But what may allow these alternative discourses to remain potent is that Skipwith himself does not make the homoerotic elements of his relation to Castlehaven explicitly legible, and hence does not usurp the prerogative or agency of the master through which they typically remained silent. His actions, then, never quite become buggery, the specific (and in this case specifically homoerotic) action that forms the basis of prosecution for Broadway and Fitzpatrick.

Fitzpatrick, however, confesses explicitly to carnal relations with Castlehaven, making legible in the mouth of the servant what was usually illegible as a power of the master. He was, of course, apparently encouraged to do so by Lord Dorset of the prosecution, and he wisely averred that although emission occurred, penetration did not. Nevertheless, this legalistic specification about the act itself was not allowed to stand, for the Lord Steward declared that the law did not distinguish between penetration and emission in the crime of buggery: "It is *Buggery* by Law; for the Law of this Land makes no distinction of *Buggery*, if there be *Emissio Seminis*."[27] But as Bruce Smith makes clear in his discussion of Coke's earlier legal clarifications of buggery in his *A Booke of Entries* (1614), convictions for buggery were to be secured around proof of penetration.[28] As this was not the case, the proof of Castlehaven's sodomy had to come via another path, the one we have seen at work in satire: the construction of an actively soliciting servant figure who embodies sodomitical desire.[29] It is not simply that Fitzpatrick's speaking about his sex acts reveals him as a "sodomite"; it is, rather, that his speaking about them can be seen to constitute an inversion of the usual order of things and so provides the occasion for him to be inscripted as an active agent, a "sodomite" as the source of transgression.

The trial seems to have activated a narrative of the minion's "agency" that we have seen in the satires, specifying unequivocally, apparently in the absence of empirical proof, that Fitzpatrick voluntarily indulged in homoerotic, and sodomitical, licentiousness. In assuring the jurors that there were no legal loopholes through which to free Fitzpatrick, the judge ruled that:

> "forasmuch as every accessory to a felon is a felon in law; so he [Fitzpatrick] being a voluntary prostitute, when he was not only of understanding and years to know the heinousness of the sin, but also of strength to have withstood his lord, he therefore was so far forth guilty."[30]

What is clear here is that the law, if not being exactly misapplied, is being cynically manipulated – by Dorset, who seemingly neglected to inform Fitzpatrick of his complicity in a felony, and by the Lord Chief Justice, who seems necessarily to define Fitzpatrick as a "voluntary prostitute" who could have resisted his lord's imprecations. Where, one might ask, does this ascription of voluntarism comes from in the convoluted proceedings of this trial?[31] Though admittedly his words are sometimes inconsistent on the point, Fitzpatrick himself repeatedly casts his accusations in the form of what the Earl "made" him do. And his gallows speech articulates his powerlessness in ways that surely must have obtained at least partially for any servant in the period. He says:

> "[that] he had fallen or run into these sins, (and especially that which he came to die for) by reason he had neglected, and not so duly, as he should have done, repaired to his ghostly father, to make confession, and take instructions from him. That after he did make confession and his sins known to the priest, he was not only sorry for them, but also resolved never to come into my lord's house again; *but it was through frailty, and because he was not furnished of another place*".[32]

Clearly, it is possible to commit buggery and not be morally culpable, but the prosecutors seem to be going to some lengths to understand Fitzpatrick as complicit in Castlehaven's guilt.[33] They thus transform his testimony into a confession, a wholly voluntary admission of a wholly voluntary crime. The judge can entertain no suspicion about Fitzpatrick's willingness to commit sodomy, for to do so would obligate him to prove that Castlehaven forced his servant if he wanted to obtain a conviction for sodomy. If he couldn't prove this, Fitzpatrick would most likely go free. And if Fitzpatrick were freed, his own confession of sex with Castlehaven would stand to "reveal" what every-one, including presumably the judge, pretended not to know: the erotic compulsions of the ruling class with regard to their servants. To preserve the status quo, then, it seems the judges had to construct some sense of individual intentionality around Fitzpatrick's actions that would demarcate them as sodomy, for only in so doing could they safely re-construe the system(at)ic illegibility of homoeroticism in master-servant relations.

One could argue that Fitzpatrick was executed because he confessed to a "crime," but it is a crime that was, it would seem, committed routinely, hardly "criminal" at all except in the revelation of the agency of an underling. In other words, Fitzpatrick's very speaking of the crime constitutes the crime of which he is guilty, and that, in turn, secures the "proof" of the sexual acts of Castlehaven himself. How this happened, I would propose, is best revealed in the (il)logic of the satires in which underlings could be represented as expressing sexual desires that provided evidence of their wills, their agency. Thus they could become the loci for a paranoid, homophobic scapegoating of individuals who were presumed to have voluntarily assisted the corrupting of their masters.

The subject servant – sodomy, satire, and silence

What all this suggests is that the texts of the Castlehaven trial can arguably be shown to articulate some sense of a sodomite as "subject." Read in the context of early modern satire, it seems clear that sexual acts, and specifically homoerotic ones, were important to the meanings of the trial, and perhaps indicators of the kinds of stress that sodomy exerted on more normative social arrangements. Of course, one cannot talk about sexual subjectivity in the modern sense, and I certainly do not mean to say that these works prefigure modern homosexual subject positions. Nothing in the satires or in the records of the trial suggest that the sexual crimes described were the result of a social identity based in sexual-object choice. And while both texts reveal homo-erotically specific senses of sodomy, they do not do so in absolute distinction from heteroerotic possibilities. Broadway's sexual crimes apparently included both buggery with a man and the rape of a woman. Nevertheless, efforts to read these texts as if they were solely about the social disorder that sodomy symbolized in the period tend to overlook their apparent concern with problems of agency and the problematic positions of individuals who could not speak about their

own acts and desires. To conclude, then, I will make a few brief sugges-
tions about what it may tell us about early modern same-sex arrangements if we take seriously individuals who were discursively
represented as "subjects" of sodomy.

Doing so allows us to understand better how and why the Lord Chief
Justice accused Lawrence Fitzpatrick of voluntary participation in
sodomy. In the grossest of senses, such a charge is logical. Short of
physical force, one must presume the "consent" of both partners in so
challenging a sport as sodomy. As Herrup makes clear, early law presumes that both partners are equally culpable.[34] But the literalness of
the law on this point only obviates the sense that it was regulating
bodies – specific men involved in particular acts. If sodomy were only a
symbolic crime, then what did the law's concern with bodies mean?
And if sodomy appears only or primarily in the midst of other social or
political disruptions, what did it mean that the judges appealed to
individual agency to press the case against Fitzpatrick? By creating a
space of intention around his sodomitical acts, the judges created not
only a sodomitical body but a juridical space of control around homoerotic sex itself.

It was a discourse that helps explain not only the cases of Fitzpatrick
and Broadway, but the many scapegoated ingles, minions, and
catamites of the satires as well.[35] Both types of text – the Castlehaven
records and early modern satires – imagine a sodomite (in the very
specific sexual sense) who can speak, can feel desire. He thus becomes
localized as a voluntary, willful transgressor. The image marks his body
as a site of containment, and, at the same time, disguises the force with
which any real social or sexual agency on his part is effectively dissolved. The individual who may or may not have willingly engaged in
sexual activity was made to stand as the symbol of social disorder not
necessarily of his making. It is significant in this regard to recall that
Fitzpatrick articulates quite a different account of himself when he
argues that social circumstances led him to commit the crimes he did.
Such an explanation, however, hardly produces a body that can serve
in its voluntary corruption as a symbol of social disorder contained.[36]

I would also argue that the space of imagined sodomitical agency
had a role to play in other, more normative discourses of power in the
period as well. We have tended to think of institutions such as mastery
or friendship as spaces of potential desire between men. These spaces
are not problematic (in DiGangi's formulation) or not visible as such
(in Goldberg's formulation) so long as the activities that took place
within them were not disruptive and so long as serving or lower-born

men did not use the intimacy created through erotic access to gain control of their superiors (the issue which was, it seems, dramatized in Marlowe's *Edward II*). But such formulations do not account completely for the ways mastery regulates not only social service but also (homoerotic) desire. Indeed, it seems possible to say that mastery regulates the servant partly through control of his desire, allowing and disallowing him to act and articulate that desire not on his own terms but on terms defined socially and politically by others.

We might expect nothing less in the early modern period, but we need to see more fully the paradoxes of power in this position. The minion or favorite in early modern ideology seems to have occupied a place similar to the woman in Petrarchan poetry, with perhaps one notable difference. The Petrarchan conventions at least imagined that the woman so fully contained by them had a body, could exhibit desire of her own (albeit always of the poet's imagination). In some senses, her desire – or lack thereof – was the occasion for the poetry. That is not so clear about the minion or servant, as his desire seems to be the thing that others would control exclusively. Within the arrangements of service, the minion may have engaged in sexual activity and may even have felt desire for his master. But these potentialities dissolved into transgressive sodomy if the minion himself articulated them as desire. As such they made him available for punishment. Any homoerotic desires he may have had could only be legitimately constituted by his master. It is not enough to see his position in purely social terms, for the social and sexual blend so fully that sex remains fully within the scope of a minion's service.

Perhaps the question to raise in this context is not "can the sodomite speak?" but "can the servant?"[37] Class or status issues are clearly inherent in the problem of "voluntary" sodomy as I have described it. One might go so far as to say that voluntary sodomy, sodomitical subjectivity, is located in the place of service, even as it reflects back onto the master. Such a situation implies the extent to which coercion was necessarily part of the erotic institutions of mastery. We perhaps do not need the Castlehaven material or the satires to reveal what seems, from our own perspective, perfectly clear. But parsing more carefully the power relations implicit in the handling of sexually available underlings in them does reveal the complementary relations of silence and speaking in early modern (homo)eroticism.

The kinds of power relations that I have attempted to tease out of the discursive treatments of servants, favorites, minions, and ingles (who are all connected in their potential erotic subjection to more powerful men) reveal a potent discourse of silence. Certainly, silence about sex, homoerotic sex, seems to have been presumed on the part of the servant or underling. But it may also be that such silence authorized a (homo)erotic compulsion enabled by and contained in the space of mastery, even perhaps rendering it invisible as compulsion. If I can't speak what is being done to me or even what I am doing willingly, then, in some sense, I seem to be doing nothing at all or something else altogether. And perhaps I am.

But if it has seemed necessary to recover the ways silence and presumptions to mastery have guided sexual access to women in the early modern period, it may also be worth seeing how they may have directed sexual access to men as well. To do so, however, we need to explore what does not seem to exist in the period or what exists only under erasure, sexual "subjects." In our effort to discover the historical specificity of the past, we cannot let their silence become our own.

Notes

I want to thank Cynthia Herrup for helping me locate and understand some of the early sources of Lawrence Fitzpatrick's trial even before she had completed and published her recent book.

1. Gayatri Spivak, "Can the Subaltern Speak?" in C. Nelson and L. Grossberg (eds.), *Marxism and the Interpretation of Culture* (Urbana, IL: University of Illinois Press, 1989), pp. 271–313.
2. See especially Chapter 1, "Word and Symbol," in Alan Bray, *Homosexuality in Renaissance England* (London: Gay Men's Press, 1982), pp. 13–32.
3. Jonathan Goldberg, *Sodometries: Renaissance Texts, Modern Sexualities* (Stanford, CA: Stanford University Press, 1992), pp. 18ff.
4. Goldberg, *Sodometries*, p. 243.
5. Bruce R. Smith, *Homosexual Desire in Shakespeare's England: a Cultural Poetics* (Chicago and London: University of Chicago Press, 1991), p. 267.
6. Gregory W. Bredbeck, *Sodomy and Interpretation: Marlowe to Milton* (Ithaca, NY: Cornell UP, 1991), pp. 145–148.
7. Bredbeck, *Sodomy and Interpretation*, p. 148.
8. For a detailed summary of the trial, see Chapter 2, "A Debauched Son of a Noble Family," in Cynthia B. Herrup, *A House in Gross Disorder: Sex, Law, and the 2nd Earl of Castlehaven* (New York and Oxford: OUP, 1999); pp. 5–62.
9. Fitzpatrick's given name is variously reported in the sources. Although Herrup is probably more correct in preferring "Florence," I use "Lawrence" in deference to my primary source, *Cobbett's State Trials* (see note 10).
10. "The Trial of Mervin Lord Audley, Earl of Castelhaven, for a Rape and Sodomy," in Thomas B. Howell (ed.), *A Complete Collection of State Trials,*

33 vols. (London: Hansard, 1809), Vol. 3, cols. 413, 412, known as *Cobbett's State Trials*. Most references in the text are to this widely available volume. Whenever necessary, however, notes to seventeenth-century sources will be used to help corroborate the historical or linguistic validity of quotations. For a history of early sources, see Herrup, *A House in Gross Disorder*, Appendix C, "Geneology of Manuscripts and Pamphlets," pp. 165–9.

11. Cynthia Herrup, "The Patriarch at Home: the Trial of the 2ⁿᵈ Earl of Castlehaven for Rape and Sodomy," *History Workshop Journal* 41 (Spring 1996): 8. In a similar vein Bruce Smith argues that "what angered the [House of] Lords the most was not the sexual crimes that Castlehaven committed against the person of his wife and servants but the political crime he attempted against the social order of which the lords were a part and over which they presided" (*Homosexual Desire*, p. 52). On the disjunction between the criminalization and persecution of sodomy and specific sodomitical sexual acts in the legal discourse of the period, see also Janet Halley, "Bowers v. Hardwick in the Renaissance," in Jonathan Goldberg (ed.) *Queering the Renaissance* (Durham, NC: Duke University Press, 1994), pp. 15–39.

Other recent work on the Castlehaven case explores, as this chapter does, early modern ideologies of sex and power. Nancy Weitz Miller suggests that the case reveals the paradoxes of early seventeenth-century ideologies of rape and female chastity in "Chastity, Rape, and Ideology in the Castlehaven Testimonies and Milton's Ludlow Mask," *Milton Studies* 32 (1996): 153-68; and Frances E. Dolan looks at it in relation to dramatic and non-literary texts that define the crimes against hierarchical and household authority known as petty treason: *Dangerous Familiars: Representations of Domestic Crime in England, 1550–1770* (Cornell, NY: Cornell UP, 1994), pp. 81–6.

See also: Barbara Breasted, "Comus and the Castlehaven Scandal," *Milton Studies* 3 (1971): 201–24; Rosemary Karmelich Mundhenk, "Dark Scandal and the Sun-Clad Power of Chastity: the Historical Milieu of Milton's *Comus*," *Studies in English Literature* 15.1 (Winter 1975): 141–52; and Leah Sinanoglou Marcus, "The Milieu of Milton's *Comus*: Judicial Reform at Ludlow and the Problem of Sexual Assault," *Criticism* 25.4 (Fall 1983): 293–327.

12. *The Poems of John Marston*, ed. Arnold Davenport (Liverpool: Liverpool University Press, 1961), Satire 3, 78.

13. *The Poems of John Marston*, 112.

14. See "Knights in Shifts", Chap. 5 in Smith, *Homosexual Desire*, pp. 160–87.

15. *The Works of Thomas Middleton*, ed. A.H. Bullen Vol. 8. (London: John C. Nimmo, 1886), p. 133.

16. Everard Guilpin, *Skialetheia or A Shadowe of Truth in Certaine Epigrams and Satyres*, ed. D. Allen Carroll (Chapel Hill, NC: University of North Carolina Press, 1974), p. 46–7.

17. *The Complete Poems of John Wilmot, Earl of Rochester* ed. D.M. Vieth (New Haven: Yale University Press, 1968), p. 117.

18. Caroline Bingham, "Seventeenth-Century Attitudes toward Deviant Sex," *Journal of Interdisciplinary History* 1.3 (Spring 1971): 457. Early manuscripts elaborate this point more precisely than the account in *Cobbett's State Trials*. In BL Harleian MS 1330, a French law summary, Fitzpatrick is said to

have stated that his confession was solicited by Archibald Douglas, husband of Lady Eleanor Davies Douglas, Castlehaven's fourth sister, and that it was made against his lord in service to the king–at the request of the privy counsel and not to accuse himself (see 62r). Early notes on the trial contained in BL Sloane 1709 repeat the point: Fitzpatrick says that "what evidence he had formerly given it was for the king against his Lord, the Earle of Castlehaven, no further" (77r; orthography regularized). The first narrative histories of the case, Hammond L'Estrange's *The Reign of King Charles* (London, 1655) and William Sanderson's *A Compleat History of the Life and Raigne of King Charles From Cradle to his Grave* (London, 1658), corroborate Bingham's idea that, in Sanderson's words, Fitzpatrick "somewhat was under hand used no doubt" (p. 160).

19. See Chapter 3, "The Homoerotics of Mastery in Satiric Comedy," in Mario DiGangi, *The Homoerotics of Early Modern Drama* (Cambridge: CUP, 1997), pp. 64–99.

20. That it did make a difference seems clear because of the attention lavished on his gallows speech in accounts of the trial. In contrast to the simpler confession of the Protestant Broadway, Fitzpatrick persists in Catholic proselytizing, even attempting to effect Broadway's conversion. Twenty-four years later, L'Estrange makes something of the contrast between the confession of the "Romish" Fitzpatrick and that of Broadway, which was "ingenuous, Christian, and sincere" (*Reign of King Charles*, p. 119).

21. *Cobbett's State Trials*, col. 416. But also compare *The Tryal and Condemnation of Mervin, Lord Audley Earl of Castle-Haven* (London: 1699; rpt Randolph Trumbach (ed.) *Sodomy Trials: Seven Documents*, New York and London: Garland Publishing, Inc. 1986): " ... and though you are not Condemn'd for that enormity, you caus'd your Daughter to be abused, and having Honour and Fortune to leave behind you, would have the spurious Issue of a Varlet to Inherit both" (p. 26). Except for BL Add Ms 22,591, all the early manuscripts I have referred to use the word *varlet*, making clear that the reference is to Skipwith. The word would have signified a person of a low or knavish disposition throughout the seventeenth century, and may also have been used – as in Shakespeare's *Troilus and Cressida* – as a term of (homo)sexual slander. By the eighteenth century, the word's imputation of seriously bad qualities began to be lost, and printed versions of the trial seem to begin to prefer "harlot." BL Add Ms 22,591 seems to use "harlott," though one might construe the orthography as confusing. Certainly, however, the word appears clearly in *The Case of Sodomy in the Tryal of Mervin Lord Audley ... printed from an original manuscript* (London: John Morphew, 1708), p. 24.

22. Bingham, "Seventeenth Century Attitudes": 465.

23. *Cobbett's State Trials*, col. 410. Although Cobbett attributes testimony to "Walter Bigg," on the basis of several early manuscripts and histories, other early sources (and Herrup) identify this testimony with Walter Tyte, steward of Castlehaven's household.

24. *Cobbett's State Trials*, cols. 411–2.

25. Herrup remarks this oddity, but given her emphasis on Castlehaven and his household, she does not explore it.

26. *Cobbett's State Trials*, cols. 412.

27. This detail is taken from the 1699 tract, *The Tryal and Condemnation*, p. 24, but it derives from earlier sources, for instance, BL Harleian Ms 1330/61v-62r.

28. Smith actually says that convictions for buggery were secured around proof of penetration, the use of force, and the fact of a victim's being underage, and his argument has been disseminated rather widely in the field (*Homosexual Desire*, pp. 51–2). Herrup, however, argues that "penetration alone determined the felony" (*A House in Gross Disorder*, p. 28). In either case, Fitzpatrick would not have been technically guilty.

29. Two early histories of Castlehaven's trial perhaps provide a clue to what is happening, for they inscript Skipwith into a familiar discursive relationship to Castlehaven. Both Sanderson and L'Estrange identify Skipwith through the same language for a male favorite that we have seen in the satires. L'Estrange calls him Castlehaven's "Ganymede," and states explicitly that the Earl committed sodomy upon him (*Reign of King Charles*, p. 115). Sanderson calls Skipwith a "minion" and a "Ganimede," and he draws Castlehaven's moral portrait as a variation on the sodomite familiar to us through satire: after describing Castlehaven's interactions with Amptil and Skipwith in rather salacious detail, Sanderson writes: "And to boot with his Ganimedes, he kept Blandina a common Whore in his house for all Comers, at sometimes four of the each after other, and himself the last, Spectatours all" (*A Compleat History*, p. 158). The word "minion" is used as well to describe Skipwith in at least one manuscript version of the trial, which also uses, as do many of the other early accounts, the word we find in *Cobbett's State Trials*, "ffavourites" (BL Landsdowne MS 213/187v). Skipwith clearly falls within the legible purview of sodomy, but unlike Fitzpatrick or Broadway, he does not become the actively soliciting agent of it. Hence his fate is remarkably different from theirs.

30. "The Trial of Lawrence Fitz-Patrick and Gyles Broadway," in *Cobbett's State Trials*, Vol. III, col. 420.

31. The specific language of volition appears in early sources. BL Sloane MS 1709, for instance, records the words of Chief Justice Hyde as they are found in *Cobbett's State Trials*. The earliest apparent source for the judicial articulation of Fitzpatrick's voluntary complicity in sodomy seems to be BL Harleian MS 1330/61v-62r. This summary of the trial records Fitzpatrick's attempt to use Irish practice to allow the approver of a crime to go free. Justice Jones argues against him, saying that such a plea has no value in England (62r), but in the elaboration of his argument, he says that Fitzpatrick's participation in sodomy, even lacking penetration, brings him within the realm of Onanism, which certainly seems capable of being construed as voluntary. Justice Croke argues that a confession is sufficient in a crime of this nature. The centrality of the question of Fitzpatrick's culpability in the Harleian MS suggests how legally problematic his case was. Of importance to my argument, this summary contains no sympathetic rendering of the various ways in which Fitzpatrick may have been compelled – both by Castlehaven himself and the justices. Cynthia Herrup first pointed out to me the significance of this manuscript.

32. *Cobbett's State Trials*, col. 422; italics added. See also BL Sloane MS 1709/79r.

33. If we compare his position to the Countess of Castlehaven's, the assertion of Fitzpatrick's "voluntarism" seems even more telling. When Castlehaven's

attorney asks to be resolved whether or not "it being proved that the party ravished were of evil fame, and of an unchaste life, it will amount to a Rape," the judges reply that "it is the enforcing against the will which makes the Rape; and a common whore may be ravished against her will, and it is Felony to do it" (*Cobbett's State Trials*, col. 414). Miller points out that in spite of this ruling, the judges seem to concur with Castlehaven's account of his wife's sexual disreputability, and that the legal tradition through which a raped woman was viewed as a spoiled or stolen commodity effectively erased the issue of her "consent" in rape trials ("Chastity, Rape and Ideology": 157–8). Nevertheless, the ruling in this instance is that the Countess's "will" is separate from that of her ravishers and that she can be forced against it. Unlike Fitzpatrick, she is not seen as the willing source of corruption.

34. Herrup, *A House in Gross Disorder*, p. 28.
35. It may be true of Castlehaven as well, but given the limitations of my focus on Fitzpatrick, I leave these implications unexplored.
36. It is worth noting that this discourse of the speaking, desiring sodomite may have found a different kind of social expression than the one I am exploring in the molly houses of late seventeenth-century London.
37. I am grateful to Jeffrey Masten for the suggestion that I reformulate my question in this way.

8
(Per)versions of Sappho

Jody Greene

> Of female poets who had names of old,
> Nothing is known but only told,
> And all we hear of them perhaps may be
> Male-flattery only, and male-poetry
>
> Abraham Cowley, "On the Death of
> Mrs. Katherine Philips, 1667."[1]

Introduction

It was not until the first quarter of the eighteenth century, nearly a century after their continental neighbors, that the majority of English readers were introduced to the dangerous pleasures of reading Sappho. Although scattered versions of Sappho had been available in translations from both Ovid and Longinus since the middle of the sixteenth century, such versions did not reach a wide audience until a curious outbreak of English Sapphism in the years 1711–13.[2] In those three short years, Joseph Addison, Ambrose Philips, Alexander Pope, and even Edmund Curll found themselves engaged in the production and circulation of what Joan DeJean calls "Sapphic fictions." In the introduction to *Fictions of Sappho*, DeJean takes note of this remarkably intense flurry of English interest in Sappho, only to dismiss it as at once belated and derivative:

> The English discovery of Sappho reproduces so closely the structure of her entry into the French tradition a half-century earlier that an analysis of its unfolding would have been repetitive, without being essential to an understanding of the future of Sapphic fictions.[3]

Yet we know from the history of Sappho's own poetry, if not from reading Freud, that there is no such thing as an indifferent repetition, and that even the most minor transformations in the English 'unfolding' of Sapphic fictions must be understood as symptomatic of differences in the cultural, literary, and linguistic fields.[4] In what follows, then, I challenge DeJean's summary dismissal of the significance of English Sapphism, both for the history of Sapphic fictions more generally, and for the history of English letters.[5] I do so, in part, by offering an overview of some of the versions and perversions of Sappho that circulated in English from 1680 to 1713, with a particular emphasis on the years 1711–13. Moreover, I depart from earlier accounts by considering these poetic productions not as documents in the social history of lesbianism, as recent criticism by Emma Donoghue and Harriette Andreadis has done, nor as part of the history of women's writing in English, as Germaine Greer does, but rather as problematic players in a very different sort of history: the history of the almost exclusively masculine enclave of English neo-classicism.[6]

Whatever its significance for the history of Sapphic fictions as a whole, the history of English versions and perversions of Sappho is certainly significant – and perhaps even essential – for our understanding of England's relation to the ancient world, as well as to its continental neighbors, at the opening of the eighteenth century. It is also a surprisingly fruitful – if somewhat queer – perspective from which to observe competing ideologies of masculinity circulating in the early modern period, in England and beyond.[7] Rather than constituting two separate analytical lenses through which to view the history of English Sapphism, however, the history of English neo-classicism and the history of masculinity come together in the Sapphic archive in compelling and inextricable ways. The period from the Restoration to the mid-eighteenth century – what was once called the Augustan age – was simultaneously the heyday of English neo-classicism and the great age of English Sapphism. It seems worthwhile to ask what role Sappho played in the broader elaboration of neo-classicism, and also how our understanding of English neo-classicism changes when we take into account translations of Sappho. Who chose to translate Sappho and who did not? What sort of readership did English translators of Sappho envision and attract? What did it mean for "male-poetry," as Cowley calls it,[8] to engage with the one and only female poet who actually had a name, of old? And finally, what sorts of pleasures – and dangers – might be attached to such acts of transgendered translation? If, as Carolyn Williams has argued, the study of classical antiquity was a virtual "male monopoly" in the Augustan period, pervaded and defined by "an atmosphere of wholesome masculinity," what changes were wrought in the atmosphere when these male monopolists collectively applied themselves to the study of Lesbian poetry?[9]

In a 1999 article in *Representations*, Dror Wahrman has challenged scholars of the early modern period in general, and the long eighteenth century in particular, to rethink the relationship between the cultural history of gender and the history of neo-classicism. It is now widely accepted that the eighteenth century witnessed the end of a series of epochal shifts in the cultural understanding of the relationship between sex and gender, ultimately resulting in a modern sex/gender system from which we are only now, perhaps, beginning to recover. Wahrman argues, following Thomas Laqueur, that these shifts can be traced to the gradual emergence of a binarized notion of sexual difference.[10] With the increasing concretization of sex as an immutable, natural category, the argument goes, gender was temporarily unmoored from its own earlier position of fixity. "The consequent autonomy of gender from the dictates of sex," Wahrman writes, "created *a space for play*, that is, a space for imaginable dissonances of gender (over) supposedly stable sexual bodies."[11]

Whether we can in fact attribute the seeming instability of gender in this period exclusively to its relationship to a newly solidified category of sex, as Wahrman does, or whether we might look as well to other explanatory paradigms, including the rise of consumer culture, as others have convincingly done, is not absolutely essential to the argument at hand.[12] I concur with Wahrman's privileging of the eighteenth century as "*a space for play*" in the domain of gender, and above all, with his insistence that we expand the archive from which we draw examples of gender instability. For, as Wahrman notes, our ability to assess just how far-reaching these transformations in gender ideology may have been will require us to move beyond the relatively self-contained archival sites from which we have hitherto drawn:

> Unsurprisingly, the evidence adduced in support of these arguments has often tended to cluster around cultural sites that could be expected to foreground experimentation and playfulness, fluidity and instability – such as theater and masquerade, perceptions of onstage and offstage cross-dressing, ballads about women passing as men, drama, and fiction.[13]

Wahrman's singular contribution to debates about gender in the eighteenth century is his conviction that we should move beyond these more obviously experimental cultural sites to "domains of culture that were less obviously performative and playful." The site he chooses is English translations of Juvenal, along with "the Augustan world of classical learning more generally."[14]

In addition to its renowned lack of playfulness, Augustan literature offers an unusual perspective from which to explore the history of gender and especially of masculinity precisely because it presents itself as impervious to such frivolous concerns. The rediscovery of the classics was undertaken as a refuge from a range of cultural upheavals – specifically, upheavals in normative gender roles – going on elsewhere in eighteenth-century English culture and literature. By virtue of its status as a homosocial enclave, almost entirely barred to women, classical learning, in Wahrman's terms, "could be expected to be least amenable to fluid notions of gender, and if anything, most committed to oppose them."[15] In fact, as Page duBois has recently argued in a work provocatively titled *Trojan Horses: Saving the Classics from Conservatives*, the Augustan retreat to classical literature as a refuge from social transformation itself has a long history – a history that extends to this day. We have always turned to the classics, she notes, to find "timeless nuggets of eternal wisdom" through which we might transcend the contingencies of historical and social change. These magic pellets of classical wisdom are simultaneously put to use – despite their ostensible timelessness – to validate our current obsessions and calm our most immediate fears.[16] Forces of cultural conservatism have been particularly adept at claiming the ancient past as their own, appropriating a sanitized version of this past in the service of broader conservative projects. It is the job of scholars both of classicism and of neo-classicism, duBois insists, not only to resist such appropriations, but also to offer competing versions that untidy, unsanitize, and uncensor the messy world of antiquity.

We might begin such a project by turning not to Plato or Aristotle but to Sappho, whose symptomatic omission from the current reclamation of the ancient world is a sure sign, according to duBois, that she deserves our attention. The same argument might be made of the study of English neo-classicism, which has been similarly loath to take note of the figure of Sappho, who is nonetheless firmly lodged at the heart of the Augustan literary tradition. Putting Sappho back into the picture of English neo-classicism – and into the history of "Western civilization" more generally – is not an additive gesture, but a fundamentally transformative one, a gesture that threatens to destabilize not only the "wholesome masculinity" of the neo-classical tradition, but virtually everything else that is wholesome about it, as well. In a passage from

Trojan Horses that echoes and consolidates many of the conclusions put forth in her earlier work, *Sappho is Burning*, duBois lays out the stakes of rethinking our cultural ancestry through the figure of Sappho:

> I would set Sappho and other Greek thinkers like her against anti-quarianism and the representations of the Greeks as monolithically male, Aryan, militarist, agrarian, and conservative. Let her stand with other Greek figures for something other than autochthony, a racialized fantasy of purity, a closed male citizen body, the subordination of women and slaves, the restriction of women to reproduction, and citizen immobility and stability. Her work, still very Greek, points in another, more daedalic direction – toward a polymorphous eroticism, toward pleasure and poetry, toward same-sex love, devotion, memory, toward hybridity, Asian, African, and European beginnings, toward nomadism and wandering and migration and the fertilization of one culture by another.[17]

When English writers of the seventeenth and eighteenth centuries came into contact with Sappho, when the culture of English neo-classical letters was "fertilized" by the Sapphic corpus, neither the Augustans nor Sappho would escape unscathed.

The traffic in Sappho

"Nothing [was] known" of Sappho in eighteenth-century England, as Cowley points out, but what had been "told" by earlier "male-poets." One might even be tempted to say that, like gender in Judith Butler's influential formulation, Sappho is "an imitation without an origin."[18] The question for early modern participants in the Sapphic tradition was where to insert themselves in the chain of imitations, those fragmentary accounts of Sappho – not all of them flattering – passed down through the Greek rhetoricians, through New and Old Comedy, and through poets such as Theocritus, Catullus, and Ovid. These partial and incomplete shards of her work – alongside influential fictional representations of the poet, most notably in Ovid's *Heroides* – were by themselves more than enough to keep most commentators and translators busy, as they tried to sort through the troubled legacy of a debased sexual outlaw who was nonetheless credited with having invented lyric poetry. Sappho's sexual indiscretions, according to literary and cultural tradition, did not end with the same-sex eroticism with which she is now universally identified. In the traditions of Greek comedy, Sappho's name seems to have been synonymous with a kind of predatory female sexuality, indiscriminate in its objects. The *Heroides* offered a Sappho who had renounced her lesbian past, but had become instead a lecherous old maid, pining after a beautiful young man, Phaon, and solacing herself through both poetic narcissism and other, more fleshly means of self-gratification.[19] Any poet who decided to insert himself into the tradition of Sapphic texts had to negotiate and avoid being sullied by one or more of these infelicitous sexual reputations.

The potential danger of tangling with Sappho – as well as the impossibility of escaping the poet's sexual reputation – is summed up neatly by Maynard Mack in an essay on Pope's early manuscripts. In a discussion of the many female figures who crop up in Pope's youthful poetry, Mack begins, "In the poems, we encounter Sappho (the poetess abandoned by Phaon, not her seedy modern sisters)."[20] By the latter phrase, one has to assume that Mack is referring to the championing of Sappho as a foremother of modern-day lesbianism. Yet Mack's apparent distinction between the available versions of Sappho is not ultimately all that helpful, since "the poetess abandoned by Phaon" – that is, the fictional Sappho of the *Heroides* – maintains almost all of the "seedy" elements associated with Sappho in modern as well as early modern versions of the poetess. In some ways, in fact, the Ovidian Sappho is even *more* "seedy" than her modern counterpart, since in addition to a professed taste for girls, the Ovidian Sappho, as we shall see, can be read as a melancholic, a whore, and a self-gratifier, as well. Mack is here trying to combine the two versions of Sappho he approves of – the lyric poet(ess) called by Plato "the Tenth Muse" and the Ovidian character – while abjecting all of the other versions of Sappho, and above all the lesbian Sappho who appears here as a modern invention. The poetess, however, will not so easily be disentangled from her seedy sisters. Mack, like Pope before him, risks contamination by Sappho the moment he acknowledges her presence in literary history.

As the quotation from Mack suggests, early modern translators interested in Sappho had available to them two poetic genealogies, one derived from the fragments attributed to Sappho herself and the other – by far the more frequently engaged – derived from Ovid's fifteenth epistle in the *Heroides*, "Sappho to Phaon," also known as the *Epistula Sapphus*. The first tradition – the "authentic" Sapphic – comprising the "Hymn to Aphrodite" and the famously triangulated fragment known as the "Second Ode" gives voice to homoerotic or at least erotically pluralist desires. The second, Ovidian tradition speaks in a more consistent voice, that of Sappho lamenting the loss of her young male lover

Phaon (although there are references in some versions of the poem to Sappho's prior dalliances with women). These two traditions are exemplified respectively at the start of the eighteenth century by rival poets Ambrose Philips and Alexander Pope – already familiar to each other as competitors in the Pastoral wars of 1708 and 1709 – each of whom attempted to inaugurate his own Anglo-Sapphic tradition. The figure of Sappho allowed each of these authors to mark out his poetic legitimacy through a combination of faithful translation and subtle innovation, as well as through fitting himself into the long line of imitators of each of these Sapphic genealogies.

In acting out their poetic rivalry through the medium of Sapphic poetry, Philips and Pope were following exactly in the footsteps of their continental precursors, as DeJean convincingly argues. For centuries, she makes clear, translating Sappho – or rather, translating those male poets, above all Ovid, who have passed her legacy down – has consti-tuted a veritable rite of passage for aspiring male poets. By inserting themselves in the long line of Sapphic imitators, young poets "strive for literary manhood," simultaneously engaging their contemporaries and their poetic predecessors. The female poet "is reduced to the status of mere accessory to a double act of male poetic bonding, with other members of the literary collective and with the male precursor."[21] More often than not, De Jean rightly notes, versions of Sappho produced under these circumstances are characterized by overt misogyny. Anxieties of influence are displaced onto the poetic object rather than onto other poets, deflecting the competitive energies of the all-male literary arena onto the female poet/mediator.

DeJean's account, then, offers a paradigm for understanding the role played by translations of Sappho in the elaboration of masculine liter-ary subjectivity in the seventeenth and eighteenth centuries. This para-digm, indebted as it is to the work of feminist critics Luce Irigaray, Gayle Rubin, and Eve Kosofsky Sedgwick, focuses on Sappho's status as currency in an exclusive exchange between masculine subjects.[22] I want to dwell at some length on this account of Sappho's role in early modern letters, because it offers as compelling a model for understand-ing the English neo-classical literary scene as it does for DeJean's French one. In addition, this model can account for and expose the misogyny which seems to be the inevitable residue of masculine subject formation in a patriarchal literary tradition such as that of Augustan England. More cynically put, if we want to understand the means through which literary men consolidated their love, intimacy, and friendship in England between 1550 and 1800, as the title of this volume has it, as well as the strategies by which they jockeyed for position and renown within their literary fraternity, we need only look at the ways they trafficked in Sappho – particularly, the Ovidian Sappho.

At the same time, however, this is not the only archive to which we might look to understand the importance of the poetess for early modern men of letters. Other, more 'daedalic' versions of Sappho (to use duBois' term), less easily assimilable than the Ovidian one, were simultaneously circulating in Augustan England, troubling the norms of neo-classical literary culture and threatening to rock the very foundations of "literary manhood." It is to these unsettling versions of Sappho that I turn in my concluding section, for a somewhat different, somewhat less predictable account of what happens when Sappho comes between men.

By far the most common archive in which Augustans encountered Sappho was in their reading of Ovid's *Heroides*, a series of verse epistles addressed by abandoned women to the men who abandoned them. Penelope, Ariadne, Dido, Medea: the greatest female figures of classical literature – the greatest human ones, anyway – sing out their love and their loss in these masterful poetic productions. Male poets have found the singing of Ovid's heroines as irresistible as that of any siren: time and again for the past two thousand years, translating the *Heroides* has constituted a poetic rite of passage, a virtuoso performance in which the male poet simultaneously displays his classical learning, his mastery of poetic form, and the quasi-magical ability to metamorphose into or blend with another subjectivity that is required of any poetic translator – especially, of course, a translator of Ovid. That the *Heroides* require the male poet to speak in the voice of a woman – to enact a cross- or transgender performance – only makes the poetic challenge that much more invigorating. As a result, the *Heroides* are, perhaps, the most sublime example of "male-poetry" in the entire neo-classical corpus.

Among the *Heroides*, the most frequently translated is the one now encountered as the last, "Sappho to Phaon" or "Sapho to Phaon" (the alternative spelling of the poet's name is common in early modern English as well as French). As Howard Jacobson, the most influential commentator on the *Heroides*, has pointed out, "Of the *Heroides*, the *Epistula Sapphus* has easily been the most discussed."[23] Jacobson goes on to offer two equally suggestive reasons why critical attention should have been so preoccupied with Sappho's lament. On the one hand, and perhaps paradoxically, Sappho's letter was missing from the rest of the *Heroides* for most of the last two millennia, only reappearing in the fifteenth century, rejoining the rest of the epistles in the sixteenth, and finally assuming its place as the last of the letters in 1661.[24] As Jacobson points out, this long separation has raised considerable questions about the poem's provenance: "the hazards of transmission have affected this poem with ambiguous paternity and the result has been a long-standing dispute as to its authenticity."[25] Despite its semi-illegitimate status, however, and despite even its doubtful authenticity, the *Epistula Sapphus* has been translated even more frequently than the rest of the *Heroides*, and even after rejoining them, has been available as a unique translation exercise in its own right. Alexander Pope is only the most famous of those who embarked upon a translation of "Sapho to Phaon" while resisting the appeal of Helen, Penelope, and the rest of Ovid's heroines.

Jacobson's second explanation for the critical attention lavished on the *Epistula Sapphus* may go some way to explaining, as well, its recurring interest for poet-translators. "Equal stimulus for interest in the poem," he writes, "has been its wealth of information about Sappho."[26] The last letter of the *Heroides*, that is, has as its protagonist not a fictional female but a historical figure, and, most importantly, a poet in her own right. Here, literature and history uncannily collide. Unlike the rest of Ovid's pining ladies, Sappho *could* conceivably have written her own heroic epistle, her own letter of love and loss, and it is this patina of "authenticity" – the word recurs again and again in discussions of Sappho – that gives the *Epistula Sapphus* its unique allure. Critical tradition has it that the letter actually contains words and phrases from the Sapphic lexicon, along with a range of rhetorical figures – most notably, figures of repetition – characteristic of her poetry. Even Ovid's elegiacs – the metrical pattern in which all of the *Heroides* appear – in this letter seem interrupted or broken by echoes of Sappho's own choppy and difficult Sapphic meter. And why wouldn't Ovid use Sappho's own words, her style and her characteristic rhetorical patterns, Jacobson reasons, if they were available to him?

> He will use Briseis' words in her letter, Dido's in hers, though of course through the mediation of Homer and Virgil. We might well expect, when he had access to the heroine's *ipsissima verba* – as only with Sappho – that he would exploit the opportunity.[27]

Whether or not the *Epistula Sapphus* in fact contains the words of the historical Sappho, Jacobson concludes, Ovid "wanted this poem to ring, in so far as was possible, Greek, exotic, sapphic."[28] Readers believed that when they encountered "Sappho to Phaon," they were, in effect, getting two for the price of one, the opportunity to experience the style and possibly the words of Ovid *and* of Sappho. It is this particular pairing that rendered translating the final epistle of the *Heroides* simply irresistible.

The appeal of "Sappho to Phaon" as a crowd-pleaser can be seen in an outpouring of translations and imitations that spanned the period from 1680 to 1712. In 1680, Jacob Tonson brought out a formidable edition of the *Heroides, Ovid's Epistles Translated by Several Hands*. Among those several hands was Dryden's. He contributed three of the epistles, while his well-known essay on translation, one of the benchmarks of English neo-classical literary criticism, formed the preface to the work. Immediately after Dryden's Preface, at the head of the volume, the first epistle to appear was that of "Sapho to Phaon," translated in this instance by Sir Carr Scrope, a Dryden associate and minor Tory poet. The poem's appearance out of place – it was the first rather than the fifteenth and last of the Epistles – must have been designed to add to the volume's allure. Among the abandoned ladies of the *Heroides*, Sappho is clearly a bestseller.

Nonetheless, the poem in Scrope's version is less than half of its original length: 96 lines, compared to the original 220. Germaine Greer calls it "perfunctory."[29] Some of the more notorious passages in the Ovidian original are left out, including the poem's quite explicit reference to Sappho's lesbianism.[30] "But though the concern might be to protect the ladies from perversion," Greer continues, "it is not to protect them from corruption, for Carr Scrope's intention is fundamentally pornographic."[31] As Sappho nostalgically recalls the joys she and Phaon shared, a distinctly unOvidian poetic idiom takes over:

> Then tender words, short sighs, and thousand charms
> Of wanton arts endeared me to his arms;
> Till, both expiring with tumultuous joys,
> A gentle faintness did our limbs surprise.

> (ll.24–8)

In this passage, with its echoes of Rochester and Behn, it is easy to see the sort of cultural cross-fertilization referred to by duBois at work. Scrope's libertine aesthetic mutes and even censors the darker preoccupations of the Ovidian original, rendering the poem fit for a mixed audience.[32]

In the months following Tonson's publication of Scrope's bowdler-ized epistle, as Greer has documented,[33] the volume as a whole, and the *Epistula Sapphus* in particular, became a major source of ammuni-tion in the ongoing battles between rival Whig and Tory literary fac-tions. Sappho's status as currency here leaked out of the refined world of neo-classical poetics to reach a more explicitly political literary market. Within weeks a Whig response to the Tonson volume appeared, written by one Matthew Stevenson and paid for by the Earl of Dorset, entitled *The Wits Paraphras'd*. Of all the protagonists of the heroic epistles lampooned here, Sappho fares the worst.

> While Phaon to the hot-house [Sicily] hies,
> With no less fire poor Sapho fries.
> I burn, I burn, with nodes and poxes,
> Like fields of corn with brand-tail'd foxes.

These lines – jauntily reduced from pentameter to tetrameter – make one grateful Swift never set his hand to the *Heroides*. More damning and more revealing than the ascription of the pox to Sappho, however, is a later section that begins, "Grunting all day I sit alone," and contin-ues with a description of Sappho in a kind of onanistic reverie. The line between rapturous memorial longing and masturbatory fantasy – tenuous since Ovid's original poem – has here been summarily broken. Sappho may have been cleansed of her lesbianism, but she has also degenerated from a whore to one who has no choice but to satisfy her overwhelming urges "alone." In addition, she has been left a parody of a poet – one who "grunts" rather than sings.

In the next round of this particular battle, a year later, Alexander Radcliffe shot back a burlesque entitled *Ovid Travestie*. Despite the poem's return to a more sedate pentameter, things for Sappho otherwise only got worse.[34] In Radcliffe's version, the link between Sappho's poetry and her powers of seduction is made explicit – very explicit: "Then you not only liked my Airy Voice," she says to Phaon, "But in my Fleshly part you did rejoice" (ll.45–6). Moreover, the masturbatory qualities of the epistle once again come to the fore. She recalls a particularly graphic sexual encounter with Phaon thus:

> Into the cellar by good luck we got,
> What we did there, I'm sure you ha'n't forgot:
> There stands, you know, an antiquated Tub,
> 'gainst which, since that, I often stand, and rub.

> (ll.95–8)

Finally, Sappho is made to voice her consciousness of her own ugliness and physical diminutiveness – a consciousness we should bear in mind as we proceed toward Pope's contribution to this genre:

> I am not very beautiful, – God knows;
> Yet you should value one that can compose;
> Despise me not, though I'm a little dowdy,
> I can do that – same – like a bigger body.

> (ll. 25–8)

Sappho's sexual availability – rather than her poetic gift – compensates here for her physical repulsiveness. In this series of linked texts, then, "the poetess abandoned by Phaon" looks just as seedy as her "modern sisters." She has shed her reputation for same-sex dalliance only to be condemned as an ugly narcissist, a whore, and a masturbator.[35]

When Alexander Pope entered the fray in 1712 with his "Sapho to Phaon," he certainly went some way towards yanking the poem back out of the depths to which it had sunk. His version appeared for the first time in the eighth edition of the Tonson volume, although, interestingly, it supplemented rather than replaced the bowdlerized Scrope version.[36] Thus immediately after the Scrope poem we find "Sapho to Phaon, Wholly Translated. By Mr. Pope." The poem, in Pope's signature heroic couplets, does not merely restore the poem to its original size, but expands it to 259 lines, some 40 lines more than the original. Moreover, this is not the only restoration effected by Pope. He mitigates the aggression toward Sappho that had been steadily mounting in the competing Whig/Tory versions of the poem, replacing it with an urbane and chummy nod to Sappho's polymorphous preferences. For Sappho's same-sex dalliances return here, and do so right at the opening of the poem: "No more the *Lesbian* Dames my Passion move,/ Once the dear Objects of my guilty Love" (ll. 17–18). In case we missed it the first time, the reference is repeated close to the end of the poem: "Ye *Lesbian* Virgins and ye *Lesbian* Dames,/ Themes of my Verse, and Objects of my Flames,/ No more your Groves with my glad Songs shall ring" (ll. 232–4). Pope maintains, though in a much more oblique form, the image of Sappho as both a sexually aggressive woman and a narcissist, but adds to her list of perversions – or rather returns to it – the *frisson* of lesbianism, that perennial staple of collective male fantasy. As Greer puts it, Pope's Sappho thus offers "elegant titillation with a spice of perversity."[37]

That Pope's version still retains the traces of that earlier aggression – not to mention the masculine competitiveness – is nonetheless clear from the only surviving manuscript of the poem, which Pope, probably in 1711, sent to his friend Henry Cromwell for comments and criticisms. On the page preceding the poem, Pope added a little obscene epigram, presumably poking fun at Cromwell's notorious easy living. The epigram reads:

> Poor Gellius keeps, or rather starves two Maids,
> Seldom he feeds, but often f——s ye Jades.
> He stops one Mouth that tother may not mutter,
> So what they want in Bread, they have in Butter.[38]

This epigram was never printed with the poem; nonetheless, it offers a remarkably concise commentary on the early eighteenth century's reading of Ovid's epistle. The epigram begins and ends by drawing an analogy between the female sexual organs and the mouth that is already implicit in Ovid's "Sappho to Phaon" and in its many translations, most notably in a phrase like "grunting all day I sit alone."[39] The "grunting" of Sappho's poetic voice here collapses into the quasi-bestial murmur of sexual gratification. Yet the third line of the epigram makes explicit what readers of the *Epistula Sapphus* already know – that is, that what is at stake here is not a confusion of Sappho's two mouths but a replacement of one by the other. "He stops one Mouth that tother may not mutter" puts female sexuality and female voice into a relationship of mutual exclusion. The line is thus reminiscent of Scrope's Sappho, who remembers how Phaon, "snatching kisses, stopp'd me as I sung" (l. 21). The careful reader will notice that Scrope's version, unlike Pope's, actually makes anatomical sense. Sappho *would* be unable to speak while being kissed by Phaon, whereas the "jade" of the epigram might in fact be able to carry on a conversation while being "stuffed" by Gellius. Nonetheless, the point of the two lines is identical: Sappho's garrulousness in the *Epistula Sapphus*, as all male poets seem tacitly to agree, is a direct result of the fact that she no longer has Phaon around to stuff her nether mouth. Male potency – poetic and otherwise – is achieved through the silencing of the female voice. Perhaps the most perfidious aspect of this textual tradition is its figuring of this silencing not as a loss but as a gift – the gift of phallic satisfaction in exchange for the loss of female language. If you want to keep a woman from muttering – and you do – the best solution is to keep her, and to keep her well fucked.

Immediately below the epigram, also in Pope's hand, we find the phrase "Written first 1707." This seemingly banal notation nonetheless constitutes yet another piece of evidence confirming the poem's location in an intricate network of relationships between and among men. The dating of the poem in 1707, almost certainly an outright lie, is nonetheless intimately bound up with the "male poetic rivalry" that has fueled this entire chain of perversions of Sappho. It is impossible to know whether Pope in fact began the poem in 1707, but the question that concerns us is why he felt compelled to state the fact on the man-uscript he was sending to Cromwell in 1711 in the unlikely company of his obscene epigram. We might ask as well why, if he began the poem in 1707, Pope was only now, four years later, interested in showing it to his friend.

Pope certainly resurrects his Ovidian translation, and perhaps fabri-cates it altogether, in direct response to another version of Sappho that was circulating late in 1711, at just the time he seems to have sent the manuscript to Cromwell. No evidence has ever surfaced as to why Jacob Tonson suddenly decided that he needed a new version of the *Epistula Sapphus* in 1712, yet commentators have tended to conclude that it was Tonson who approached Pope to request a new translation of the poem. Perhaps it was Pope who, hearing about the forthcoming version by a rival poet – Ambrose Philips – could not resist offering his own contribution to the Sapphic corpus. Pope's placement of the poem in 1707 not only reminds Cromwell and others that this predates other versions of Sappho circulating in 1711, especially Philips's, but also, I think, places it very deliberately before 1708 – that is, before the Pastoral controversy that pitted these two young poets against each other in front of an audience of their literary betters.[40] In order to short-circuit any suggestion that his Sappho – or rather, his Ovid – is simply a belated and possibly mean-spirited response to Philips's own Sapphic production, Pope insists on the autonomy of his "Sapho to Phaon," on its precedence, but also on its origins outside of the rather sordid com-petitiveness of the literary market-place. Unlike those Whig and Tory polemicists who unabashedly flaunted the status of their translations of Ovid as mere salvos in a war of words, Pope here betrays a distinct ambivalence about allowing his poetic productions to become mere instruments through which to negotiate his literary reputation.

To return to DeJean, Pope here seems loath to acknowledge but unable to avoid 'striving for literary manhood' through competitive relationships with other poets, with Ovid and Sappho as well as with Philips, and even with a figure such as Henry Cromwell. By placing

himself in the Ovidian tradition of Sapphic translations, and by aligning himself with the hybrid figure Mack calls "the poetess abandoned
by Phaon," Pope was clearly constructing for himself a venerable literary ancestry designed to boost his poetic credentials. Whatever vague
discomfort he may have experienced as the price of this "initiatory
rite," and however high the costs for the figure of Sappho on whose
poetic corpus such rites were enacted, Pope, like so many of his contemporaries did achieve a kind of poetic "coming of age," a consolidation of
his identity as a poet through the mediation of the Tenth Muse.[41]

Yet Sappho did not always play such a straightforwardly enabling
role for those poets and other literary figures who came into contact
with her in the eighteenth century. As the passage from duBois quoted
at the end of my first section suggests, however relentlessly the figure
of Sappho has been written over, however frequently she has been
asked to play the role of handmaid in the elaboration of a culturally
conservative, patriarchal, and misogynist literary tradition, the polymorphous, feminine and feminist, even queer aspects of the Sapphic
archive always threaten to erupt, troubling the seamless absorption of
the poet into a homogenized and homogenizing neo-classicism. For
Ambrose Philips, Edmund Curll, and above all Joseph Addison, Sappho
proved a somewhat more disturbing figure than she had done for
many of their contemporaries – a figure who upset both the "wholesome masculinity" of Augustan literature and its sense of itself as the
rightful inheritor of an unproblematic, unbroken poetic legacy extending from the Greeks and Romans to themselves. Even more alarming
than the dangers of encountering these other versions of Sappho, these
men found, were its pleasures – pleasures that can only, in the end, be
described as distinctly perverse.

Perversions of Sappho

In the fall of 1711, Addison published a series of three *Spectator* papers
devoted to the subject of Sappho. Within these papers appeared
Philips's translations of the two best-known Sapphic fragments, the
"Hymn to Aphrodite" and the "Second Ode". The first, translated from
Dionysius of Halicarnassus and called by Philips "An Hymn to Venus,"
appeared in *Spectator* no. 223 (15 November 1711). In the second
Sappho paper, no. 229, published a week later, Addison included no
less than three translations of the "Second Ode" as it was recorded in
Longinus's treatise *Of the Sublime*: Catullus's, the most famous of all

Latin versions; Boileau's, the quintessential French neo-classical contribution; and finally, Philips's own effort. Addison crows that Philips's translations mark an entirely new era in the history of Sappho and of English letters: "these two finished pieces," he mistakenly writes, "have never been attempted by any of our Countrymen."[42] Their status as the putative first English translations of Sappho is matched by their qualitative pre-eminence over versions in any other language – especially, French: "the Translation has preserved every Image and Sentiment of *Sappho*," Addison writes of the "Hymn to Aphrodite," "without any foreign or affected Ornaments."[43] Philips's rendering of the "Second Ode" is singled out for yet more praise: "this Translation is written in the very Spirit of *Sappho*," he writes, "and as near the *Greek* as the Genius of our Language will possibly suffer." Whereas Boileau's version is dismissed as "rather an Imitation than a Translation," Philips's Sappho is almost no translation at all.[44] Unmediated by temporal or linguistic difference – or as nearly so as English will "suffer" – Philips's translations are authentically Sapphic productions.

In his praise for Philips's fidelity to the Sapphic original, Addison sets aside the problem of the mediating roles played by Dionysius of Halicarnassus and Longinus in the recording of these two Sapphic odes. Yet he is not unaware of the complexities of the reception history of the poems, as the *Spectator* papers on Sappho make clear. Indeed, the whole of *Spectator* no. 223, along with parts of the other two papers on Sappho, offer an extended meditation on the vicissitudes of poetic transmission. Addison writes at the opening of *Spectator* no. 223:

> When I reflect upon the various Fates of those multitudes of Ancient Writers who flourished in *Greece* and *Italy*, I consider Time as an Immense Ocean, in which many noble Authors are entirely swallowed up, many very much shattered and damaged, some quite disjointed and broken into pieces, while some have wholly escaped the Common Wreck; but the Number of the last is very small.

Following this unusually frank acknowledgment of the precariousness of the West's artistic heritage, Addison quotes from the *Aeneid*, one of those few texts that has come down to us in one piece: "*Apparent rari nantes in gurgite vasto*," or, in Dryden's translation, "And here and there above the Waves were seen/ Arms, Pictures, precious Goods, and floating Men."[45] Literary history, in Addison's analogy, and history in general, is here turned into a kind of shipwreck, in which only fragments of a lost whole are left floating above and just below the surface.

Time, here figured not in linear or cyclical terms, but as an undifferentiated ocean, cannot be trusted to preserve the things of the past, even
the "noble Authors," intact. Survival is relatively arbitrary, and those
remnants that come to us may be damaged, disjointed, mutilated, or
swallowed up altogether. To study or translate the classics is thus, in
Addison's formulation, to enter into a melancholic relationship in
which one holds onto these fragments of the past while being forced to
acknowledge that they are only a poor substitute for the original, lost
whole. In addition, in the encounter with what is left of the ancient
world, one cannot help but be aware that one's own poetic productions will be subject to a similar fate, as they, too, are lost or broken
apart in the "Immense Ocean" of literary history.

As duBois notes in *Sappho is Burning*, this vision of the past and its
accompanying unease seem to afflict all those who come into too close
contact with Sappho. She writes, "when we read a fragmentary text like
Sappho's, we may be conscious of the possibility of dismemberment, of
the fragility of wholeness, of corporeal and psychic integrity."[46] It is no
coincidence, then, that Addison's remarks come in the course of a consideration of Sappho; nor is it surprising that he should give Sappho
pride of place in his piecemeal historical pantheon: "Among the mutilated Poets of Antiquity," he writes, "there is none whose Fragments
are so beautiful as those of *Sappho*."[47] In *Spectator* no. 229, he lends
support to his own preference for Sappho by comparing the "Second
Ode," the best-known of all Sapphic fragments, to the Belvedere torso,
another well-known fragment of the ancient world from which, he
writes, "*Michael Angelo* declared he had learned his whole Art." These
two "mutilated Figure[s]," Addison concludes, have held more appeal
for the greatest artists and poets than many of those ancient works that
have come down to us undamaged.[48] Why this should be the case,
however, and how it is that artists should come to learn their "whole
Art" from these part objects, Addison fails entirely to speculate.[49]

It does seem to be the case, however, that Addison finds Sappho's
mutilated figures beautiful not despite, but because of, their fragmented status. How are we to understand this romance of the partial
and the mutilated – what duBois calls, "the aesthetics of the fragment,"
in the context of an Augustan literary tradition that does not elsewhere
dwell on the pleasures of the shattered and the damaged?[50] In fact,
English neo-classicism, especially as practiced by Dryden and Pope,
seems drawn almost exclusively to those figures – Virgil, Ovid, and to a
lesser degree Homer – who have "escaped the Common Wreck." Here,
in these brief moments in the *Spectator* papers, Addison seems to be

flirting with an alternative aesthetic project and an alternative relationship to the classical world, one that would require acknowledging not only the existence of fragmentation, but its pleasures as well. Against a vision of the classical past as "a disciplined wholeness" to which we must conform and submit, Sappho's fragments, in Addison's tentative formulation, seem to promise something both more beautiful and more undisciplined.[51]

Yet Addison almost immediately breaks off from his elaboration of the pleasures of this alternative Sapphic aesthetics in *Spectator* no. 223 to express his ambivalence about the effects such an orientation to the ancient world might have on his readers:

> I do not know, by the Character that is given of her Works, whether it is not for the Benefit of Mankind that they are lost. They were filled with such bewitching Tenderness and Rapture, that it might have been dangerous to have given them a Reading.[52]

The first sentence of the passage – with its unspecific phrase, "the Character that is given of her works" – seems to anticipate a fairly conventional dismissal of Sappho and her works as unfit for civilized readers. The sexual improprieties attached to the figure of Sappho loom up for a moment, only to dissipate, as the second sentence specifies how it is that the loss of her works could possibly be "for the Benefit of Mankind." Unadulterated Sappho, Addison suggests, might just have been too much to bear, too "bewitching," too "tender," inclined to incite "Rapture." It is, he concludes, a kind of necessary evil that only tiny scraps of her poetry remain, buried in the works of other – male – poets and critics. For Sappho preserved entire would have been considerably too hot to handle: she is called by ancient critics the Tenth Muse, he records, but she also has another, more inflammatory reputation: "by Plutarch," Addison remembers, she "is compared to *Cacus* the Son of *Vulcan*, who breathed out nothing but Flame."[53]

What we are left with, then, in Addison's deeply uneasy version of Sappho, is a thoroughgoing ambivalence about the poet's legacy as well as her effect in the present on those who read and translate her. In the presentation of the work itself, moreover, Addison will turn his back on Sappho's bewitching charms, substituting for his original assessment of the poet a series of disciplinary gestures designed to render Sappho less "dangerous" – the word is his – than she might otherwise have been. Most importantly, in the way he frames the poems Addison employs a series of techniques that downplay the very fragmented condition he elsewhere seemed to valorize in Sappho's works.

Rather than leaving the poems disjointed and indeterminate, Addison places them inside a larger, more coherent narrative, a narrative in each case tailored to render Sappho more palatable – or at the very least more appropriate – for his English audience. Before turning to a fuller exploration of these techniques, however, it seems important to pause, once again, over Addison's opening remarks in *Spectator* no. 223. For even if Addison is successful in containing Sappho's incendiary potential, his earlier acknowledgment of the unavoidably fragmented relationship to the classical past will remain untouched. Addison may be capable of mitigating the threat posed by Sappho's tenderness, as well as by her rapture, but he will be unable to repair the recognition of fragility that he himself precipitated at the start of this highly unusual meditation on the pleasures of antiquity.

No sooner has he allowed Sappho to appear and to speak than Addison has to kill her off in order to shut her up. In an interesting and altogether fanciful merger of the Ovidian Sappho with the historical one, Addison claims in *Spectator* no. 223 that the "Hymn to Venus" was in fact written on the occasion of Sappho's unrequited passion for Phaon, in an attempt to get Aphrodite to intervene and force the young man to return Sappho's advances. In Addison's account, moreover, the poem fails to achieve its goal of provoking divine intervention – a failure that has mortal consequences:

An Inconstant Lover, called *Phaon*, occasioned great Calamities to this Poetical Lady. She fell desperately in Love with him, and took a Voyage into *Sicily* in Pursuit of him, he having withdrawn himself thither on Purpose to avoid her. It was in that Island, and on this Occasion, she is supposed to have made the Hymn to *Venus*, with a Translation of which I shall present my Reader. Her Hymn was ineffectual for the procuring that Happiness which she prayed for in it. *Phaon* was still obdurate, and *Sappho* so transported with the Violence of her Passion, that she was resolved to get rid of it at any Price.

There was a Promontory in *Acarnania* called *Leucate*, on the Top of which was a little Temple dedicated to *Apollo*. In this Temple it was usual for despairing Lovers to make their Vows in secret, and afterwards to fling themselves from the Top of the Precipice into the Sea, where they were sometimes taken up alive . . . . *Sappho* tried the Cure, but perished in the Experiment.[54]

While the story of Sappho's love for Phaon and the leap from the Leucadian cliff are both taken from the *Epistula Sapphus*, in Ovid's version Sappho does not actually make the leap, and certainly does not perish in the process. Marginally more subtle – though no less damning – than this act of blatant aggression towards the poet is Addison's insistence that the "Hymn to Venus," however bewitching, was wholly "ineffectual" in its attempt to enlist the goddess of love in Sappho's cause. "In Pity come and ease my Grief," Philips's Sappho implores Venus, "Bring my distemper'd Soul Relief;/ Favour thy Suppliant's hidden Fires,/ And give me all my Heart's desires."[55] Whereas the Philips poem leaves open the question of whether Sappho's prayers will be answered, the framing Addisonian narrative has already prepared us for Sappho's disappointment. Her desires emphatically will not be granted. A beautiful poet she may be – especially, according to Addison, in Philips's version – but an ineffectual one as well.

Addison's framing of the Second Ode is even more telling than his treatment of the "Hymn to Venus." For, notwithstanding his praise for Philips's unique ability to channel the Sapphic voice, Addison insists upon one very particular departure from earlier versions of the poem, a departure designed explicitly to render the poem less dangerous than it might otherwise have been. In the "Second Ode," a scene of triangulation unfolds in which the poetic speaker – female in the Greek original – watches a male rival watching their mutual female beloved. At the beginning of *Spectator* no. 229, before any of the three versions of the poem he prints, Addison momentarily strikes a cautionary note: "Whatever might have been the Occasion of this Ode," he writes, "the *English* Reader will enter into the Beauties of it, if he supposes it to have been written in the Person of a Lover sitting by his Mistress."[56] Rather than leaving the gender of the poetic speaker unmarked, as Boileau does, Addison insists on a heterosexual structure of desire: a male poetic speaker watches a man watching a woman with whom the speaker is in love.[57] It is notable that Philips's poem does not itself mark the gender of the speaker; rather, Addison's note is necessary to make the poem fit for "the *English* Reader" – as opposed, we might assume, to the French one, a French reader already stuck with a translation that is imprecise (an "imitation"), excessively ornamented, and marred by sexual indeterminacy. The local poetic rivalry precipitated by Sappho within the English neo-classical scene now threatens to become an international incident, as competing versions of the poetess focus and bring to the surface underlying tensions centering around everything from poetic style to sexual politics.[58]

To insist on placing this poem in a paradigm of compulsory heterosexuality, moreover, creates more problems than it solves, since the last stanzas of the poem, as recorded in Longinus, are almost universally understood to contain a description of female orgasm.[59] In Willis Barnstone's version, entitled "Seizure," the poem reads:

> . . . as I look at you my voice
> is empty and
>
> can say nothing as my tongue
> cracks and slender fire is quick
> under my skin. My eyes are dead
> to light, my ears
>
> pound, and sweat pours over me.
> I convulse, greener than grass,
> and feel my mind slip as I
> go close to death.[60]

Here, by way of contrast, is Philips's version of the same lines:

> For while I gaz'd, in Transport tost,
> My Breath was gone, my Voice was lost:
>
> My Bosom glow'd; the subtle Flame
> Ran quick though all my vital Frame;
> O'er my dim Eyes a Darkness hung;
> My Ears with hollow Murmurs rung:
>
> In dewy Damps my Limbs were chill'd;
> My Blood with gentle Horrours thrill'd;
> My feeble Pulse forgot to play;
> I fainted, sunk, and dy'd away.

Until the last two lines, the Philips version seems almost consistent with the original. Though the sense of "convulsion" has been lost, and though one of the most famously vexing and beautiful of all Sapphic phrases – χλωροτέρα δὲ ποίας ἔμμι: "greener than grass I am" – has disappeared completely, the image of a body and consciousness abandoned to and split apart by desire remains, despite the ordered couplets. The most important change, however, comes in the last two lines, in which "I go close to death" becomes "I fainted, sunk, and dy'd away." Fainting, the complete loss of consciousness, replaces the more threatening sense of altered consciousness captured in the Barnstone translation. Moreover Philips's "sunk, and dy'd away" comes dangerously close to a description of the after-effects of a male orgasm.

Detumescence replaces convulsion, especially when we remember that the Philips version came to its readers – its *"English* reader," at least – framed by Addison as a description of male, rather than female experience. It is immediately after these lines that Addison's assessment of the poem – "as near the *Greek* as the Genius of our Language will possibly suffer" – appears. The English language, it seems, will not suffer an open discussion of female orgasm, a discussion the French version at least flirts with in phrases such as, *"je tombe en de douces langueurs."*[61] Philips's English version, especially as framed by Addison, refuses the ambiguity of the *petite mort* of the final lines, insisting on fainting, rather than coming, as an appropriate outcome to this scene of frustrated desire.

In case we are still in any doubt about what exactly is taking place in the "Second Ode," Addison ends *Spectator* no. 223 with a digression, the sole purpose of which is once again to shore up the poem's heterosexual credentials by insisting on the speaker as a male subject. In order to prove that the "Phrenzies of Love" as described in the poem are indeed "an exact Copy of Nature" – that is, male nature – Addison includes the following story from Plutarch:

> That Author in the Famous Story of *Antiochus*, who fell in love with *Stratonice*, his Mother in Law, and (not daring to discover his Passion) pretended to be confined to his Bed by Sickness, tells us, that *Erasistratus*, the Physician, found out the Nature of the Distemper by those Symptoms of Love which he had learnt from *Sappho's* Writings. *Stratonice* was in the Room of the Love-sick Prince, when those Symptoms discovered themselves to his Physician; and it is probable that they were not very different from those which *Sappho* here describes in a Lover sitting by his Mistress.[62]

The physician knows how to diagnose the patient's condition – he is "love-sick" – on the basis of the symptoms described in Sappho's poem. In Addison's representation of the story, however, he is not content – as physicians for centuries had been – with a mere analogy between the condition of Antiochus and that of the (female) speaker of the "Second Ode," that is, between the symptoms of male and of female love-sickness. "Forgetting" that the original poem featured a female protagonist, Addison concludes that Antiochus' symptoms were similar to those *"Sappho* here describes in a Lover sitting by his Mistress." Whereas the essay begins by insisting only that the English reader "suppose" a male protagonist, and that he do so only if he

wants to enter into the poem's "Beauties," Addison has now completely reassigned the poem a heterosexual love-plot. Here, as elsewhere, Addison's ambivalence about the dangers of exposing the
English reader to Sappho eclipses his earlier appreciation of the poet's
charms. In order to protect his readers from perversion, he must resort
to a whole range of framing devices designed to allay the myriad
dangers of reading Sappho.

Edmund Curll, unsurprisingly, had no such qualms when he offered
the public his own version of the works of the Tenth Muse. In 1713, in
a typically opportunistic move, Curll capitalized on the mini-craze for
Sappho by bringing out *The Works of Anacreon and Sappho, Done from
the Greek by Several Hands, with their Lives Prefix'd*. The Sappho section –
a mere ten pages long – simply reprints the Ambrose Philips poems
from the *Spectator* word for word, but frames them in an entirely new
and entirely contradictory way. First, there is an anonymous life of
Sappho, composed either by Curll himself or by one of his hirelings.
Where the *Spectator* papers had simply passed obliquely over the vexed
issue of Sappho's tendencies, the Curll biographer unabashedly reintro-
duces the issue by bringing up the subject of Sappho's female friends:

> On the Account of whom, her Character suffer'd so much, from the
> charge of Dishonest and Unnatural Pleasure. It being a constant
> Tradition that her Amorous Humour was not satisfied with the
> Addresses of Men; but that she was willing to have her *Mistresses*
> too, as well as her *Gallants*.

In these lines, Curll jauntily goes where English readers and critics
have never so explicitly gone before – that is, straight to the topic of
Sappho and her "Lesbian Dames." Immediately after this sensational
biographical tidbit, though, Curll continues:

> Indeed the incomparable *French* Lady [Mme. Dacier], who has lately
> adorn'd [Sappho's] Relicks, is very ingeniously singular in defending
> her from this unhappy Imputation. But however she may defie the
> rest of the World, yet, since Mr. *Dacier* has declar'd, for the common
> Opinion, she will certainly submit to the superior Judgement of her
> Husband.[63]

The logic of this passage betrays a kind of divided consciousness in its
relation to women – notably, to female literary figures and to the issue
of female autonomy. On the one hand, Sappho's equal preference for

women and men is frankly presented, without censure. Furthermore, later in the biography, the "Second Ode" is described as "an Amorous Ode address'd to one of the Young Maids that she admir'd."[64] Sappho, it seems, is free in this version to exercise her erotic preferences as she likes. On the other hand, the cost of this equanimity seems to be the superfluous aside about the competing interpretations of her life put forth by the Dacier couple. Mme. Dacier's attempt to "defend" Sappho from charges of lesbianism here comes off as prurience. "Incomparable" though her learning may be, she will still be required, in this instance, to "submit" to her husband, and in particular to his "superior judgement."[65] The price for recognizing one female figure's autonomy – Sappho's freedom of erotic choice – is another female figure's subjugation.

Only pages later, moreover, in a moment that seems to run exactly counter to the *laissez-faire* attitude of the life, we find printed above the "Second Ode" Addison's cautionary note explicitly denying – or at the very least refusing to recognize – the poem's lesbian content. Originally separated by two pages from the poem, the note has now become attached to it, paradoxically forcing all readers into an awareness of the poem's complicated gender and sexual positionings, precisely by denying that they are complicated at all. How are we to read the seeming disjuncture in the Curll edition between the biography and the presentation of the poem itself? And how, to return to an earlier point, are we to read the Addisonian refusal to expose the English public to Sappho's taste for girls, against his recommendation that they expose themselves to the rapture her poetry provokes? Surely the last of these reading experiences, which threatens to precipitate an entire psychic unraveling (a form of "subjective dismemberment," as duBois calls it), is more 'dangerous' than the first.

In the blatant contradictions of the Curll volume, as in its Addisonian precursor, the incoherence precipitated by the eighteenth-century English encounter with Sappho emerges. Fissures in the norms of masculinity and femininity, in ideologies of sexuality, and in neo-classical poetics, to name only a few, seem spontaneously to erupt when Sappho comes on the scene. Moreover, Sappho seems to have a fracturing effect on critical and theoretical sensibilities, as well. How ought we read – let alone make sense of and communicate – the history of representations of Sappho in early modern England? On the one hand, it seems necessary to point out, and to keep pointing out, the sometimes numbing misogyny of this literary tradition, not to mention its scathing representation of both lesbianism and heterosexual femininity. As Sappho gets passed from male poet to male poet, she becomes increasingly disheveled, mutilated almost beyond recognition, except that we are constantly being reminded of who she is, and, indeed more insistently, of who she was. Male poets seem perfectly capable of achieving literary manhood without dragging their male predecessors – Homer, Virgil, Ovid – through a similar process. What is it, then, that makes the public humiliation of Sappho so perversely irresistible?

On the other hand, it is possible and even necessary to think beyond the misogyny of this material, beyond the casual amusement this misogyny still seems capable of generating, in order to perform a different kind of work, what I think of as queer work. In calling this form of analysis queer, I draw on ideas put forth by Louise Fradenburg and Carla Freccero, whose introduction to the volume *Premodern Sexualities* offers both an account of and a model for what it means to do queer work on premodern cultural artifacts. Such an analytical stance entails, among other things, abandoning epistemological certitude, the desire for truth, in our historical endeavors. It means, as well, theorizing pleasure, both the forms and expressions of pleasure that we encounter in the past and the pleasure we ourselves take in reading, thinking, and writing about early modern texts. Fradenburg and Freccero write:

> One of the central challenges queer perspectives offer to historical practice is their insistence that the purpose of recognizing pleasure's role in the production of historical discourse is not necessarily to launch yet another renunciation of such pleasure. We take queer theory to be a pleasure-positive discourse, despite the fact that its own discussions of pleasure and aversion have been at times quite complicated and heated; and one of the most important analytical challenges offered today by queer positionalities is their reconsideration of the very stances of epistemological certitude that have played so large a role in the definition and proscription of dangerous pleasures, indeed of pleasure *as* dangerous.[66]

In the context of translations of Sappho, then, a queer methodology might prompt us to ask what sorts of pleasure neo-classical poets and critics derived from their encounters with Sappho. Such pleasures might include, but certainly would not be limited to, the intimacy, in the "Hymn to Aphrodite," of speaking as a woman to another woman; the strange delight, in the "Second Ode," of narrating the experience of female orgasm, "greener than grass"; and the mixed pain and pleasure, in the *Epistula Sapphus*, of being abandoned, in the sense of being left behind to mourn but also in the sense of losing all control, of being unrestrained, shameless, enraptured. These are queer pleasures indeed, pleasures available to and perhaps unavoidable for men writing in the Sapphic tradition.

In *Sappho is Burning*, duBois writes that in the encounter with Sappho, "pleasure comes from an appreciation of the disintegration the poet describes, the undeniable pain of eros, of a disordering desire that shatters the tongue, that brings the I to a place near death."[67] Addison, approaching this "place near death," drew back from the edge, catapulting Sappho over the cliff in his stead. Yet he left behind an unusually personal, unusually powerful record of this encounter with Sappho, a record that captures both the desire Sappho's works can incite in male poets and critics and the fear and loathing that desire seems to precipitate. Addison's account of Sappho, like all of the other English versions produced at the start of the eighteenth century, certainly seems to bear out the thesis, advanced by both duBois and DeJean, that male poets and critics have turned to Sappho again and again as a means of consolidating their identities as literary men, a consolidation effected against the backdrop of Sappho's fragmentation. Yet in the process, these men exposed themselves to the very disintegration and disarticulation they were seemingly trying to overcome. What we see so vividly in Addison's account, however, and what makes that account so undeniably perverse, is not simply the recognition of the inevitability of fragmentation but rather the sheer pleasure, the very queer pleasure Addison takes in the acknowledgment of his own mutilation.[68]

Finally, what if the perversions of Sappho to which I allude in my title, are not only those perversions visited upon her, but also those performed by her, on all poets and readers who come in contact with her *oeuvre*? What if, that is, simply by virtue of their encounter with Sappho, male poets and critics become queer men? Sappho contaminates, as Alexander Pope recognized when he had her say, in his "Sapho to Phaon," "I'm my own Disease." The versions of Sappho produced between 1711 and 1713 suggest that this disease – this cultural contamination – has the capacity to spread as each new generation of "male-poets" is exposed to the fragments of Sappho.[69] In 1787, for instance, a commentator named Joseph Berington had this to say about another of these Sapphic fictions:

Never, I believe, was there a more dangerous production. It presents poison to the hand of inexperienced youth, and the cup which holds it is all of burnished gold. It would have been well, I believe,

for the common interests of virtue and innocence, had this seduc-
tive poem never seen the light.[70]

Berington, however, is not writing about a poem attributed to Sappho,
nor is he referring to any of the surviving versions of Sappho produced
in the ancient world. The poem in question is "Eloisa to Abelard," a
heroic epistle in the Ovidian strain published in 1717. The author of
the poem, a poem that itself would have much to say on the topic of
fragmentation and mutilation, was none other than Alexander Pope.

Notes

1. Abraham Cowley, "On the Death of Mrs. Katherine Philips, 1667," quoted
   in Germaine Greer, "The Enigma of Sappho," *Slip-Shod Sybils: Recognition,
   Rejection, and the Woman Poet* (London: Viking, 1995), p. 135.
2. The first English translation of Ovid's *Heroides* – including the epistle
   "Sappho to Phaon" – was George Turberville, *Heroycall Epistles of the Learned
   Poet, Publius Ovidius Naso* (London, 1567). Longinus was translated in 1652
   by John Hall, *Dionysius Longinus of the Height of Eloquence. Rendered out of the
   Original by J.H. Esq.* (London, 1652) and the translation included Sappho's
   "Second Ode." For the best modern synopses of the appearance of Sappho in
   early modern England, see Greer, *Slip-Shod Sybils*, pp. 130–45 and 450–7nn,
   and Lawrence Lipking, *Abandoned Women and Poetic Tradition* (Chicago and
   London: University of Chicago Press, 1988), especially pp. 80–3. Selected
   English translations of Sappho are collected in Peter Jay and Caroline Lewis
   (eds.), *Sappho Through English Poetry* (London: Anvil Press, 1996).
3. Joan DeJean, *Fictions of Sappho, 1546–1937* (Chicago: University of Chicago
   Press, 1989), p. 5.
4. To take only the most obvious example of such a difference, English, unlike
   the Continental languages into which Sappho had previously been translated, is a language without genders. Not only are the vast majority of
   nouns ungendered, but adjectival and verb forms do not reflect the gender
   of the subject or speaker of a given utterance. English translators could and
   did capitalize on this linguistic characteristic to blur the gendered identity
   of both the poetic speaker and the addressee in their versions of Sappho's
   poetry, especially the love poetry. Some examples are discussed below.
5. I use the terms "Sapphic" and "Sapphism" somewhat loosely throughout
   the essay to refer to any and all cultural productions that make reference to
   the figure of Sappho, whether as author or as subject matter.
6 Emma Donoghue, *Passions Between Women: British Lesbian Culture,
   1668–1801* (New York: HarperCollins, 1993); Harriette Andreadis, *Sappho in
   Early Modern England: Female Same-Sex Literary Erotics, 1550–1714* (Chicago
   and London: University of Chicago Press, 2001); and Greer, *Slip-Shod Sybils*.
   Donoghue and Andreadis both consider Sappho's place in the history of lesbianism. Andreadis opens her recent book by stating that she is interested
   in Sappho's "iconic status ... with respect to female literary creativity, and,

more particularly, in relation to female same-sex erotic love" (p. xi). While the second chapter of the book does attempt an overview of representations of Sappho in English after 1550, the main force of the argument is an attempt to recover 'the history of female same-sex erotics' (p. 1). DeJean (*Fictions of Sappho*) is interested, as I am, in what Sappho has to do with the cultural history of masculinity, but my analysis departs from hers in a number of ways. Most obviously, she looks for the most part only at the French tradition of Sapphic fictions. In addition, while her reading of the sort of poetic rivalries precipitated by Sappho influenced the first and second parts of this paper in essential ways, she seems less interested in understanding the sorts of pleasure male translators take in their engagement with Sappho. Finally, for DeJean, the history of masculine appropriations of Sappho is primarily a history of the consolidation of poetic subjectivity. Whether male translators of Sappho 'come of age' through their engagement with other male translators of Sappho, or whether they participate in that small group of poets who "identify with the original woman writer," translating Sappho offers them a means of solidifying their identity. I am interested, following Page duBois, in the ways in which engaging with Sappho produces disidentification and the disintegration of subjectivity – a disintegration that carries with it its own perverse pleasures. Page duBois, *Sappho Is Burning* (Chicago: University of Chicago Press, 1995) and *Trojan Horses: Saving the Classics from Conservatives* (New York: New York University Press, 2001).

7. It is also, of course, a crucial site from which to assess ideologies of femininity, and I touch on this topic in what follows; however, in the context of a volume on the history of masculinity and of queer men, it seems more immediately relevant to focus on what Sappho has to do with the history of relations between men.

8. Cowley in Greer, "The Enigma of Sappho".

9. Quoted in Dror Wahrman, "Gender in Translation: How the English Wrote Their Juvenal, 1644–1815," *Representations* 65 (1999): 4. See Carolyn D. Williams, *Pope, Homer, and Manliness: Some Aspects of Eighteenth-Century Classical Learning* (London: Routledge, 1993).

10. Thomas Laqueur, *Making Sex: Body and Gender from the Greeks to Freud* (Cambridge, MA: Harvard University Press, 1990).

11. Wahrman, "Gender in Translation": 2.

12 Among those who have argued most persuasively for the relationship between the rise of consumer culture and the development of new forms and expressions of masculinity in the eighteenth century are: G.J. Barker-Benfield, *The Culture of Sensibility: Sex and Society in Eighteenth-Century Britain* (Chicago and London: University of Chicago Press, 1992); Laura Brown, *Ends of Empire: Women and Ideology in Early Eighteenth-Century English Literature* (Ithaca, NY: Cornell University Press, 1993) and Neil McKendrick, John Brewer, and J.H. Plumb (eds.), *The Birth of a Consumer Society: the Commercialization of Eighteenth-Century England* (Bloomington: Indiana University Press, 1982).

13. Wahrman, "Gender in Translation": 3.

14. Ibid.

15. Ibid.: 4.

16. DuBois, *Trojan Horses*, p. 20.

17. Ibid., pp. 72–3.

18. Judith Butler, *Gender Trouble: Feminism and the Subversion of Identity* (New York: Routledge, 1990), p. 138.

19. Howard Jacobson writes of Ovid's version, "calling Phaon back to her in dreams, Sapho masturbates to a climax. Ovid will not allow her any love that is not selfish." "Heroides 15: Sappho," *Ovid's Heroides*, (Princeton: Princeton University Press, 1974), p. 70.

20. Maynard Mack, "'The Last and Greatest Art': Pope's Poetical Manuscripts," *Collected in Himself: Essays Critical, Biographical, and Bibliographical on Pope and Some of His Contemporaries* (Newark: University of Delaware Press, 1982), pp. 322–47. See also Mack's *Alexander Pope: a Life* (New Haven: Yale University Press, 1985), p. 323.

21. DeJean, *Fictions of Sappho*, pp. 6–7.

22. Luce Irigaray, *This Sex Which is Not One*, trans. Catherine Porter (Ithaca, NY: Cornell University Press, 1985); Gayle Rubin, "The Traffic in Women: Notes Toward a Political Economy of Sex," in Rayna Reiter (ed.), *Toward an Anthropology of Women* (New York: Monthly Review Press, 1975), pp. 157–210; Eve Kosofsky Sedgwick, *Between Men: English Literature and Male Homosocial Desire* (New York: Columbia University Press, 1985).

23. Jacobson, *Ovid's Heroides*, p. 277.

24. For an account of the textual history of the *Epistula Sapphus*, see Greer, *Slip-Shod Sybils*, p. 125ff.

25. Jacobson, *Ovid's Heroides*, p. 277.

26. Ibid., p. 278.

27. Ibid., p. 281.

28. Ibid., p. 286.

29. Greer, *Slip-Shod Sybils*, p. 139.

30. Near the start of the poem, Ovid's Sappho laments that Phaon has so stolen her heart that he has made her forget those "*aliae centum, quas non sine crimine amavi*" (those hundred other girls whom I have loved, not without blame [l. 19]). These lines are simply absent from the Scrope version. The line and its subsequent translation history are further complicated by an ongoing controversy over whether the Ovidian original read "*quas non sine crimine*" or "*quas hic sine crimine*" – that is, "those whom I have loved, not without reproach" or "those whom I have loved without reproach." The controversy is discussed in Jacobson, *Ovid's Heroides*, pp. 292–3.

31. Greer, *Slip-Shod Sybils*, p. 139.

32. The volume opens with a dedicatory epistle to one "Louisa Lenos," suggesting that despite its pretensions to high literary status – most notably marked by Dryden's critical preface – the volume was intended for female as well as male readers.

33. Greer, *Slip-Shod Sybils*, pp. 139–44.

34. The poem is reprinted in full in Jay and Lewis, *Sappho Through English Poetry*, pp. 87–90.

35. Despite the almost total disintegration of the *Epistula Sapphus*, in poems such as these, into an obscene ditty, fit for a men's room wall, the charges leveled against Sappho in these works are all easily traceable to the Ovidian original. For the most comprehensive account of the character of the Ovidian Sappho, see Jacobson, *Ovid's Heroides*.

36. [Jacob Tonson] *Ovid's Epistles. Translated by Several Hands. The Eighth Edition* (London, 1712).
37. Greer, *Slip-Shod Sybils*, p. 144.
38. Maynard Mack reprints the manuscript of the poem in its entirety in *The Last and Greatest Art: Some Unpublished Poetical Mansucripts of Alexander Pope* (Newark: University of Delaware Press, 1984), along with the Gellius epigram. The poem has interest, he states here, as "the only surviving auto-graph of a substantial translated work" (p. 72). In his introduction, Mack hesitates over the question of whether the epigram was in fact meant to refer to Cromwell, although he concludes that one may "reasonably guess" that Pope had Cromwell in mind when he attached it to the manuscript. In his life of Pope, Mack avoids any discussion of the embarrassing epigram, and in fact devotes less than a paragraph (in a work of almost a thousand pages) to Pope's translation of "Sapho to Phaon." Here and elsewhere, the poem seems to fit uneasily, if at all, into the canon of Pope's works, though Aubrey Williams, *The Poetry and Prose of Alexander Pope* (Boston: Houghton Mifflin, 1969) does include it in his work, which constitutes the most important classroom edition of Pope's poetry.
39. For a fuller elaboration of the interchangeability of women's "mouths" in Early Modern literature, see Barbara Spackman, "*Inter musam et ursam moritur*: Folengo and the Gaping 'Other' Mouth," in M. Migiel and J. Schiesari (eds.), *Refiguring Woman: Perspectives on Gender and the Italian Renaissance* (Ithaca: Cornell University Press, 1991), pp. 19–34. For further informative explorations of the relationship between women's embodiment and women's speech, see Ann Rosalind Jones, "Surprising Fame: Renaissance Gender Ideologies and Women's Lyric," in N.K. Miller (ed.), *The Poetics of Gender* (New York: Columbia University Press, 1986), pp. 74–95 and Peter Stallybrass, "Patriarchal Territories: the Body Enclosed," in M.W. Ferguson, M. Quilligan, and N.J. Vickers (eds.), *Rewriting the Renaissance* (Chicago: Chicago University Press, 1986), pp. 123–42.
40. For an overview of the Pastoral controversy, see Mack, *Alexander Pope*, pp. 214–18. The controversy began in 1709, when Jacob Tonson published pastorals by Philips and Pope in the same volume of his *Miscellany*. Inevitably, the poems were compared, although the comparison did not become public or explicit until *after* the publication of both Philips's and Pope's versions of Sappho. In *Guardian* papers published in April 1713, Philips was elevated to the status of an equal to Theocritus and Virgil, while Pope was barely mentioned.
41. DeJean, *Fictions of Sappho*, pp. 6–7. See also Elizabeth D. Harvey, "Ventriloquizing Sappho, or, The Lesbian Muse," in *Ventriloquized Voices: Feminist Theory and English Renaissance Texts* (London and New York: Routledge, 1992), pp. 116–39.
42. The "Second Ode" had appeared at least twice previously, first in John Hall's translation of Longinus (1652). The next appearance seems to have been in Aphra Behn, *Miscellany, Being a Collection of Poems by Several Hands* (London, 1685). The poem appears under the heading "Verses made by Sapho, done from the Greek by Boyleau, and from the French by a Lady of Quality." This is the only English version I have run across from this period by a woman – if it is indeed by a woman – and the translation is unique

and interesting in a number of other ways, including the fact that (unlike the Boileau poem from which it is supposedly taken) the poem is restored to something close to Sapphic meter.

43. Joseph Addison et al. *The Spectator*, ed. Donald F. Bond, 5 vols (Oxford: Clarendon Press, 1965.), Vol. II, p. 367.
44. Addison's remarks here seem to contain a nod to Dryden's essay on translation, which was itself published in the 1680 Tonson edition of the *Heroides*.
45. Addison et al., *The Spectator*, Vol. II p. 365 n.2.
46. DuBois, *Sappho Is Burning*, p. 21.
47. Addison et al., *The Spectator*, Vol. II, p. 365.
48. Ibid., p. 390.
49. For a rather different account of the way in which the fragmentation of women's bodies is a precondition for male lyric poetry, see Nancy J. Vickers, "Diana Described: Scattered Women and Scattered Rhyme," *Critical Inquiry* 8 (Winter 1981): pp. 265–79.
50. DuBois, *Sappho Is Burning*, pp. 31ff.
51. Ibid., p. 26.
52. Addison et al., *The Spectator*, Vol. II, p. 366.
53. Ibid.
54. All of the third Sappho paper (*Spectator* no. 233) is devoted to a fantastic catalogue of all of those, both male and female, who have made the leap from the Leucadian cliff. Interestingly, in contrast to the narrative in *Spectator* no. 223, Sappho does not die from her fall in the last of the *Spectator* papers, but she does disappear. Addison recounts her impetuous launch from the cliff, after which, he continues, "many, who were present related, that they saw her fall into the Sea, from whence she never rose again; though there were others who affirmed, that she never came to the bottom of her Leap; but that she was changed into a Swan as she fell, and that they saw her hovering in the Air under that Shape" (II, p. 408). Leaving open the question of whether or not she in fact perished in this version of the narrative, Addison goes on to transform her disappearance into the condition of possibility for the further emergence of a male poetic career. According to *Spectator* no. 233, the poet Alcaeus, himself in love with Sappho, arrived to take the leap on the very evening after Sappho had thrown herself off the cliff. Hearing about her demise, "and that her Body could be no where found, he very generously lamented her Fall, and is said to have written his Hundred and twenty fifth Ode upon that Occasion" (II, p. 409). These are almost the last words of the last of the Sappho papers, and they seem to leave us with the most appropriate of morals: sad and unfortunate though the loss of Sappho may have been, it is redeemed by the knowledge that "male-poetry" lives on and thrives as the fruit of Sappho's sacrifice.
55. Addison et al., *The Spectator*, Vol. II, p. 369.
56. Ibid., p. 390.
57. The structure of desire here, in which a male subject's relation to his beloved is triangulated through the desire of another male subject, is also, in Sedgwick's sense, a homosocial one. Heterosexuality and homosociality are not, then, mutually exclusive, but comfortably coexist. Neither,

however, leaves space for the lesbian desire that has so deliberately been banished from this scene.

58. See Penelope Wilson, "Classical Poetry and the Eighteenth-Century Reader," in Isabel Rivers (ed.), *Books and Their Readers in Eighteenth-Century England* (New York: St. Martin's Press [now Palgrave Macmillan], 1982) pp. 69–96.

59. The poem has also been passed on in medical texts as a technical description of a seizure. For a description of both traditions of transmission, see Lipking, *Abandoned Women*, pp. 59–63.

60. Willis Barnstone (trans.), *Sappho and the Greek Lyric Poets* (New York: Pantheon, 1988), pp. 67–8.

61. Addison, et al., *The Spectator*, Vol. II, p. 391.

62. Ibid., p. 393.

63. [Edmund Curll], *The Works of Anacreon and Sappho, Done from the Greek by Several Hands* (London, 1713), p. 65.

64. Ibid., p. 69.

65. In case this seems like a coincidence, note that Addison does exactly the same thing regarding Mme. Dacier in *Spectator* no. 229, Vol. II, p. 391.

66. Louise Fradenburg and Carla Freccero (eds.), *Premodern Sexualities* (New York and London: Routledge, 1996), p. xviii.

67. DuBois, *Sappho Is Burning*, p. 75. Leo Bersani, "Is the Rectum a Grave?" in Douglas Crimp (ed.), *AIDS: Cultural Analysis, Cultural Activism* (Cambridge, MA: MIT Press, 1988, 1993), pp. 197–223, develops the concept of gay *eros* as "self-shattering." His analysis of the pleasures of relinquishing control and ceding the integrity of the self offers a productive counterpoint to the analysis offered by duBois in *Sappho Is Burning*.

68. Gary Taylor, *Castration: an Abbreviated History of Western Manhood* (New York and London: Routledge, 2000) entertains the possibility that castration might, after all, have certain advantages. See especially the chapter "Contest of Males: the Power of Eunuchs," pp. 33–47.

69. Disease offers a powerful metaphor for cultural transmission, yet there are obvious dangers to employing any language of pathology to describe queer desire. Nonetheless, I retain the use of this complex of imagery because it appears in the texts under discussion here, and because it does so without descending into either panic or extreme prejudice. Put otherwise, the response to the spread of English Sapphism does not seem to be to try to stop the proliferation of Sapphic texts. Moreover, the main symptom of the Sapphic virus seems to be pleasure – a kind of pleasure that readers know is "dangerous" but that they persist in passing on to others. For this reason, though not without some trepidation, I retain the metaphor of disease in my discussion of these cultural productions.

70. Quoted in James E. Wellington, ed. Alexander Pope, *Eloisa to Abelard. With the Letters of Heloise to Abelard in the Version by John Hughes* (1713). (Miami: University of Miami Press, 1965), p. 33.

Index